Experimental Sociology

Experiments have gained prominence in sociology in recent years. Increased interest in testing causal theories through experimental designs has ignited a debate about which experimental designs can facilitate scientific progress in sociology. This book discusses the implications of research interests for the design of experiments, identifies points of commonality and disagreement among the different perspectives within sociology, and elaborates on the rationales of each. It helps experimental sociologists find appropriate designs for answering specific research questions while alerting them to the challenges. Offering more than just a guide, this book explores both the historical roots of experimental sociology and the cutting-edge techniques of rigorous sociology. It concludes with a tantalizing peek into the future and provides a roadmap to the exciting prospects and uncharted territories of experimental sociology.

DAVIDE BARRERA is Associate Professor of Sociology at the University of Turin and Research Fellow at Collegio Carlo Alberto. His interdisciplinary research focuses especially on cooperation and trust. His work has appeared in prestigious journals such as *Socio-Economic Review, Sociological Methods & Research, Social Networks, European Sociological Review*, and more.

KLARITA GËRXHANI is Professor of Socio-Economics at the Vrije Universiteit Amsterdam, Research Fellow of Tinbergen Institute and KNAW member. Her interdisciplinary research bridges economics and sociology, occasionally venturing into social psychology. She has published in highly ranked journals such as *Journal of Political Economy, American Journal of Sociology, Harvard Business Review, Annual Review of Sociology, Social Networks, Experimental Economics*, and more.

BERNHARD KITTEL is Professor of Economic Sociology at the University of Vienna. His research interests include distributive justice, labor markets, and welfare states, integrating perspectives from sociology, political science, and economics. He has published in high-ranking journals and is coeditor of *Need-based Distributive Justice* (2020) and *Priority of Needs?* (2024).

LUIS MILLER is Research Scientist at the Spanish National Research Council. He uses experiments and behavioral models to understand social and political behaviors in divided societies. He has published in highly ranked journals such as *PNAS, Political Analysis, Journal of Conflict Resolution, Sociological Methods & Research, European Economic Review*, and more.

TOBIAS WOLBRING is Professor of Economic Sociology at Friedrich-Alexander-University Erlangen-Nürnberg. His research is located at the intersection of sociology, economics, and psychology. He has published textbooks and papers in high-ranking journals, was a visiting professor in Hong Kong and Utrecht, and has received various awards including the Robert K. Merton Award.

Methodological Tools in the Social Sciences

SERIES EDITORS

Paul M. Kellstedt, *Associate Professor of Political Science, Texas A&M University*

Guy D. Whitten, *Professor of Political Science and Director of the European Union Center at Texas A&M University*

The Methodological Tools in the Social Sciences series is comprised of accessible, stand-alone treatments of methodological topics encountered by social science researchers. The focus is on practical instruction for applying methods, for getting the methods right. The authors are leading researchers able to provide extensive examples of applications of the methods covered in each book. The books in the series strike a balance between the theory underlying and the implementation of the methods. They are accessible and discursive, and make technical code and data available to aid in replication and extension of the results, as well as enabling scholars to apply these methods to their own substantive problems. They also provide accessible advice on how to present results obtained from using the relevant methods.

Other Books in the Series

Eric Neumayer and Thomas Plümper, *Robustness Tests for Quantitative Research*

Nils B. Weidmann, *Data Management for Social Scientists: From Files to Databases*

William Roberts Clark and Matt Golder, *Interaction Models: Specification and Interpretation*

Michael A. Bailey, *Polling at a Crossroads: Rethinking Modern Survey Research*

Experimental Sociology
Outline of a Scientific Field

Davide Barrera
University of Turin & Collegio Carlo Alberto

Klarita Gërxhani
Vrije Universiteit Amsterdam & Tinbergen Institute

Bernhard Kittel
University of Vienna

Luis Miller
Spanish National Research Council

Tobias Wolbring
Friedrich-Alexander-University Erlangen-Nürnberg

CAMBRIDGE
UNIVERSITY PRESS

Shaftesbury Road, Cambridge CB2 8EA, United Kingdom

One Liberty Plaza, 20th Floor, New York, NY 10006, USA

477 Williamstown Road, Port Melbourne, VIC 3207, Australia

314–321, 3rd Floor, Plot 3, Splendor Forum, Jasola District Centre, New Delhi – 110025, India

103 Penang Road, #05–06/07, Visioncrest Commercial, Singapore 238467

Cambridge University Press is part of Cambridge University Press & Assessment, a department of the University of Cambridge.

We share the University's mission to contribute to society through the pursuit of education, learning and research at the highest international levels of excellence.

www.cambridge.org
Information on this title: www.cambridge.org/9781316515228

DOI: 10.1017/9781009099653

© Cambridge University Press & Assessment 2025

This publication is in copyright. Subject to statutory exception and to the provisions of relevant collective licensing agreements, no reproduction of any part may take place without the written permission of Cambridge University Press & Assessment.

When citing this work, please include a reference to the
DOI 10.1017/9781009099653

First published 2025

A catalogue record for this publication is available from the British Library

A Cataloging-in-Publication data record for this book is available from the Library of Congress

ISBN 978-1-316-51522-8 Hardback
ISBN 978-1-009-09651-5 Paperback

Cambridge University Press & Assessment has no responsibility for the persistence or accuracy of URLs for external or third-party internet websites referred to in this publication and does not guarantee that any content on such websites is, or will remain, accurate or appropriate.

Contents

List of Figures, Tables, and Boxes	*page* viii
Preface	ix
1 Introduction	1

PART I The Philosophy and Methodology of Experimentation in Sociology

2 The Development of Experimental Sociology	13
3 What Makes Sociological Experiments Different from Other Experiments?	29
4 Experiments and Causality	40
5 Experimental Designs and Typologies	52

PART II The Practice of Experimentation in Sociology

6 Laboratory Experiments	69
7 Field Experiments	81
8 Vignette Experiments	95
9 Natural Experiments and Quasi-experiments	106

PART III Methodological Challenges of Experimentation in Sociology

10 Validity	119
11 Incentives	132
12 Ethics and Deception	144
13 Experimental Sociology – Quo Vadis?	154
References	159
Index	192

Figures, Tables, and Boxes

Figures

3.1	Macro–micro–macro model	*page* 31
5.1	The role of theory in experimental sociology	53
10.1	Types of validity	121
10.2	Generalizability continuum	128

Table

7.1	Different types of subjects' compliance/noncompliance	87

Boxes

8.1	Why should women get less?	98
8.2	Buying a used car	99

Preface

Sociology has a long tradition of interest in experimental work but an equally long history of skepticism toward and outright rejection of the approach. While neighboring disciplines, such as psychology, economics, and political science, have gradually developed discipline-specific standards of experimental methodology, after intense debate about the pros and cons of various decisions, sociology remained largely silent on methodological issues. Instead, sociological experimentalists implicitly took over the standards from the neighboring disciplines toward which they were oriented. This orientation allowed them to relate to established literature and to conduct their experiments according to the standards of the addressed discipline. However, the drawback of this strategy was that they implicitly accepted the conceptualizations specific to the disciplinary perspective of those neighbors. To the extent that sociology asks different questions and emphasizes different aspects of human behavior, sociological experiments guided by the conceptualizations of neighboring disciplines are drawn away from the core of sociological interests.

Against the backdrop of this concern, Bernhard Kittel and Klarita Gërxhani initiated the Annual Conference in Experimental Sociology (ACES) in 2017. The first conference took place in Vienna, Austria, in 2018, organized by Bernhard Kittel, and involved just a handful of European scholars conducting experimental work. Klarita Gërxhani organized ACES 2019 at the European University Institute (EUI) in Florence. The number of participants roughly doubled, partly because scholars using field experiments joined the venue. Axel Franzen (University of Berne) and Andreas Diekmann (University of Leipzig and ETH Zurich) organized ACES 2021 at Monte Verita in Ascona, Switzerland, extending the scope to researchers using survey experiments. ACES 2022 was hosted at Utrecht University, the Netherlands, by Wojtek Przepiorka, Vincent Buskens, and Rense Corten, where the venue became sizable with several parallel sessions. ACES 2023 was hosted by Luis Miller and Amalia Alvarez-Benjumea at the CSIC in Madrid, Spain, and we (cautiously) predict a long-term continuation of this initiative.

This book is thus the outcome of more than an effort of five scholars who are enthusiastic about experiments. We thank the editors, Paul

Preface

M. Kellstedt and Guy D. Whitten, for encouraging the publication of this book in the Series Methodological Tools in the Social Sciences of Cambridge University Press. We would like to thank the participants at the ACES conferences for the many contributions and discussions that helped us to sharpen our understanding of the various views on standards of experimental work in sociology. Our particular thanks go to Licia Bobzien, Jordi Brandts, Andreas Diekmann, William Foley, Johanna Gereke, Siegwart Lindenberg, Wojtek Przepiorka, Werner Raub, Arthur Schram, Brent Simpson, and two anonymous reviewers for reading the whole or parts of the manuscript, alerting us to issues that we overlooked and offering us a multitude of comments which helped us improve the argument in the book. The order of authorship is alphabetical, and the contributions are too intertwined to separate responsibilities.

1 Introduction

Experimentation rests on manipulation and control. Researchers derive expectations – hypotheses – about causal relationships between variables from theoretical reasoning. To test these expectations, they systematically change single properties of the independent variable, that is, the variable hypothesized to be the cause, and observe the effect of this change on the variable hypothesized to respond to that change, the dependent variable. In the simplest possible experiment, the independent variable can take on two values, for example, present or absent, and the dependent variable may be measured on any scale. The main aim of experiments is to compare the effect of different states of the explanatory variable, which are implemented in separate treatments, on the dependent variable. If a change in the independent variable that results from experimental manipulation in a treatment condition is followed by a change in the dependent variable, the latter is interpreted as a consequence of the former.

The inference to be drawn about the causal effect of a change in the independent variable on the dependent variable depends on the confidence one can place in the assumption that no other factor has interfered with the focused relationship, known as the ceteris paribus clause. Thus, researchers need to make arrangements that prevent interferences by other factors. The most thorough arrangement ascertaining this condition is to shield the observation of the causal relationship from the environment such that no other factor may have caused the observed effect.

The closest approximation to this arrangement is the experiment, most notably the laboratory experiment. It is an approximation because shielding the observation from exogenous factors requires a thorough understanding of the causal relationships at work. The relevant factors depend on the specific research questions asked in a particular discipline. For example, gravity may be most relevant for certain questions asked in physics but can typically be neglected in the social sciences. The most important challenge for social sciences is the fact that humans are living and thinking agents of their own destinies. As participants in a laboratory experiment, humans bring along their own attitudes, perceptions, behavioral routines, and experiences. Humans vary in psychological predispositions and sociodemographic and socioeconomic characteristics. While these traits are the focus of many experiments, mostly engaged with research questions that relate to psychological and sociopsychological theories, they are often considered nuisances in other experiments that are motivated mainly by theories developed at the intersection with economics. In many laboratory experiments, participants are subjected to the rules of the experimental protocol and receive clear instructions about what they are expected to do. Depending on the research context, humans appear in different roles. In order to clarify the role that we address in a specific argument, we differentiate between humans, agents, participants, and subjects. We speak of humans if we refer to members of the species in general terms. Humans become individual agents in theoretical models. In the context of experiments, we speak of participants if we refer to human beings and of subjects if we refer to their role in an experiment.

Participants in experiments interpret their experiences in the laboratory, and this interpretation may affect their behavior in the experiment. Unlike the kind of objects studied in many natural sciences, it would thus be a more than heroic assumption to treat humans as independent, interchangeable, and homogeneous "units of analysis" who respond identically to treatment variations. High-energy physicists accelerate an arbitrary set of protons and shoot them into the electronic detector to study subatomic particle interactions. No serious observer would question this practice because all agree in assuming that it does not matter which proton is used in the experiment. As far as they can judge, one is like the other.

In contrast, selecting participants in social science experiments cannot be assumed to be inconsequential for the outcome. This caveat constitutes a challenge for the kind of inferences experimentalists wish to make in the social sciences. Although it is impossible to fully eradicate the problem, experimentalists have developed ways to cope with it. Most fundamentally, two arrangements are often jointly employed in laboratory experiments to minimize the effect of human heterogeneity on the outcomes of experiments: randomization and incentivization. Randomization, the random allocation of participants to treatments, is crucial for equalizing the composition of the groups that are assigned to different treatments ex ante. As said earlier, participants bring their attitudes, perceptions, behavioral routines, and experiences to the laboratory. This heterogeneity of individual profiles is randomly allocated to the different groups, which implies that in expectation, group averages and other statistical measures must be equal. Hence, if no group were treated, the expected outcomes of different groups would be the same. Randomization thus shields the focused experimental test from exogenous interfering factors. The argument behind incentivization – originated in economics – is that providing homogeneous incentives for behavior within conditions minimizes individual heterogeneity in behavior. Money is a uniformly recognized medium of exchange, where, for example, € 10 can buy more of a good than € 5. Thus, one can assume that ceteris paribus, obtaining € 10 is preferred to € 5 by all participants. To the extent that earning money is a motivation of participants, they can be expected to respond in identical ways to the stimulus provided by the incentive. Whether incentives are a crucial element of the experimental design or undermine the aim of the experiment depends on the research interest. The more the research question focuses on individual characteristics, the more distortionary the effect of incentives. In contrast, the more individual characteristics are considered a nuisance to be controlled, the more beneficial incentives are.

The laboratory provides a setting in which randomization and incentivization can be ensured to a large degree. In other types of experiments, such as field experiments, control of the assignment procedure and the incentives is more difficult to achieve by the experimenter, but often such control is not necessary or even desirable for solving the problem of causal inference. We will discuss problems of causality in Chapter 4, different experimental designs in Chapter 5, the types of experiments and their ways of dealing with the inferential challenge in Part II, and issues of incentivization in Chapter 11.

Throughout the book, we define an experiment as a research procedure in which the researcher controls the phenomenon under investigation by introducing at least one unique factor that differentiates at least two otherwise identical conditions. Thereby, key features of experimental design are the manipulation of a treatment, the creation of treatment and control conditions, and the random assignment of participants to these conditions. In combination with a high degree of control over the experimental environment and interfering factors, experimental designs give researchers traction in identifying causal effects. Whether the experiment replicates a formal model, tests the implication or assumptions of a verbally formulated theory, or explores the empirical corroboration of one's intuition, all sociology experiments use controlled manipulation and random assignments of participants to conditions as primary instruments to infer causal relationships between phenomena.

The history of experimental sociology dates back to the early 20th century. By the 1930s, a small but vibrant community of experimental sociologists was active in developing the field. Not only were several experimental studies published in major journals, but there was also an engaged methodological discussion about various aspects of experimentation. However, by the 1950s, the method had been virtually abandoned. As we will argue in Chapter 2, this was due to some unfortunate methodological choices by the proponents of experimental sociology, with the exception of some experimental work in a small area of coalition theory. It was mainly exchange theory and status theory in the 1970s that, inspired by social psychological work, reintroduced experimental designs on interaction and group behavior into sociology. An additional inspiration came from game theory, which sparked experimental work among sociologists in the late 1970s and early 1980s.

Exchange theory and game theory, which represent different perspectives and have developed different experimental standards and traditions, frame the current debates in experimental sociology (Willer & Walker 2007; Jackson & Cox 2013; Webster & Sell 2014a; Keuschnigg & Wolbring 2015a; Mize & Manago 2022). Subject to continuous fundamental critique, experimental sociology has for long taken a rather defensive stance in its conceptual and methodological reasoning (Martin & Sell 1979). Nevertheless, it has produced a sizeable stock of findings in laboratory work, for example, on network exchange theory (Cook & Chesire 2013; Cook et al. 2013; Molm 2014; Neuhofer, Reindl, & Kittel 2015) and in game-theoretic contributions (Diekmann & Voss 2016; Raub 2017). In recent years, field experiments, which were a major element of experimental sociological work in the 1930s, have regained popularity in sociology (Wolbring & Keuschnigg 2015; Baldassarri & Abascal 2017), not to speak of the long tradition of survey experiments (Mutz 2011; Lavrakas et al. 2019). A genuine sociological contribution to social science experiments is the development of factorial surveys, also known as vignette experiments (see Chapter 8) (Rossi 1979; Jasso & Opp 1997; Auspurg & Hinz 2015a).

In the present volume, we give an overview of the principles of experimental research in sociology, where the integration of theoretical reflection and methodological implications is central. Furthermore, the volume aims to identify points of commonality and disagreement between the different perspectives within sociology and to elaborate on the rationales of each to alert experimental sociologists to potential challenges and help them find appropriate designs to answer their specific research questions. The book is conceptualized as an advanced textbook that goes beyond an instruction manual and aims to motivate readers to reflect on their experimental designs and practices in a deeper and more thorough manner. It predominantly speaks to graduate students and academics who are interested in doing experimental work.

1.1 OUTLINE OF THE BOOK

The book consists of three parts. In the first part of the book, which contains four chapters, we focus on the philosophical and methodological foundations of experimentation in sociology. In Chapter 2, we trace the development of experimental sociology over the course of a century in an attempt to reconstruct the specific perspectives, perceptions, and decisions made by its major proponents. We proceed chronologically and start by discussing the early initiatives to introduce experimental methods into sociology. Next, we focus on the methodological debate of the 1930s. In the following section, we explore the traces that laboratory experiments left in the 1950s and 1960s and then elaborate on the reintroduction of experiments through exchange theory in the 1970s and on the inspirations from game theory in the 1980s. The final section reflects on the prospects of experiments in sociology.

In Chapter 3, we present a genuine sociological perspective on experimental research and contrast it with approaches in the neighboring disciplines of psychology and economics. Many experimental studies in sociology are founded in rigorous sociology, which "often focuses on interactions, and the macro-consequences of interactions, of actors who do not act 'mindlessly.' Actions may depend in various ways on actors' 'definition of the situation' and on what they expect other actors will do" (Gërxhani, de Graaf, & Raub 2022, 3). According to Max Weber (1978 [1921/22]), the fundamental concept is social action, that is, the intentional behavior of individual agents embedded in relationships with, and directed toward, other agents. They are interdependent in their actions and thus try to anticipate the behavior of others. These considerations hint at a core challenge differentiating sociology from neighboring disciplines: Sociology aims at conceptualizing the individual and the social level of the human world in conjunction, emphasizing the social embeddedness of individual action. In this chapter, we will first highlight the specificity of the sociological perspective in contrast to neighboring disciplines, most notably economics. We will then elaborate on the implications of this perspective on the conceptualization of the research question and discuss the proposition that there exist phenomena that emerge at the social level. We will illustrate this proposition by juxtaposing economic and sociological definitions of some key concepts and the consequences of how these basic concepts are operationalized in experimental research.

Chapter 4 elaborates on the importance of causal explanations in sociological research and how the experimental method can contribute to it. Sociology is a science concerning itself with the interpretive understanding of social action and, thereby, with a causal explanation of its course and consequences (Weber 1978 [1921/22]). Empirically, a key goal is to find relations between variables. This is often done using naturally occurring data, survey data, or in-depth interviews. With such data, the challenge is to establish whether a relation between variables is causal or merely a correlation. One approach is to address the causality issue by applying proper statistical or econometric techniques, which is possible under certain conditions for some research questions. Alternatively, one can generate new data with experimental control in a laboratory or the field. It is precisely through this control via randomization and the manipulation of the causal factor(s) of interest that the experimental method ensures – with a high degree of confidence – tests of causal explanations.

Chapter 5 focuses on different research designs in experimental sociology. Most definitions of what constitutes an experiment converge on the idea that the experimenter "controls" the conditions under which the studied phenomenon is observed and analyzed. Typically, the researcher exerts experimental control by creating two situations that are virtually identical, except for one element that the researcher introduces or manipulates in only one of the situations. The purpose of this exercise is to observe the effects of such manipulation by comparing it with the outcomes of the situation in which the manipulation is absent (Guala 2005; Meeker & Leik 2007; Willer & Walker 2007; Thye 2014). One way to look at how the implementation of this rather straightforward exercise produces a variety of designs is by focusing on the relationship that experimental design bears with the theory that inspires it. Therefore, we begin Chapter 5 with a discussion of the relationship between theory and experimental design before turning to a description of the most important features of various types of designs. The chapter closes with a short overview of experiments in different settings such as lab, field, and multifactorial survey experiments.

In the second part of the book, which also consists of four chapters, we discuss these different types of experiments in more detail. We introduce principles of experimentation for the specific type of experiment, discuss their strengths and challenges, and elaborate on practical aspects of planning and conducting these kinds of experiments. Relying on some influential experimental studies, we explain how research questions and theoretical considerations guide design choices in applied research. To show how sociology can profit from the use of experimental methods, applications cover topics of general relevance in the discipline, such as social norms, social networks, social inequality, and social institutions. For example, we present lab experiments on social norms, field experiments on crime and deviance, survey experiments on the gender wage gap, and natural experiments on social institutions.

In Chapter 6, we start with laboratory experiments, the type of study that most people have in mind when talking about experiments. We first discuss the strengths of laboratory experiments, which offer the highest degree of experimental control as compared to other types of experiments. Single factors can be manipulated according to the requirements of theories under highly controlled conditions. As such, laboratory experiments are well-placed to test theories. We then introduce a sociological laboratory experiment as a leading example, which we use as a reference for a discussion of several principles of laboratory research. Furthermore, we discuss a second goal of laboratory experiments, which is the establishment of empirical regularities in situations where theory does not provide a sufficient guide for deriving behavioral expectations. The chapter concludes with a short discussion of caveats for the analysis of sociological data generated in laboratory experiments.

Chapter 7 introduces a second important type of experiments: field experiments. Field experiments have a long tradition in some areas of the social and behavioral sciences and have become increasingly popular in sociology. Field experiments are staged in a "natural" research setting where individuals usually interact in everyday life and regularly complete the task under investigation. The implementation in the field is the core feature distinguishing the approach from laboratory experiments. It is also one of the major reasons why researchers use field experiments; they allow incorporating social context, investigating subjects under "natural" conditions, and collecting unobtrusive measures of behavior. However, these advantages of field experiments come at the price of reduced control. In contrast to the controlled setting of the laboratory, many factors can influence the outcome but are not under the experimenter's control and are often hard to measure in the field.

In Chapter 8, we discuss the methodology of vignette experiments. Vignettes are brief descriptions of social objects including a list of varying characteristics, based on which respondents state their evaluations or judgments. Vignettes can be incorporated into a population survey or administered to a convenience sample in an experimental laboratory. Two elements of vignette studies are common to the definition of experiments that we put forth throughout the book: manipulation and random assignment. Vignettes allow the simultaneous manipulation of more dimensions and the inclusion of more levels per dimension than what is usually possible in other types of experiments. In addition, vignettes can generate fictitious settings in which factors that are typically correlated in real life do not correlate in the vignette samples. Similar to laboratory experiments, respondents can be randomly assigned to vignette subsets. However, sometimes – when the number of factors and levels per factor is small enough – the entire vignette set can be administered to all respondents.

In Chapter 9, we discuss natural experiments and quasi-experiments. First, we provide a broad definition of natural experiments encompassing the different types of designs social science researchers call natural experiments. A natural experiment is an observational study in which an external force assigns the treatment of interest. It is not required that this external force provides an unbiased allocation of individuals or units to treatments. Second, natural experiments are understood as as-if experiments when the researcher is able to construct treatment groups that are identical in all respects but the treatment. In practical terms, this implies testing whether treatment groups differ in observable characteristics. When some differences are found, instruments like matching methods can be used to increase the comparability between the groups. Third, the absence of random assignment generates a higher degree of uncertainty around the treatment effects. Additional analyses – tests of predetermined covariates or placebo tests – are required to reduce this uncertainty.

In the third and final part of the book, we focus on three aspects that, in our view, deserve particular attention when designing and running sociological experiments because they have generated a valuable debate between experimental sociology and the neighboring disciplines psychology and economics. These aspects are questions of internal and external validity, approaches to create adequate incentives in a decision situation, and considerations about ethics and deception.

In Chapter 10, we address the often misunderstood concept of validity. Much of the methodological discussion around sociological experiments is framed in terms of internal and external validity. The standard view is that the more we ensure that the experimental treatment is isolated from potential confounds (internal validity), the more unlikely it is that the experimental results can be representative of phenomena of the outside world (external validity). However, other accounts describe internal validity as a prerequisite of external validity: Unless we ensure internal validity of an experiment, little can be said of the outside world. We contend in this chapter that problems of either external or internal validity do not necessarily depend on the artificiality of experimental settings or on the laboratory–field distinction between experimental designs. We discuss the internal–external distinction and propose instead a list of potential threats to the validity of experiments, which includes "usual suspects" like selection, history, attrition, and experimenter demand effects, among others, and elaborate on how these threats can be productively handled in experimental work. Moreover, in light of the different types of experiments (cf. Chapters 4–8), we also discuss the strengths and weaknesses of each regarding threats to internal and external validity. We argue in this chapter that while it is true that each design contains certain features that affect the likelihood that threats to validity apply, the internal and the external validity of inferences also substantially depend on the specific research question and the exact experimental setup. Hence, developing a tailor-made experimental design (including the right choices about sampling, setting, incentives, deception, treatment, and measurement) for a research question is key for valid inferences.

Building on these clarifications on the concept of validity, we discuss the role of incentives in experimental sociology in more detail in Chapter 11. Providing the right incentives in an experiment is an important precondition for drawing valid inferences. This is a predominant view in experimental economics based on the induced-value theory assuming that monetary incentives override any other human motivation in laboratory economic experiments. A slightly less demanding assumption is that subjects can be incentivized by monetary payoffs but are also motivated by other-regarding preferences or reciprocity. On the other hand, psychologists focus on motivations that subjects bring into the laboratory as a predisposition to behavior and on the framing of the situation. Sociological research takes elements from both perspectives and emphasizes institutional, cultural, and social determinants of human behavior. An important theoretical framework for experimental work is sociological work on framing. According to sociological framing theories, subjects interpret the situation in terms of the given cues and select an action that is appropriate to the situation. The chapter discusses the implications of these three views on the design of experiments in sociology.

In Chapter 12, we address questions related to the use of deception in experimental sociology and discuss ethical as well as practical considerations. Experimental practices have developed in different scientific disciplines following different historical trajectories. As a consequence, standard experimental procedures differ strikingly between disciplines. One of the most controversial issues is the use of deception as a methodological device: Deception is generally permitted and widely used in social psychology experiments and business research, but it is strictly forbidden in experimental economics, where all major economic journals enforce a ban on experiments involving deception. In the sociological scientific community, there is no clear consensus on the matter. Importantly, the disagreement is sometimes based on ethical considerations, but more often, it is based on pragmatic grounds: the anti-deception camp argues that deceiving participants lead to invalid results, while the other side argues that deception has little negative impact and, under certain conditions, can even enhance validity. In this chapter, we (1) discuss the historical reasons leading to the emergence of such different norms in different fields, (2) analyze and separate ethical and pragmatic concerns, and (3) propose some guidelines to regulate the use of deception in sociological experiments.

Chapter 13 summarizes the main points of the book and reflects on possible ways ahead for experimental sociology.

PART I
The Philosophy and Methodology of Experimentation in Sociology

2 The Development of Experimental Sociology

Discussions about the development of experimental sociology typically start by referring to the marginal status that experiments have in the field and the recent rise of their role in the social scientists' toolbox (Jackson & Cox 2013; Mize & Manago 2022). While this is certainly true, this narrative undervalues the long tradition that experimental methods have in sociology, which can be traced back to the early twentieth century. It is also true that these early studies do not fulfill today's standards of social scientific experiments. But neglect of these early attempts would misrepresent the role that sociologists had in the development of the experimental social sciences.

2.1 THE EMERGENCE OF EXPERIMENTAL SOCIOLOGY FROM THE NINETEENTH CENTURY UNTIL THE 1920S

Auguste Comte (1798–1857) is not only considered a founding father of sociology as an academic discipline, but he is also identified as the first to have reflected on the potential contribution of experiments to the creation of sociological knowledge (Chapin 1917a). In Comte's reflections, the objections typically raised against experiments in sociology are still present today. He doubted that a "direct experiment," that is, a single intervention in the social process, can be of any "scientific value" because of the complex interplay of social forces, which renders impossible the isolation of "either the conditions or the results of the phenomenon" (Comte 2000 [1896], 205). Instead, he suggested that "indirect experiments" can be valuable: "Whether the case be natural or factitious, experimentation takes place whenever the regular course of the phenomenon is interfered with in any determinate manner. The spontaneous nature of the alteration has no effect on the scientific value of the case, if the elements are known. It is in this sense that experimentation is possible in Sociology" (Comte 1875, 83). More specifically, Comte argued that the analysis of pathological cases may be regarded as "the true scientific equivalent of pure experimentation ...", which "consists in the examination of cases ... in which the natural laws ... are disturbed by any causes, special or general, accidental or transient; as in revolutionary times especially, and above all, in our own" (Comte 1875], 83). In modern terminology, what Comte calls for is the analysis of "natural experiments" (for details, see Chapter 9).

Yet, the "proper" introduction of experimentation to sociology is thanks to two individuals, the American sociologist Francis Stuart Chapin (1888–1974) and the Russian sociologist Pitirim Alexandrovich Sorokin (1889–1968) (Brearley 1931). Chapin had written extensively about experimental methodology and developed designs for experimental field interventions (frequently using quasi-experimental designs), which would nowadays be called "social experiments" (Rieken & Boruch 1978; Greenberg & Shroder 2004).

In Chapin's very early introduction of the experimental method to sociology, an experiment is defined as "simply observation under controlled conditions," whereby it is "human interference with the conditions that determine the phenomenon under observation" (Chapin 1917a, 133). The procedure is "to vary only one condition at a time and to maintain all other conditions rigidly constant" (Chapin 1917a, 133). He thus moved one step beyond Comte by identifying human interference with the conditions as the crucial element distinguishing experiments from mere observation. Starting from the premise that "[s]ociety is the only official sociological experimenter" (Chapin 1917b, 247), Chapin discussed the founding of utopian societies in the American Midwest in the 1820s (Chapin 1917a) and the introduction of social legislation in Germany in the 1880s (Chapin 1917b) as two variants of sociological experiments. Both variants, however, consist of singular and complex phenomena and thus do not lend themselves well to the "verification" of theories, the stated aim of experimentation (Chapin 1917a, 133). He almost rhetorically asked whether sociologists have "ever actively interfered with the determining conditions of a social problem to the extent of attaining control of the conditions" (Chapin 1917b, 246) and gave the response that "[t]he data of sociology are so complex and observations show such great variation, that precise methods seem impossible" (Chapin 1917b, 247). Instead, Chapin put his bets on the newly emerging discipline of statistics because "[t]he statistical method helps to analyze out conditions of cause and effect, and assists in overcoming the difficulties presented by the complexity of data." He then concluded that "the statistical method bears to scientific method in sociology much the same relation that the experimental method bears to precise methods in physical science" (Chapin 1917b, 247).

Sorokin took a different path to experimental sociology. Like Chapin, he argued that if sociology is meant to be a "nomographic" science, "which intends to develop rules describing the functional and causal relationships in the field of social phenomena," then the discipline's problems must also be studied experimentally (Sorokin 1928a, 186, translated by author). However, his ideas of sociological experiments did not relate to the macro level of societies but focused on individuals in their social environment. In one of the very first reported sociological experiments, which might be termed "proto-laboratory," Sorokin (1928b) studied the effect of social distance on altruism in a narrowly circumscribed social setting. Students were asked to donate money to buy teaching material for their department, assist students of another department who became victims of a flood, and support foreign universities in danger of closure due to a famine. Note that in this sequence, both the social distance and the severity of the need increase, which does not allow establishing whether one or the other factor is causal. Nevertheless, the result was overwhelming in-group favoritism, with strongly declining donations as the social distance increased despite the increasing gravity of need. In the same paper, Sorokin also studied the extent to which this behavior is congruent with the stated general attitudes toward the satisfaction of needs but found that the stated attitudes did not correlate with the donated amounts. He concluded that "the above result clearly shows how unscientific it is to judge people, groups, or historical periods by their words" (Sorokin 1928b, 9, translated by author). From today's perspective, what is stunning in this study is how much of the current thinking about other-regarding preferences (Cooper & Kagel 2016) was already being addressed about ninety years ago.

In other experiments, Sorokin explored work efforts under various conditions. For example, to study work incentives in capitalist and socialist economic systems, he asked children to complete a set of tasks, and the earned sum was paid out either to the participant or to a friend (Sorokin 1928a; Sorokin et al. 1930). He put much effort into concealing the fact that the game suggested to the children was actually a study – a procedure that would be criticized as deception according to modern standards (for more details, see Chapter 11) – and into maintaining as many aspects of the setting constant across subjects in order to control for confounders. The sessions took place in the children's habitual environment, a design that might nowadays be described as a lab-in-the-field experiment. The study of young children was motivated by the aim to control for contextual conditions, among which he considered imbuement by socialist or capitalist bias in the course of socialization. While in the initial paper he did not find substantial differences between treatments (Sorokin 1928a), in a second paper on the same topic, which included a larger number of participants, he found that "'individual remuneration' stimulates a greater efficiency of work than 'group remuneration'" (Sorokin et al. 1930, 782) – a result that, according to Sorokin, militated against a core assumption of communism.

2.2 THE 1930S AND 1940S: HESITATIONS AND CRITIQUES

The beginnings of experimental sociology, discussed in the previous section, already highlight the many facets of the upcoming debates on experimental methods in sociology. One of the major themes in these methodological debates throughout the early years was the concern about whether the requirements of experiments can be attained in the analysis of sociological questions. Well aware of phenomena emergent at the social level that Durkheim (1982 [1895]) had identified as "social facts," both Chapin (1936) and Sorokin (1931) emphasized in their programmatic statements the importance of social forces that go beyond individual action and problematized the implications of the complexity of social constellations for experimental work.

Chapin and Sorokin agreed in their view that, against both the ideographic and the normative position, the quest for generalizations based on the empirical observation of repeatedly occurring and uniform social phenomena should be the aim of sociology (Sorokin 1931, 23; Chapin 1936). For Sorokin, the subject area of sociology consisted "in nothing but a study of those traits and relationships which are common to all social phenomena" (Sorokin 1931, 23), thus searching for an overarching theory in which the partial theories addressed by more specific social sciences such as economics or political science are embedded. In his presidential address to the American Sociological Society, Chapin (1936) laid out a research program and a methodology for the study of intended action and its unintended consequences emanating from the interrelationships between individuals and their actions. In turn, in a sweeping critique of social planning, Sorokin (1936) rejected the very idea that forecasting social phenomena is possible at all.

The implications of sociology's focus on human *interactions*, which differentiates the discipline from neighboring disciplines, have been a major concern for the design of experiments throughout these early years. The concern was that sociology can claim, to a lesser degree than psychology and, later, economics, to study unitary, homogeneous, and, ultimately, exchangeable "units of analysis" that interact with their social environment but are independent in their decisions (Carr 1929). This interest in interactions is contrasted with psychology's focus on, what Carr called, human *reactions* to environmental stimuli, and it raises the question of under what conditions sociologists can use experiments. Carr distinguished three "levels of accessibility" an observer can refer to – the "face-to-face situation," the "crowd situation," and the "distance contact, or public, situation" (Carr 1929, 66) – and suggested that only the first is amenable to experimentation. According to Carr, two challenges stand out: the problem of inducing people to interact naturally in an artificial setting and the problem of producing a complete transcript of all interactions that have happened between the involved participants.

He claimed that, with respect to the former, the crucial difference between interaction in ordinary life and in the laboratory is that in ordinary life, action is "an instrument for the effectuation of our desires and purposes" (Carr 1929, 66) while it is not necessarily so in an experiment. His solution was to "recognize the functional nature of interaction. ... It does not greatly matter what the objective is ... but given any sort of common goal, the unreality vanishes and interaction becomes the perfectly unconscious instrument of adjustment that it normally is" (Carr 1929, 67). As for the problem of recording interactions, he first enumerated the possibilities of transcripts being recorded by the interacting participants themselves, by an observer, or by a mechanical means of record. Carr discarded the first two possibilities because they are necessarily incomplete, subjective interpretations of portions of the events taking place in the interaction and because they distract participants or observers from the actual interaction being studied. The problem of record, as Carr conceptualized it, thus boiled down to the technical and budgetary problems of producing a movie of the interactions.

It took several decades and methodological innovations before both problems were mitigated, although the issue still cannot be considered fully settled today. Induced value theory (Smith 1976) eventually provided the fundament for the assumption of unitary motivations (for more details, see Chapter 11). Furthermore, the massive reduction in costs of video production due to the development of small and powerful computers, together with new systems of score notation of interactions (Nullmeier & Pritzlaff 2010), allowed for the production of detailed transcripts in experiments. Today, written communications are automatically recorded in modern computer laboratories, which provide a complete transcript of all events occurring in the course of an interaction (Kalwitzki, Luhan, & Kittel 2012). However, at the turn of the 1930s, these developments were beyond imagination.

In particular, Chapin's response documents an ambivalent stance toward experiments. In these years, Chapin completed his approach to controlling potentially intervening factors. He argued that the experimental method assumes the researcher to be able to identify the causal factors and to hold these factors constant (Chapin 1931). In methodological terms, Chapin contrasted direct and indirect control. Direct control is the "manipulation of objects or persons present to sense perception," whereas "indirect control of the factors in a situation" is exercised "by manipulation of the symbols of the objects or persons not present to sense perception" (Chapin 1931, 551).

The belief that matching on all relevant variables is the only practical technique for isolating the causal effect is paramount in his writings. For example, to test the effect of class size on academic achievement, he proposed pairing students in a small class with students in a large class with respect to mean intelligence and mean academic grade (Chapin 1931). Describing a design for the study of "authoritarian" and "equalitarian" family group patterns (Chapin 1932), he suggested controlling for a list of manifest and latent structural patterns, such as the number of parents living in the same household, the number of children in the household, the sex distribution of siblings, the age distribution of siblings, illness, the presence of further relative or unrelated persons in the household, and more. He considered these aspects to be "objective factors in the sense of being susceptible to verification by independent observers on the basis of sensory experience" and "[c]onsequently they may be controlled by matching or equating on these factors in the subject and control groups" (Chapin 1932, 204).

However, in a comment to this article, Angell (1932, 207) disagreed with Chapin. He claimed that Chapin's approach did not require identifying and isolating all significant variables, which Angell considered to be impossible due to the complexity of social phenomena. Moreover, Angell argued that even if this were possible, it required controlling for "four or five variables at the very least," creating "a situation which makes this method inapplicable unless one can bring together a very large number of cases" (Angell 1932, 209). Implicitly, the salience of this objection was acknowledged by Chapin a few years later when he recited a study by one of his doctoral students who investigated the effect of school attendance on economic well-being based on 671 graduates and 523 dropouts from high school and commented that "matching eliminated so many cases that the sample dwindled in size at an alarming rate after each new control was set" (Chapin 1938, 790). However, Chapin continued to propagate his "technique of selective control" for some years (Chapin 1940b, 1950) and summarized his view on experimentation in sociology in a book based on his journal articles (Chapin 1947).

Chapin's studies all make use of some "natural" allocation of subjects to the treatment or the control condition. In that sense, they would not classify as "true" experiments according to modern standards but would be examples of natural experiments in which no targeted interference with the conditions either by the researcher or by some administrator has taken place (Dunning 2012; see also Chapter 8). Chapin (1938, 795) labeled this approach an "ex post facto experiment." Somewhat closer to what might count as precursors to modern randomized controlled trials (RCTs)[1] were

---

[1] So-called randomized controlled trials are typically designed to test a policy intervention and are often conducted in the field (Deaton & Cartwright 2018). In a

intervention studies. Chapin repeatedly referred to Dodd (1934) as a best-practice example in experimental sociology. In this study, Dodd analyzed the effects of hygienic education on hygienic practices in a village in rural Syria by matching the village to another village selected out of a shortlist of villages based on nine factors. The experimental village received several visits from a traveling clinic, which instructed families in hygienic practices. In contrast, the control village was supposed to be "isolated from any influence spreading from the clinic" due to its geographical location (Chapin 1938, 787). Despite all precautions, Dodd admitted that the indirect spread of information may have compromised the independence between the experimental and control villages. Chapin added that the nine factors "supposedly held constant" may not have been adequately measured, and thus controlled, in practice, which once more highlighted the difficulties involved in the method of selective control (Chapin 1938, 788).

In addition to the problem of control, experiments were then also criticized for other methodological reasons. Angell (1932) deplored the risk to which subjects were exposed, the self-consciousness of humans who responded to the fact that they were participating in an experiment, and the fact that experiments with humans could never be repeated under exactly the same conditions. The problem of self-consciousness has entered the literature in the form of the "Hawthorne effect," which resulted from a series of economic experiments on the effect of lighting on productivity (Roethlisberger & Dickson 1939). These studies have been described as the "most well-known early sociological experiments" (Jackson & Cox 2013, 30), although their initial research question did not contain any sociological element, and the subsequent interpretation of the unforeseen results highlighted social psychological effects. Productivity turned out to be less affected by lighting than by the presence of researchers and by the fact of being treated, which was interpreted by many participants as a sign of appreciation. With respect to the methodology of experimentation, these studies had a huge impact by alerting experimentalists to the possibility of treatment bias.

Still, it took a few more years until new fundamental assumptions challenged the hegemonic position that Chapin and his method of selective control had obtained in the small field of experimental sociology.

---

strict sense, all the experimental design types discussed in the second part of this book, with the exception of natural and quasi-experiments, are randomized control experiments. However, the term RCT has been popularized in the social sciences in a more restricted sense involving field experimentation and policy orientation.

2.3 THE 1950S AND 1960S: THE ASCENT OF MODERN EXPERIMENTAL SOCIOLOGY

The third scholar who has been attributed the status of a pioneer in the field is Ernest Greenwood (1945), who, in his PhD dissertation supervised by Paul Lazarsfeld, wrote the first systematic and comprehensive review of experimental methodology in sociology (Oakley 1998). Greenwood extensively discussed Chapin's work in a highly appreciative tone. However, the volume is, in fact, a crushing critique of that approach, culminating in the assessment that "[U]nder ideal conditions the ex post facto experiment yields results as valid as the projected type. Actually this almost never happens" (Greenwood 1945, 145).

One of the methodological questions Greenwood raised was how control can actually be achieved. He first discussed the problem of identifying relevant factors and then proceeded to present Chapin's approach for selecting factors to be equated for control. He distinguished the exact equation of values on a factor (precision control), which results in rapid shrinkage of the number of cases available for analysis, from the equation of the frequency distribution of a factor in groups to be compared (frequency distribution control). He explained that Chapin's method of precision control is actually an operationalization of Mill's method of difference and that Mill himself had doubted whether this ideal could ever be reached in practical research. Then, he remarked that the statistician Ronald A. Fisher (1971 [1935]) had, after much reflection on the possibility of exactly equalizing factors, "reached negative conclusions as to its feasibility" (Greenwood 1945, 87). It is at this point that Greenwood (1945, 88) introduced a new paradigm to experimental sociology (Willer & Walker 2007, 37) by exclaiming, "[W]hat can be done so that this unavoidable inequality shall not destroy exactness of the experimental design? Fisher has an answer: Randomize!"

Chapin conceded that randomization is a feasible solution under laboratory conditions but objected that these conditions – which are the random selection of subjects from a population, the random assignment of subjects to treatments, the control of the treatments by the experimenter, and homogeneity tests prior to analysis – are only seldomly met in practice because "much social research is unavoidably and perhaps desirably, conducted in *situ*" (Chapin 1950, 26). A further problem with Fisher's randomization solution, which Chapin (1940a) claimed to be particularly challenging for field experiments (for more details, see Chapter 7), is the rather long period between the initial observation and the observation of outcomes, which generates potentially differing dropout rates in the treatment and the control group (see also Taves 1953). His concerns about the feasibility of randomization relate to three instances of an experimental design that we can reformulate in modern parlance. First, the selectivity of experimental subjects, for example, due to access restrictions or the requirement of voluntary participation in the experiment, is a challenge to the generalizability of results because behavior in the experiment may correlate with the willingness to participate. Second, the nonrandom assignment of subjects to treatments potentially undermines the internal validity of findings. Often, in policy evaluation studies, this assignment will be guided by program-specific or political reasons, which may bias the composition of treatment and control groups. Finally, Chapin points out that the differential dropout of subjects from the experiment, which is unavoidable, may bias the results toward those who stay in the experiment.

It appears that the impasse that Chapin's reservations about the use of randomization and probability theory have led to has resulted from the assumption that most sociologically interesting questions necessarily require field studies and cannot be analyzed in the laboratory. This assumption goes back to Comte but has been undisputedly accepted by Chapin as well as many other experimental sociologists of that time. It is noteworthy that, despite programmatic statements to the contrary, the experimental work published in the 1930s and 1940s was mostly driven by social problems and was rather applied than related to theory-testing in its ambitions. With the ascent of structural functionalism as the hegemonic social theory in the 1950s and the simultaneous dominance of behavioralism in empirical research, the disjuncture between sociological theory and research became even more pronounced.

As a result, experimental sociology was eventually overtaken by experimental economics, which was initiated in the late 1940s by Chamberlin (1948) and whose practitioners opted for randomization (Weimann & Brosig-Koch 2019). The random allocation of subjects to treatments proved to be a much more powerful and flexible methodology to identify causal effects. In the report on their first experiment on oligopoly, Sauermann and Selten (1959, 429) state that they "arbitrarily" allocated subjects to treatments and positions. Smith (1962, 112), who participated as a student in Chamberlin's experiment and was thus inspired to study competitive behavior on the market, explicitly used the term "random" when describing the allocation of subjects to treatments (Bergstrom 2003).

In the meantime, some sociological work inspired by the sociology of small groups, such as the triad, which is considered the most foundational social constellation (Simmel 1950 [1908]; Yoon, Thye, & Lawler 2013), developed by applying the newly developed theory of games (von Neumann & Morgenstern 1944). Researchers started to elaborate theory-led hypotheses amenable to laboratory research. In particular, a theory of coalition building in the triad took shape (Mills 1954; Strodtbeck 1954; Caplow

1956, 1959; Gamson 1961b) and was tested using laboratory experiments (Vinacke & Arkoff 1957; Gamson 1961a).

Robert Bales (1950), who pioneered interaction process analysis for small groups in the Laboratory of Social Relations at Harvard University, provided further inspiration for the design of experiments and conceived a detailed coding scheme for recording interaction profiles. Mills (1954) devised an experiment to test Simmel's (1950 [1908], 135ff.) proposition that a triad tends to segregate into a dyad and a third player and that with rising solidarity in the dyad, the relationships tend to become more robust. Mills (1954, 657–658) suggested that the study of small groups might capture social phenomena that are also relevant at the level of society, whereby he explicitly referred to one of the major contributions to structural-functionalist thinking (Parsons & Shils 1951). The experimental design bears much resemblance to Sorokin's approach, although his work is not mentioned. In order to study the reaction of subjects to coalition changes, Mills organized group discussions whereby two of the three group members were confederates of the experimenter who played the roles of an adversary and of an ally of an experimental subject. In one treatment, the subject started in a coalition and lost her ally. In contrast, in the other treatment, the two confederates formed a coalition, and one of them changed position and proposed forming a coalition with the subject. Participants were selected on the basis of status and personality measures. Mills observed the subject's reactions to changes in the coalition structure and did not find the hypothesized effects.

Theodore Caplow (1956) related Simmel's reflections to game theoretic arguments. He derived hypotheses about the likelihood of coalition formation between two of the three group members in a competitive game. He also introduced power differences by attributing different weights to the players. Vinacke and Arkoff (1957) tested Caplow's theory by contrasting two hypotheses: According to the utility maximization assumption of game theory, players should rationally aim at winning the game and condition their strategies on their expectations about the other players' strategies. The alternative hypothesis was that each player's strategy depends on "the conditions that obtain at the point where play begins, that is, in terms of how the player interprets the position of himself in relation to the other two players" (Vinacke & Arkoff 1957, 407). In the experiment, 90 students were divided into groups of three and played a board game, the purpose of which was to reach "home" first. No mention is made of monetary incentives. The players' speed depended on their weight. A die was rolled, and the outcome was multiplied by the players' weight so that once the type of triad was defined and the weights allocated, the outcome of the game was determined by factors external to the coalition formed. Players could cumulate strength by forming a coalition, and the focus of the study was to determine the coalition formed in different types of triads. The results supported the hypothesis that players' perceptions of power patterns influenced coalition formation in the ways predicted by Caplow. In contrast, the results rejected the game theoretical predictions for most types of triads, supporting the view that "people tend to act according to their perceptions of a situation, and not according to what a fully informed theorist might expect" (Vinacke & Arkoff 1957, 413).

The design of this experiment was innovative insofar as it simply disregarded the concerns that had dominated the discussion initiated by Chapin, and it contained many facets of what we nowadays consider state-of-the-art in the experimental social sciences (Willer & Walker 2007). For example, an elaborated theoretical argument from which the authors derived two competing arguments motivated design choices and treatments. Care was taken to obtain randomly composed groups, weights were randomly allocated, and group compositions remained constant. Groups played a series of six games, whereby the sequence of the games and the turns of the players were systematically varied to cancel out order effects. Although the design shared with Sorokin a focus on questions that can be studied in the laboratory, it went beyond Sorokin's research by putting social interaction within the group center stage.

The next important step in the development of experimental sociology was taken by William Gamson, who won the American Association for the Advancement of Science (AAAS) Prize for Behavioral Science Research in 1962 for his experimental work. As the 85th president of the ASA in 1994, he was the third sociologist in that position who engaged in experimental work. In a generalization of Caplow's theory of coalition formation to larger groups, which became known as Gamson's law of proportionality, Gamson (1961b) used the results of Vinacke and Arkoff (1957) to show the congruency of his model with the data in groups of three. In a follow-up paper on his contribution to coalition theory, Gamson (1961a) extended the group size to five in order to test whether the theory also holds for groups larger than the triad. The aim of the game that was played in the laboratory was to win resources ("jobs") by gaining a majority in a vote under the condition that no player has a sufficient number of votes to win the vote alone. He sorted members of two student fraternities into groups of five with a fixed ratio of three to two, thus profiting from a difference in social distance within each group, whereby one fraternity could form a majority. He then varied the distribution of weights ("votes") in different rounds ("conventions"), producing incentives for building coalitions that cut across the fraternal affiliations. The experiment showed that the theory predicted well the initial choices of members of the winning coalitions but failed to predict the choices of those players who were not members of such a coalition (Gamson 1961a, 573). Fraternal affiliation turned out to matter, but not in a consistent way.

This study might be identified as the first truly modern sociological experiment. In addition to the design elements used by Vinacke and Arkoff, Gamson incentivized strategic behavior in coalition building by introducing a tournament in which the participant who had accumulated the largest number of points in a series of rounds was awarded a monetary prize. Moreover, guided by derivations from theory, he meticulously traced individual behavior and its implications for group outcomes. Moreover, not least, the paper is the first to, albeit only briefly, exploit the transcripts as "a rich source of insight into the thinking processes of the subjects as they plotted and planned their future strategies and discussed the reasons for their past actions" (Gamson 1961a, 572). This line of research has been further developed and extended into a theory of social decision-making (Ofshe & Ofshe 1970, see also Burhans 1977).

2.4 THE 1970S AND ONWARDS: INSPIRATIONS FROM SOCIAL PSYCHOLOGY

By the 1970s, the founders of experimental sociology were practically forgotten, although some of them are still cited now and then (Rieken & Boruch 1978; Oakley 1998; Diekmann 2008; Jackson & Cox 2013; Baldassarri & Abascal 2017). Instead, sociologists started to look outside of their own discipline for methodological inspiration. Building on programmatic work on the formalization of sociological theory (Berger, Zelditch, & Anderson 1966), experimental sociology in the United States developed along research programs at the intersection of sociology and social psychology. One program built on expectations states theory and used carefully designed experiments to test formally derived hypotheses on the development of status beliefs (Berger, Ridgeway, & Zelditch 2002).

Another theory program, which is one of the most long-standing and concise research programs in the Kuhnian sense developed by sociologists, is social exchange theory (Blau 1964; Emerson 1976) with its offspring network exchange theory (Cook & Emerson 1978; Molm & Cook 1995; Willer 1999). Motivated by the idea of developing sociology as an "exact" science in the Popperian sense (Willer 1967, 1992), it relies on laboratory experiments in the well-established social psychological tradition (Willer & Walker 2007). Despite, or perhaps because of, much disagreement and debate about the details, the program has developed in a stepwise, cumulative manner in which each additional element has been carefully integrated into a common framework (Cook & Chesire 2013; Molm 2014; Neuhofer, Reindl, & Kittel 2015). The program has been focusing on small-group research, and after the group of researchers institutionalized their deliberations in the early 1980s, it became integrated by an annual conference and a yearbook entitled "Advances in Group Processes" (Zelditch 2014a).

The starting point of this research program has been an attempt to formulate a system of propositions rigorously deduced from first principles that focus on the power structure of relations between actors (Emerson 1972a, b). Power is an emergent phenomenon at the social level, and its analysis requires a different approach than the study of individual preferences and behavior. From its first formulation in the early 1960s (Emerson 1962), the research program has had a strong experimental twist, although the first mention of an experiment by Emerson (1964) is restricted to a cursory note in the conclusion of the paper in which results of an experiment are listed without any reference to its design and procedures.

The specific research interest in structures of relations requires experimental designs to generate and target variation at the social level (Molm 2014). Similar to experimental economics designs, subjects need to have control over resources that are valuable to other subjects. In addition, in order to achieve specific outcomes, they are dependent on the actions of others. However, Molm (2014, 206) claims that sociological experimentalists must also be able to "manipulate dimensions of the structure and process of exchange and measure their effects on exchange outcomes (e.g., power use, behavioral commitment, and affective ties)." These sociological studies differ from the emerging standard in experimental economics in their understanding of what an outcome is (Falk & Heckman 2009; Bardsley et al. 2010; Weimann & Brosig-Koch 2019).

The canonical design developed by Cook and Emerson (1978) implemented networks with different structures. Subjects, whose task is to allocate a fixed sum of points, are located in the nodes of a network whose edges constitute communication channels between subjects. At the end of the experiment, points are exchanged into local currency. The presence or absence of edges generates different network structures. Subjects interact with each other after a preparatory session in which they are assured that they are indeed interacting with each other, not with the computer, and that there is no deception involved. The experiment is administered in isolation rooms so that subjects do not know with whom they are actually interacting. Two types of power differences are introduced by selectively opening communication channels (edges) between the nodes in the network and by varying the value of edges to the subjects in the nodes. This design became the workhorse of experimental social exchange theory and stimulated a plethora of variations on the theme, cumulatively developing an understanding of social structures and interactions in small groups (Molm & Cook 1995; Cook & Chesire 2013; Cook et al. 2013).

The scholar who brought modern experimental research to European sociology is Siegwart Lindenberg, who moved to the Netherlands from the United States in 1973. Having cooperated with, inter alia, sociologists Georg Homans and Harrison White and psychologist Robert Bales, his own first experiments, conducted at Harvard University, related to the cognitive representation of social structure, and specifically to the processes of grouping, ordering, and nesting social entities and their effects on beliefs, perceptions, and behavior. For example, focusing on end-anchoring and linearity in the cognitive representation of order, he tested the hypothesis that "people tend to order (linearly) towards the least preferred (or least valued) state" (Lindenberg 1977, 212). The data supported the hypothesis, and he interpreted the results as showing that "values can directly influence the direction of ordering" (Lindenberg 1977, 219). This ordering effect makes people who place themselves high on this ordering, say, rich people, perceive more fine-grained differences between people with regard to wealth or income than people who place themselves low on the ordering. In more recent field experiments, Lindenberg has studied the influence of the social environment on norms and self-regulation and has developed a sociological theory on framing effects (Lindenberg 2013; see also Chapters 6 & 10).

2.5 THE 1980S AND ONWARD: INSPIRATIONS FROM GAME THEORY

For sociologists, the theory of collective action (Olson 1965) constituted a particularly interesting challenge because it made strong behavioral claims for a social interaction situation in which more than two individuals are involved and group phenomena emerge (Simmel 1950 [1908]). Sociologists Gerald Marwell and Pamela Oliver were among the pioneers of the experimental examination of predictions derived from the logic of collective action. Their work inspired the canonical design of public goods experiments in economics (Ledyard 1995, 130). Marwell systematically explored the various assumptions underlying this logic. In joint work with coauthors, he showed that the effects of free riding were weaker than expected and that groups produced substantial amounts of a public good, despite the compelling logic of the problem of collective action (Marwell & Ames 1979). In subsequent work, he and coauthors tested various details, such as the effects of group size, of financial stakes, or of the divisibility of the public good on collective action (Alfano & Marwell 1980; Marwell & Ames 1980). These experiments fulfilled many of the standards that were gradually developing in experimental economics at that time. They involved a substantial effort to select subjects and to randomize their allocation to treatment and control conditions. Subjects were incentivized by monetary payoffs, which depended on their own and others' decisions. Marwell's experiments pioneered a design that has since become standard in online experiments: Subjects participated from home, and the experimenter interacted with them by mail and phone, spreading the experiment over several days as all interactions had to take place sequentially.

Paralleling these efforts, Oliver (1980) studied the effect of selective incentives for coalition building – namely, punishment options – on the likelihood of collective action in a power-imbalanced apex game described by von Neumann and Morgenstern (1944). Oliver was less interested in the exact division of payoffs than in the coalitions formed. Under the punishment condition, more coalitions formed and punishments were given if subjects cooperated with the apex player, instead of forming a coalition against this player. Oliver (1984) studied the effect of rewards and punishments on cooperation, finding a positive punishment effect but no reward effect. Furthermore, she observed evidence of a second-order dilemma as punishment also instigated retaliatory spirals. Subjects were seated in separate cubicles in the laboratory in order to ensure complete anonymity. Interactions took place by means of paper slips on which decisions were noted, which were read out loudly by the experimenter. It was only the presence of a confederate of the experimenter, who played according to a predefined script and whose presence was not disclosed to the subjects, that was a departure from the current standard in experiments.

In the meantime, a small but vibrant community in German sociology had started to discuss rational choice and game theory and the possibilities of a mathematical representation of social theory (Diekmann & Voss 2016). Like in social exchange theory, the aim was to develop a scientific fundament for the analysis of social interactions and society (Opp 1970; Hummell 1972a, b). While this community did not yet engage in experimental work in the 1970s, it generated a research field in which formal theory provided hypotheses amenable to systematic testing in the laboratory and thus prepared the ground for the later move to experimental research.

As far as can be reconstructed, the credit for the first experiment by a European sociologist in Europe goes to Andreas Diekmann. Working with Anatol Rapoport at the Institute of Advanced Studies in Vienna, Austria, he engaged in developing experiments to test game-theoretic predictions (Diekmann et al. 1981). In this context, Diekmann (1985) analyzed the volunteer's dilemma, which can be seen as a variant of the public goods game. He explored the model empirically by conducting a survey experiment in which he showed that the bystander effect increases with group size (Diekmann 1986). Participants were asked to choose between contributing and defecting in a volunteer's dilemma, which was represented in strategic form as a game between self and hypothetical others, with the number of others ranging from two to ten. Although "it was announced that points could be converted to money" (Diekmann 1986, 191), in the end, all participants received the same lump sum payment. In a follow-up experiment in a laboratory, Diekmann (1993) tested the predictions from three competing game-theoretic theories. In that experiment, Diekmann used a larger sample, increased the group size, and made real payoffs dependent on actual outcomes. After these initial experiments, Diekmann focused on work using other methods but returned to experimental methodology in the early 2010s at ETH Zürich and became a mentor of experimental sociology in Europe.

A second stream of research that contributed to the development of modern experimental sociology from the perspective of game theory was Werner Raub's and his associates' theoretical work on the problem of cooperation and the credibility of a commitment to play the cooperative strategy in social dilemmas (Raub & Voss 1986). Raub modeled a hostage game as a special case of the prisoners' dilemma, in which both sides can invest in a hostage that is lost in case they do not fulfill their commitment. The model was corroborated by the data (Raub & Keren 1993, 64). The experiment was monetarily incentivized and used design features from the network exchange literature. Subjects were told that they played against another subject, who, in fact, was a computer who played the rational strategy (Raub & Keren 1993, 56). Building on these initial explorations, Raub & Weesie (1993) developed a research program on the mechanisms of cooperation at the Interuniversity Center for Social Science Theory and Methodology Research (ICS), a cooperation of sociology departments at several Dutch universities. Although this center had built a reputation for a rigorously theory-testing approach to sociology, Raub's experimental ambitions were only reluctantly accepted. These circumstances were responsible for the development of an approach at Utrecht University that became one of the hallmarks of sociology: building a robust understanding of a social phenomenon by testing the same hypothesis with different designs and methods. In this way, experiments became acceptable as one way of collecting data for testing game-theoretic models alongside other methods. By the early 2000s, Raub had established Utrecht as a stronghold of experimental sociology rooted in game theory, and the group has since produced a continuous stream of experimental work (Raub 2017).

The efforts of these pioneers have motivated a new generation of sociologists to engage in experimental work. Moreover, there have been recent initiatives – culminated in the organization of the Annual Conference of Experimental Sociology (ACES) – to create a more structured platform where sociologists applying the experimental methodology can come together to exchange their work and share views in the further development of the field.

3 What Makes Sociological Experiments Different from Other Experiments?

Writing explicitly about sociological experiments rests on the presupposition that such experiments differ from experiments conducted in other social sciences. In this chapter, we aim to identify the particular features that result from the specific perspective that sociologists take on social reality emphasizing the interrelatedness of individual behavior and socially emergent phenomena. We first highlight core elements of the sociological perspective by contrasting it with the perspectives of other disciplines and then discuss the implications for the conceptualization of experiments in sociology.

3.1 SOCIOLOGY AND THE NEIGHBORING DISCIPLINES

In sociology, no paradigm has solved or at least become hegemonic regarding "how to understand and explain" individual human action. In his famous definition of human action as behavior that is guided by a subjective meaning, Max Weber (1978 [1921/22], 3) has pointed to the core challenge: The subjective meaning that individuals attach to action can only be inferred from observed behavior, including speech acts. As a consequence, the ideal–typical distinction into instrumentally rational, value rational, affectual, and traditional action motives (Weber, 1978 [1921/22]) has evolved into a variety of conceptualizations, ranging from hermeneutic methods to understand the subjective meaning to assumptions underlying formal models. Even within the narrower area of rational choice sociology, the debate about the adequate way of conceptualizing action is still unresolved (Diekmann 2022). Nevertheless, while it is true that sociology hosts many perspectives and paradigms, in recent years, a rigorous approach to testing sociological theories has developed (Kroneberg & Kalter 2012; Jann & Przepiorka 2017; Gërxhani, de Graaf, & Raub 2022). The main distinction differentiating sociological approaches from economic and psychological thinking is that the sociological perspective entails a dominant focus on the embeddedness of individual perceptions, preferences, meanings, and actions in the social context, which contributes to the generation of subjective meaning in individuals. With political science, its other close neighbor, sociology shares the interest in social aggregates, but it departs from the core emphasis of political science on "system variables," that is, on variables describing aspects of whole societies, such as the type of government or the party system; in contrast, sociology focuses on the interrelationships between individual behavior and social aggregates (Lazarsfeld & Menzel 1961; Abell 2003).

Compared to its neighboring disciplines, sociologists thus ask their questions and formulate their theories at a different level of aggregation, the level of "interpersonal mechanisms" (Simpson & Willer 2015: 44). Hence, the difference between the disciplines is not a matter of taste or methodological standards but a conceptual one. According to Simpson and Willer (2015, 45), the social forces that bring "the behaviors of more self-interested individuals in line with group goals" can be heuristically grouped into three broad categories – rules of adequate behavior in particular situations, reputations as moral judgments among relevant others, and relations, which are characterized by network structures of mutual commitments. Institutions, social structures, and cultural practices are examples of social phenomena in which individual life is embedded.

For many modern theoretical approaches in sociology, the proposition of a mutual dependency between individual action and societal structures marks the point of departure for the development of theories (Coleman 1990; Raub, De Graaf, & Gërxhani 2022). Navigating between the "undersocialized" conception of human beings in economics and the "oversocialized" conception in traditional sociology, these modern approaches focus on the embeddedness of individual action in social structures: "Actors do not behave or decide as atoms outside a social context, nor do they adhere slavishly to a script written for them by the particular intersection of social categories that they happen to occupy. Their attempts at purposive action are instead embedded in concrete, ongoing systems of social relations" (Granovetter 1985, 487).

These insights have led to the development of the "macro–micro–macro model," which serves as an analytical tool for arranging research questions in a unified conceptual map (Coleman 1986; Raub & Voss 2017). Figure 3.1 depicts this map. In order to explain relationships between structural phenomena that emerge at the level of social groups, this model suggests elaborating the mechanisms leading from one social phenomenon to another in three steps (Bunge 2004). The first step focuses on the analysis of the social preconditions of the ways in which individuals relate to the world they live in. The explanatory variable is located on the societal level, and the dependent variable is on the level of the individual. Esser (1999,

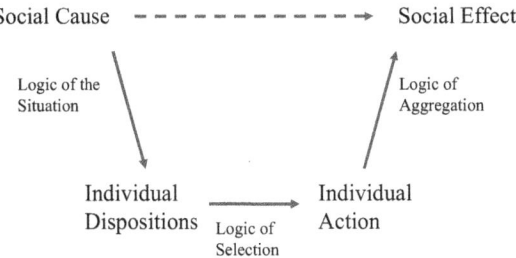

Figure 3.1 Macro–micro–macro model (Adapted from the version in Esser 1999).

91–100) identifies this step as the "logic of the situation" because it focuses on the direct influences of the social context on the formation of individual action dispositions. As a heuristic for conceptualizing the interplay of factors that potentially determine behavior, these dispositions can be grouped into three categories: desires (D), beliefs (B), and opportunities (O) (Hedström 2005, 38–42).[1] Analyzing how these action dispositions influence individual action is the second step, which is the "logic of selection" in Esser's terminology. In this step, individuals choose their actions from a set of options they perceive as conditional on their desires, beliefs, and opportunities. Both the explanatory and the dependent variables are located at the individual level. The third step aggregates individual action back to the social level, that is, focuses on how the joint activity of individuals produces emergent social phenomena. Thus, the dependent variable is a societal phenomenon, and the explanation rests on individual behavior. Hereby, a distinction is made between "parametric" aggregation, which refers to the emergence of collective phenomena resulting from mutually independent individual choices that can be described by statistical summaries, and "strategic" aggregation, which describes mutually responsive actions such as those analyzed in game-theoretical models (Abell 2003; Kittel 2006).

Contributions from experimental sociology typically focus on the mechanisms underlying one of the three steps. Research questions related to the logic of the situation search for explanations of individual beliefs, preferences, or perceived constraints. Since these latent dispositions are not

---

[1] Barrera (2014) and Diekmann (2022) note the conceptual similarity of the DBO model to the BPC (beliefs, preferences, constraints) approach advocated by Fehr and Gintis (2007) as a fundament for the social sciences altogether. The different terminology should not obscure the fact that preferences are based on desires and the constraints and opportunities are just two opposite perspectives on the perception of possibilities.

observable as such, they either have to be inferred from manifest behavior in the laboratory or field contexts or must be explicitly addressed in survey questions. The latter can, for example, be straightforwardly captured by vignette studies using factorial designs. While it is possible to experimentally manipulate beliefs and preferences in the laboratory (Chong & Druckman 2007), Jasso and Opp (1997) pioneered the use of factorial surveys in the study of the effect of norms on political action. The authors find, inter alia, that the overwhelming majority of respondents subscribe to conditional norms, which means that they consider the context when evaluating a norm. An example of a laboratory experiment on the effect of the social context on the perception of the situation is the study of the emergence of solidarity in social exchange situations by Molm, Collett, and Schaefer (2007). The authors vary the exchange structure and analyze the differences in feelings of social solidarity using a set of bipolar semantic differences scales.

Research that probes the logic of selection can be more easily done in the laboratory. Given that this step involves the psychology of choice and is also the main focus of economics, these two neighboring disciplines have produced much research on the logic of selection. For example, in the psychology of choice, most notably prospect theory, experimental research has explored the effect of framing on preference reversals (Kahneman & Tversky 1979) and the impact of social value orientations on decisions (Messick & McClintock 1968; Murphy & Ackermann 2014). In behavioral economics, extensions to the narrow self-regarding utility framework have included other regarding preferences such as altruism and reciprocity into the models (Fehr & Schmidt 1999; Bolton & Ockenfels 2000; Charness & Rabin 2002).

In sociology, most experimental work in the social exchange tradition has assumed self-regarding behavior. However, Willer, Gladstone, and Berigan (2013) have explored the inclusion of social value orientations in exchange theoretical models. Lewis and Willer (2017) subsequently tested this approach experimentally but did not find supporting evidence. Nevertheless, other experimental sociological studies show social values in individual and group decision-making. For example, Winter, Rauhut, and Helbing (2012) find that cooperative intentions can fail to produce cooperative outcomes if subjects hold different norms of distributive justice. According to a study by Schwaninger, Neuhofer, and Kittel (2019), subjects with higher scores on a measure of social value orientations are more likely to allocate part of an endowment to others who have no means to extort their share from them. In an analysis of institutional change as a solution to collective action problems, Gërxhani, Volker, and van Breemen (2021) observe that proselfs who benefit from cooperation are most likely to advance an institutional change to raise contributions, whereas the behavior of prosocials depends on their relative earnings' position. These studies reveal a rising interest in the implications of individual non-material motivations that replaces the assumption of rational, self-regarding utility maximization in earlier experimental work in sociology.

The logic of aggregation focuses on the generation of emergent social phenomena. For example, experiments have revealed the conditions under which public goods are provided (Marwell & Oliver 1993) and common pool resources are sustainably used (Ostrom, Walker, & Gardner 1992). Another example is the study by Rauhut (2013) on the effect of lying in a social group on individuals' norm violations. In the experiment, participants had the possibility to increase their payment by falsely reporting private information on the outcome of a dice roll over several rounds. In the experimental condition, participants received feedback on the reported dice roles of other subjects between the rounds, clearly pointing toward dishonest answers from their fellow participants. As an aggregate result, the treatment triggered the decay of the honesty norm and caused a substantial share of cheating (see also Diekmann, Przepiorka, & Rauhut 2015; Kroher & Wolbring 2015).

Experiments that wish to represent a distinctively sociological perspective are thus faced with the challenge of dealing with the problem of social embeddedness, which goes beyond subjective states of mind: "[T]he microlevel manifestations of social order – cooperation, trust, and prosocial behavior among individuals – also require the operation of mechanisms embedded in social settings. They are more than the direct products of individuals' altruism" (Simpson & Willer 2015, 45). Social mechanisms necessarily presuppose the presence of a social entity because they require the existence of at least three connected actors, which is the condition of phenomena that emerge at the social level (Simmel 1950 [1908]; Lindemann 2010; Yoon, Thye, & Lawler 2013), such as rules, reputations, and relations (Simpson & Willer 2015). This is because rules can be changed *ad libitum* in dyads, relations can only vary if more than two individuals are involved, and a reputation rests on a shared perception of one's behavior by at least two others. However, this is not to say that sociological experiments can only be conducted with three or more individuals because the presence of a social entity can also work through other channels such as socialization, information on the behavior of others, or the framing of the social context (see also Chapter 12).

The conception of the subject matter of sociology outlined earlier differs markedly from neighboring disciplines. Psychologists approach human behavior from the perspective of the human mind, thus focusing on the conscious and unconscious mental processes of subjects that determine individual behavior (Gerrig 2013, 2). Other subjects are relevant to the extent that they influence individual mental states, a topic covered by social psychology, "the study of the ways in which thoughts, feelings, perceptions, motives, and behavior are influenced by interactions and transactions between people" (Gerrig 2013, 447). According to this definition, social psychology also focuses on individual behavior as the outcome of interest and is often interested in group processes but puts a stronger emphasis on individual states such as motivations and psychological effects than sociologists do. Moreover, sociological approaches focus more on the wider range of embeddedness in social contexts (including institutions, etc.) and the premise that collective phenomena are generated by the actions and interactions of individuals. These differences between the two disciplines are also illustrated in the sociological and psychological approaches to group phenomena (Lindenberg 2015).

Economists, on the other hand, focus on individual decisions under scarcity and derive expectations about individual behavior from assumed, or revealed, individual preferences. For example, in a widely read textbook, economics is introduced as the science of decision-making by rational individuals: "The fundamental lessons about individual decision making are that people face trade-offs among alternative goals, that the cost of any action is measured in terms of foregone opportunities, that rational people make decisions by comparing marginal costs and marginal benefits, and that people change their behavior in response to the incentives they face" (Mankiw & Taylor 2006, 16). Rationality is defined by reference to transitive preference orders over a complete and publicly known set of alternatives (Gintis 2014). Agents are assumed to decide by maximizing subjective expected utility (von Neumann & Morgenstern, 1944), whereby the concept of utility is not restricted to self-regarding preferences but may also take costs and benefits of others into account. Other subjects' behaviors enter the equation as external constraints to be accounted for when determining the behavior that maximizes expected outcomes.

Political science, in turn, presupposes the existence of social structures by defining its field as "the systematic study of governance" (Roskin 2020). The latter focuses on power relations between humans aiming to make a collective decision within the context of a social entity structured by rules of interaction. In political economy and public choice, which are the strongholds of experimental research in political science (Palfrey 2009; Kittel & Marcinkiewicz 2012), many conceptual and theoretical inspirations come from economics (Persson & Tabellini 2000; Mueller 2003). A second important field of experimental research in political science, which has a tradition that goes back to the 1920s (Gosnell 1927), is political psychology, with a focus on voting behavior (De Rooij, Green; & Gerber 2009; Druckman, Kuklinski, & Sigelman 2009; Faas & Huber 2010).

3.2 EMERGENT SOCIAL PHENOMENA

Macro phenomena such as rules, reputations, and relations are the subject matter of sociology (Simpson & Willer 2015). If they are to be explained by the interactions of individuals embedded in a social context, then the emergence of these phenomena at the social level has implications for the way in which sociologists think about them, build theories to explain them, or use them in theories explaining other phenomena at the individual or social level. Sociologists describe collectively shared states, not individual states, the same way gas pressure describes a state of gas, not a state of the atoms composing gas. According to this perspective, many phenomena cannot be attributed to individuals but are conceptualized as traits of collectivity, which are external to the individual and constitute a context of norms that conditions individual behavior. However, in addition, such norms may be internalized by individuals through socialization or persuasion and thus shift from an exogenous factor to a value in itself that motivates behavior. For the design of experiments, this double pathway of influence poses a challenge. The researcher must find means to separate behavior driven by internal values from behavior due to adherence to a norm without conviction.

To conceptualize social phenomena, Lindenberg (1997) distinguishes between functional, cognitive, and structural interdependencies among interacting individuals. "Functional" interdependencies, which result from the fact that individual behavior often generates externalities that affect others' chances of reaching their goals or that affect the production of common goods, can be described by game-theoretical models (Crawford 2002). "Cognitive" interdependencies refer to collective identities, expectations, and perceptions. Individuals influence each other's beliefs and preferences and develop a sense of belonging to groups constituted by their roles in society, which, in turn, affect the ways in which cognitive interdependencies are formed. These group processes involving collective phenomena, such as social cognition (Happé, Cook, & Bird 2017), social identity formation (Spears 2021), collective intentionality (Jankovic & Ludwig 2017), and decision-making (Kerr & Tindale 2004; Stasser & Abele 2020), are a core focus of social psychology. Both functional and cognitive interdependencies require some form of relatedness between individuals to become effective. If there were no ties of any sort between individuals, they would neither produce externalities to each other nor develop cognitive interdependencies. These ties form the structural interdependencies that constitute social groups, and such structural interdependencies are often conceptualized in terms of relational networks (Molm 2014). Social groups differ from networks because the former necessarily entail cognitive interdependencies, which the latter lack (Lindenberg 2015, 438).

Many macro phenomena that are situated at the societal level can be studied in a nuclear form in small groups. Although societies and groups differ in size and scope, many social mechanisms are at work in both nuclear and societal environments. To the extent that this assumption holds, the experimental study of small group processes in the laboratory gives indications about the way in which the same factor constellations may affect developments at the societal level, whereby experimental evidence is much more difficult to produce.

Social groups have several characteristics that emerge at the societal level, which, although rooted in individual behavior and the interdependencies between individuals, cannot be reduced to individual behavior alone. Lindenberg (2015) discusses four emergent collective phenomena, which – though not exhaustive – are most relevant for sociological research, and we briefly reiterate them here. The first phenomenon he introduces is "social embedding." People develop shared knowledge and collective memory as well as a collective identity, a notion of "We" (Schutz 1967 [1932]) that forms the foundation of social integration (Lockwood 1964) within the group. However, while social embedding fosters integration within the group, it implies closure to the outside and thus a separation between in- and outgroups. Given that the formation of a social identity rests on socialization or ascription in many cases, individuals can influence group membership through their own decisions only to a very limited extent.

Norms are the second emergent social phenomenon in Lindenberg's list. By identifying common standards of adequate behavior within the group, norms foster social embedding in that they "are specific to the group and help create a social (i.e., group) identity, increasing groupishness and making a group special and different from other groups" (Lindenberg 2015, 436). They thus provide a regulatory fundament for individual behavior and for the sanctioning of positive and negative externalities of behavior as well as for facilitating coordination and cooperation (Opp 2015). The importance of sanctioning highlights the fundamental detachment of norms and individual behavior: Irrespective of whether people are ignorant of a norm or decide not to follow it, the existence of the norm is manifested in the fact that the breach of a norm is sanctioned with a positive probability. Accordingly, Horne and Mollborn (2020, 468) view norms as "group-level evaluations of behavior."

A third collective phenomenon is group-level motivation. On top of the positive and negative sanctions, Lindenberg (2015, 437) maintains, "it is people's ability to identify with group goals ("We" rather than "I") and the activation of this orientation through cues in the environment that are the major drivers of norm conformity." He refers to fairness of procedure and outcomes, respect for norms by others, leadership, and common tasks as examples of group-level motivators. More fundamentally, groups are claimed to develop a collective intentionality that may (Alonso 2017) or may not (Tuomela 2017) be methodologically reducible to individual intentions. Tam (2020) differentiates between groups as aggregates, which are the sum of independent behaviors; as associations, which are based on mutual expectations of individual commitment; and as "We-groups," which are based on the joint commitment to collective action. These latter groups are characterized by a mutual normative expectation of being "inseparable members with a common frame of mind" (Tam 2020, 347), and it is these sort of groups that cannot be reduced to the individual level.

Fourth, status hierarchies are an inherently social phenomenon because they are a relational property of groups. People compare themselves to others with respect to various criteria that may, for example, be ascriptive or merit-based and refer to dimensions such as gender, race, physical attractiveness, and educational or occupational attainment. Those comparisons are then translated into rank orders of relative standing in a group. Typically, higher status positions entail power and prestige that rest on performance expectations (Berger et al. 1977). These expectations also imply certain responsibilities and obligations for high-status group members within the group; for example, the anticipation of other group members that they go ahead in overcoming collective action problems (Simpson, Willer, & Ridgeway 2012).

Group-level phenomena vary in how they relate to individual behavior. Collective identity affects individual social experiences. Whether a person is treated as a group member or as an outsider is often not an issue of own decisions but an experience of others' behavior toward oneself. Although these experiences may affect individual behavior, they cannot be attributed to the individual as a choice. Adherence to norms may be internalized, but even in this case, people have the choice not to comply and to face potential sanctions. While social norms as such may be unobservable, norm compliance and sanctioning are amenable to an assessment of individual costs and benefits and can be observed at the individual level. Group-level motivation, or collective intentionality, lifts this assessment of costs and benefits to the group level. While this assessment remains mostly within an individual's mind, it needs explicit deliberation at the group level. Individual contributions to the formation of a collective intention and the process of deliberation are observable at the group level and can be studied in the context of an experiment (Kalwitzki, Luhan, & Kittel 2012). Finally, although status hierarchies rest in the relations between group members, to the extent that they translate into different expectations toward each other, they have an individual-level correlate.

3.3 EMERGENT SOCIAL PHENOMENA AND EXPERIMENTAL SOCIOLOGY

The implication of the emergent property of social phenomena for conceptualizing sociological experiments can be illustrated by first reflecting on different definitions of a core concept in this controversy – reciprocity, which is used by major proponents of economics and sociology (Kittel 2015). Behavioral economists conceive of reciprocity as "a behavioral response to perceived kindness and unkindness" (Falk & Fischbacher 2006, 294). According to this definition, reciprocity is a behavioral disposition of individuals that needs explanation because it causes a deviation from the game-theoretic predictions. Economists differentiate a weak form of reciprocity, which is individually profitable, from a strong form, which requires the choice of suboptimal strategies (Guala 2012). In stark contrast, for sociologists and social psychologists, "[r]eciprocity, the giving of benefits to another in return for benefits received, is a defining feature of social exchange" (Molm, Collett, & Schaefer 2007, 199). Put differently, sociology defines reciprocity as a social force external to the individual, a structural property of a relationship, a "social fact," which compels individuals to behave in accordance with the norm of responding cooperatively to cooperative behavior, irrespective of individual dispositions or preferences. In turn, the conceptual distinction, which guides the design of treatments, does not refer to individual dispositions – such as weak or strong – but to the relational structure: Reciprocity can be direct, targeting a specific other, or indirect, targeting a social entity.

These differences in the conceptualization of reciprocity have implications for an experiment's focus and the layout of the design. If reciprocity is seen as a behavioral response to another agent's behavior, then the other's intention becomes a crucial condition for one's own behavior. In the so-called moonlighting game (Falk, Fehr, & Fischbacher 2008), two players sequentially give tokens to the other player or take tokens away from the other player. In one treatment, the first player is in full control of his/her decision, whereas in the other treatment, the first player's move is determined by chance. The outcome variable is the amount the second player gives to or takes from the first player. The experimental results show that second players reward good intentions and punish bad intentions, although the association is not deterministic.

In contrast, if reciprocity is viewed as a socially emergent phenomenon that sets the scene for social exchange, then properties of the exchange situation become focal. To reflect this in the design of their experimental treatments, Molm, Collett, and Schaefer (2007) vary the predictability and instrumental value of reciprocity in a network consisting of one player connected to two other players. The outcomes of interest are (a) the frequency with which the players interact with the other players in response to the predictability and value of reciprocity and (b) the sentiment that players develop toward the other players, measured on bipolar semantic differences scales. In a follow-up experiment (Molm 2010), the interest is in different structures of reciprocity, differentiating (i) unilateral from bilateral flows of benefits in two-player settings and (ii) bilateral from multilateral settings. In both experiments, reciprocity is a property of the social structure, not of individual behavior.

Social psychologists likewise view reciprocity as a property of the social structure, but their research typically focuses on mechanisms that operate at the individual level when reciprocal behavior is observed. For example, in Regan's (1971) classical experiment, participants were asked to work on a task together with a partner – who was actually a confederate. In the treatment condition, while working on the task, the confederate bought a drink and offered it to the participant. At the end of the experiment, the confederate asked the participant to buy a raffle ticket from him/her. The results showed that while for participants in the control condition, the decision to buy the raffle ticket correlated with how much they liked the partner, in the treatment condition, the gesture of offering a drink created a sense of obligation to reciprocate, which led most participants to buy the ruffle ticket irrespectively of how much they actually liked the partner.

To conclude, although researchers from different disciplines may study – broadly speaking – the same phenomena, they do so by focusing on a different level of aggregation. If a phenomenon such as reciprocity is viewed from the individual perspective, it becomes an attribute of individual behavior in social interaction. The same phenomenon viewed from the social perspective is conceptualized as a property of the social interaction situation. Such a conceptualization has, in turn, implications for the key features of an experimental design aiming to study that phenomenon. In Chapter 6 on laboratory experiments and in Part III, we will further elaborate on important differences in the experimental approach of sociologists, economists, and social psychologists.

4 Experiments and Causality

4.1 EXPERIMENTATION AND CAUSALITY

Many sociological experiments are designed to answer questions such as why people cooperate, trust, or enforce social norms (Marwell & Ames 1979; Cook et al. 2005; Willer, Kuwabara, & Macy 2009). The goal of experimentation is to offer an explanation for a previously established social regularity such as cooperation, trust, or normative behavior. As in other sciences (Gneezy & List 2013; Pearl & Mackenzie 2018), in sociology, "why" questions are arguably the kind of questions that experimental studies aim to answer. The type of experiments that try to answer a why question typically test hypotheses derived from theoretical models. However, many other sociological experiments do not aim to explain the cause of an empirical regularity but to establish the existence of that regularity. This second type of experiments addresses questions as follows: Do people discriminate in the labor market, are blacks less trusting than whites, or are groups smarter than individuals (Simpson, McGrimmon, & Irwin 2007; Pager, Bonikowski, & Western 2009; Lorenz et al. 2011)? The second type searches for empirical regularities and investigates phenomena that cannot be explained by existing theories.

Whether an experiment tests the implications of a theoretical model or establishes empirical regularities has profound consequences for the way causality is conceptualized. For instance, if a researcher designs an experiment investigating whether people discriminate in the labor market or whether groups are smarter than individuals, she needs to argue why that is the case, even if the causal mechanism is not the focus of her empirical strategy. By contrast, if a researcher designs an experiment testing the implications of a theoretical model, the model itself contains the causal links and determines what the experimenter manipulates.

In a recent overview of causal inference with observational data, Breen (2022) concludes that establishing causality with observational data is a path one can take, but it remains challenging for the reasons mentioned below. In Goldthorpe's (2001, 6) words, "However valuable [the] techniques are, it is still difficult to avoid the conclusion that, in non-experimental social research, attempts to determine the effects of causes will lead not to results that "never die" but only to ones that have differing degrees of plausibility." In fact, some scholars argue that this is precisely the reason behind the increased popularity of experiments in the social sciences (Morton & Williams 2010). For instance, after reviewing the extensive literature on the role of social networks on labor market outcomes such as job entry or wages, Mouw (2006, 99) concludes, "If individuals choose friends who are similar to them, then one may reasonably suspect that the effects of many social capital variables are overestimated because of unobserved, individual-level factors that are correlated with friendship choice and the outcome variable of interest." In such situations, experimental designs are a good choice if one wants to draw causal inferences on the precise effect of social networks (Mouw 2006; Castilla, Lan, & Rissing 2013).

At the core of causality is the idea of "intervention." Woodward (2003) defines an intervention as a "surgical" manipulation of a variable that leaves the rest of the experimental system intact. In essence, this is what experimentalists do: "purposely" and "surgically" altering one or more independent variables and measuring afterward the changes produced in the dependent variable. Experimentalists are therefore interested in the "effects of causes" (e.g., how does treatment X affect prosociality), that is, the causal effect of an intervention. This focus on the "effects of causes" is often contrasted in the literature (for a review see Dawid & Musio 2022) with investigations using observational data on the "causes of effects" (e.g., what causes prosociality), that is, reconstructing how different explanatory variables contributed to a certain observed outcome.

The relationship between intervention and causality may become clearer with an example. Let us think of the well-known problem in sociology of the effect of group size on cooperation: Rational choice theory predicts that the larger the size of a human group, the lower the level of individual cooperation of its members to a collective action (Olson 1965). In an ideal experimental situation, we can intervene by altering the group size while maintaining other features of the (experimental) social system, such as communication, monitoring, or costs, constant, and study the relationship between size and cooperation. This is precisely one of the manipulations introduced by Marwell and Ames (1979) in their seminal paper on contributions to public goods.[1] Their experiment was conducted

---

[1] In an experimental public goods game, participants receive an initial endowment (tokens or money), and they secretly choose whether and how much to invest in a

using 256 school students between the ages of 15 and 17 years, and group size was varied between 4 (small groups) and 80 (large groups).[2] Group size was one of the three independent variables manipulated, the others being the distribution of interests and resources among the participants. The combination of the three leads to a 2 × 2 × 2 full factorial design (see Chapter 5 for more details on factorial designs).

In this example, the group size "causes" an increase or a decrease of cooperation if the group size is the only manipulated variable (i.e., the only difference between the treatment and the control condition), and hence, we can attribute changes in the level of cooperation to such an intervention. Notice that this approach to causality imposes two very strict requirements: "manipulability" and "identification" of the covariation between the cause (group size) and the effect (cooperation). While, in principle, observational studies may try to approximate these requirements through natural sources of (exogenous) variation (Breen 2022), an experiment is the most appropriate setting to fulfill the two conditions. In an experiment, the researcher intervenes by manipulating conditions, for instance, by varying the size of a group of people interacting in a situation, and the researcher can easily identify and measure the association between the purported cause (group size) and the effect (contribution to a public good).

How does a researcher intervene in an experiment? Experimental interventions may involve "control" and "randomization." Control refers to the capacity of the researcher to keep all the extraneous factors that could confound the investigation constant. Randomization or manipulation by "random assignment" is a mechanism through which units (i.e., participants) are assigned to experimental treatments or conditions with known probability. Because it is hard to know all the extraneous variables

---

public pot. The resources invested in this pot are multiplied by a factor (greater than one and less than the number of players), and then this "public good" payoff is evenly divided among the players. Each participant also keeps the part of the endowment that they choose not to invest. Assuming that there are no selective incentives (for example, the possibility to punish those who do not invest), the incentive structure of the game is such that contributing nothing always maximizes the individual payoff, but full contribution is the most beneficial action for the group.

[2] This classical experiment involved *deception* in that all participants were in groups of four, but half of them were told that they interacted in groups of 80. Since the experiment was conducted by telephone and mail, they could by no means know the actual size of their group. Public good games have been extensively studied in experimental economics, carefully avoiding deception, but too often without citing Marwell and Ames' (1979) seminal study. We will come back to the methodological issues surrounding deception in Chapter 12.

that could confound an investigation, experiments use random assignment to guarantee that the comparison units are indeed comparable. Statistically speaking, "randomization provides *orthogonality* of the treatment to the other causes" (Deaton & Cartwright 2018: 4). The main difference between control and randomization is that whereas actual control is a "practical" matter, randomization is only control "in expectation" and, in this sense, it is only a second best. Thus, sometimes, control and randomization are combined in so-called blocked randomized designs, which rely on the identification of subgroups and on random assignment to experimental conditions within them.[3]

Whether an experiment requires random assignment is not free of controversy. There are important sociological types of research designs – usually also called experimental – that aim to maintain a high degree of control without the researcher's explicit manipulation or intervention. These are the so-called ex post facto, quasi-experiments, or natural experiments.[4] These are important designs in sociology, which will be discussed throughout this volume, but they do not meet all defining features of an experiment in the narrow sense. In this chapter, we restrict ourselves to this narrower definition of an experiment, which involves both control and manipulation through random assignment, which is also referred to as a "randomized controlled experiment" (Titiunik 2021).

4.2 THE CANONICAL APPROACH: COUNTERFACTUAL MODEL

The canonical approach to causality in randomized experiments that formalizes this idea of causality is the "potential outcomes" or "counterfactual" approach, also known as the Neyman–Rubin causal model (Rubin 1974; Holland 1986). Descriptions of this model abound, so we will only present it briefly here.[5] In order to grasp its intuition, let us illustrate it with an example on information and cooperation. Imagine our conjecture is that people adapt their contribution levels to a project to the level shown by other group members and that, in an experiment, we manipulate whether participants receive information about the others' contribution.

---

[3] In modern observational research, an increasingly popular method of causal analysis that generalizes this approach is the use of matching estimators (Gangl 2010).
[4] Recall Chapin's (1947) reluctance to accept randomization and his insistence on control (cf. Chapter 1).
[5] For introductions, see Angrist and Pischke (2009, 2015), Cunningham (2021) and Morgan and Winship (2015). For a comprehensive treatment of the counterfactual approach, see Imbens and Rubin (2015).

The treatment is, then, "information," and we randomly assign participants to a (treatment) condition in which they receive information about others' contributions and a (control) condition in which they do not receive such information. The logic of the counterfactual approach would be as follows.

For each individual i, let Y_{i0} be the outcome (contribution) if i is not exposed to the treatment (i is not informed) and Y_{i1} be the potential outcome if i is exposed to the treatment (i is informed). The individual treatment effect (ITE) τ_i is simply defined as follows:

$$\text{ITE} = \tau_i = Y_{i1} - Y_{i0} \tag{4.1}$$

The problem is that not all variables in Eq. (4.1) are observable in practical terms, meaning we can never observe situations in which the same individual is, at the same time, exposed and not exposed to the treatment. This is also known as the fundamental problem of causal inference (Holland 1986), as it cannot be solved empirically. Causal inference – both with observational and with experimental data – in practice thus always requires deviating from this analytical ideal of Eq. (4.1) and rests on certain simplifying assumptions for identification. The fundamental problem of causal inference has two possible solutions: a "scientific" solution and a "statistical" solution (Holland 1986, 947). The scientific solution consists of obtaining Y_{i1} by comparing the outcomes of two subsequent events in which the same unit is treated versus not treated, called the individual treatment effect (ITE).

$$\text{ITE} = \tau_i = Y_{i1}^{t1} - Y_{i0}^{t0} \tag{4.2}$$

The scientific solution rests on two invariance assumptions: "temporal stability" and "causal transience." Temporal stability implies that the measurement of the untreated outcome Y_{i0} is time-invariant, that is, it is not affected by when the measurement is taken. Causal transience implies that the measurement process is transient, and it does not alter the untreated outcome Y_{i0}. The scientific solution is more common in the natural sciences because in social sciences, participants typically respond to anything that happens in their environment, and the assumption of causal transience is generally hard to maintain. Nevertheless, panel designs with two or more measurement points are increasingly used in sociological research (Halaby 2004; Allison 2009). Likewise, experiments in which the researchers place the same participants in two conditions (at different times) are relatively common. Experimental designs in which the same subjects experience both (control and treatment) conditions are called within-subjects designs. We further discuss within-subjects designs in Chapter 5.

The statistical solution consists of observing τ_i by comparing equivalent units at the same time. Such an approach is known as a between-subjects design because the treatment does not vary within but between different subjects. It is a statistical solution because τ_i is estimated as the *average treatment effect* (ATE) comparing the mean scores of two groups. Equivalence between the groups is obtained through random assignment of individual units to either the treated or untreated condition.

$$\text{ATE} = E(\tau) = E(Y_{i1}) - E(Y_{j0}) \qquad (4.3)$$

The average treatment effect is the difference between the average "potential outcome" of being exposed to the treatment (informed) and of not being treated (not informed). However, due to the fundamental problem of causal inference, measures of "realized outcomes" of Y_{i1} are only available for those units who are exposed to the treatment (informed) and of Y_{j0} for those units who are not (not informed). Thus, one can try to estimate the causal effect based on this group difference in realized outcomes, but there is an important practical caveat of this approach, namely, "selection": Treated and untreated participants can be different in aspects other than the exposure to the treatment. If this is the case, other "third" variables may confound or bias the outcome. In practice, estimates of the ATE always incorporate some bias. We will come back to this point later.

Now we would like to answer the question of why randomization is important for the counterfactual approach, and for that, let us introduce a second concept: the *average treatment effect on the treated*.

$$ATT = E(\tau_i | T_i = 1) = E(Y_{i1} | T_i = 1) - E(Y_{i0} | T_i = 1) \qquad (4.4)$$

Equations (4.3) and (4.4) need not be the same. $E(Y_{i1}|T_i = 1)$ is the potential outcome from the treatment among the treated and $(Y_{i0}|T_i = 1)$ is the potential outcome that would have been observed in the absence of treatment among those who are treated. Here lies the essence of the counterfactual approach: It tries to approximate the difference between the outcome (cooperation) when a group has been exposed to the treatment (information) and the outcome in that same group when not being exposed to the treatment. However, in most cases, these are two different groups of experimental subjects, and they may differ in characteristics unknown to the researcher.

Why is randomization crucial for the interpretation of the counterfactual model? When treatments are randomly assigned, the group that receives the treatment ($T_i = 1$) has the same "expected" outcome as if the group that does not receive the treatment ($T_i = 0$) were treated:

$$E(Y_{i1}|T_i = 1) = E(Y_{i1}|T_i = 0) \qquad (4.5)$$

Also, when treatments are randomly assigned, the group that does not receive the treatment has the same expected outcome, if untreated, as the group receiving the treatment, if untreated.

$$E(Y_{i0}|T_i = 1) = E(Y_{i0}|T_i = 0) \tag{4.6}$$

It follows from Eqs. (4.2), (4.5), and (4.6) that the average treatment effect in randomized controlled experiments can be estimated as follows:

$$\text{ATE} = E(Y_{i1}|T_i = 1) - E(Y_{i0}|T_i = 0) \tag{4.7}$$

In sum, the two comparison groups are identical "in expectation," and we have no statistical reason to believe that variables other than the treatment (information) is causing the observed difference in outcomes (cooperation) between treated and untreated participants. Random assignment is crucial for the estimation of the average treatment effect because the statistical solution assumes independence. That is, it assumes that the determination of whether units in the groups are assigned to treatment or control is independent of all variables, including the outcome variable Y, as well as all possible unobserved confounding factors (Holland 1986). Accordingly, random assignment ensures that (1) alternative causes are not confounded with a unit's treatment condition, (2) possible threats to internal validity are randomly distributed over conditions, (3) the experimental groups have the same mean score on the dependent variable before treatment, and (4) a valid estimate of the error variance – orthogonal to the treatment – can be computed (Shadish, Cook, & Campbell 2002).

But this is what happens in theory; how does the counterfactual approach work in practice? A simple way to show how a treatment effect is estimated in practice is through a linear regression model (Angrist & Pischke 2009) of the following form:

$$Y_i = \alpha + \beta D_i + X'_i \gamma + v_i \tag{4.8}$$

In this model, $\alpha = E(Y_{i0})$ is the outcome of the untreated group, and the coefficient of the dummy variable $\beta = E(Y_{i1} - Y_{i0})$ is the treatment effect (both ATE and ATT). Crucially, v_i is the bias (or disturbances) introduced by unobserved differences between the treated and untreated groups. In relatively small samples, which are typical in laboratory experiments, treated and untreated groups are likely to differ in some unobserved characteristics. The effect of unobserved characteristics upon which the groups may differ is to add random variance (noise) to the dependent variable, which is assumed not to affect the validity of the experimental inference (Thye 2014). However, in practical terms, the estimation always incorporates some disturbances or biases. This is why most sociological experiments incorporate $X'_i\gamma$, a vector of independent variables, such as sociodemographics, that may help improve the precision of the estimation of the treatment effect. Moreover, not only do these covariates make the estimation more precise, but they also help test auxiliary hypotheses concerning the effect of other independent variables on the experimental outcome or the interaction between these variables and our main treatment manipulation.

4.3 THE LIMITS OF THE COUNTERFACTUAL APPROACH

The beauty and simplicity of the counterfactual approach is that all its terms are approximated, although not necessarily observed, in experimental data with random assignment. We need to simply start from a pool of potential participants, randomly assign half of them to a treatment condition and half to a control condition, and observe the outcome of participants' interactions in, say, a public goods game. Unfortunately, things are not always as simple, and the model incorporates a number of crucial assumptions and interpretations that we need to consider before we can uncritically accept the superiority of randomized experiments in terms of causality.

First, the model assumes no "post-randomization bias"; that is, it assumes no changes in the characteristics of the groups and other potential causes of the outcome after the randomization has been implemented. Again, there is a problem here because there will always be some change (even if it is only the passing of time) between the randomization and the data collection. Still, in a most controlled version of an experiment like in a laboratory, one can imagine situations in which no substantial changes occur between the act of randomly assigning participants to treatments and actual participation and observation in the experiment. However, the post-randomization bias may be especially problematic in field experiments where researchers have less control, and there might be uncontrolled changes between randomization and the conduct of the experiment. Post-randomization bias may be conscious or unconscious. The former refers to situations in which there is cherry-picking or fabrication of the data; the latter refers to situations in which there is a poor implementation of the experiment, for instance, favoring interventions that may confirm the researcher's hypotheses. In either case, the post-randomization bias poses a threat to one of the fundamental assumptions of causal inference: the stable unit treatment value assumption (SUTVA), which states that the potential outcomes do not depend on the assignment mechanism or the subjects' characteristics. The SUTVA thus requires – among other things – that there is "no interference between units (...) leading to different outcomes depending on the treatments other units received" (Rubin 1980, 591). Importantly, social interactions between different subjects can lead to violations of the SUTVA if subjects in different experimental groups influence each other.

A second assumption of this simple model is the absence of "measurement error" introduced by the treatment. This is common to all sorts of methodological approaches. For instance, survey research pays special attention to the error introduced by the wording of the survey questions, the position of the questions in a questionnaire, or the mode of administration of the survey (face-to-face, phone, or online). Similarly, randomized experiments are subject to specific types of measurement error. Following our example on information and cooperation, the mere fact of providing information may cause unexpected changes in participants' perceptions and behaviors. Note that in many experiments, researchers compare a situation (treatment) in which they apply some intervention to a virtually identical situation (control) in which there is no intervention (see Chapter 5 on experimental designs). For instance, Aguiar, Brañas, and Miller (2008) investigated whether altruistic behavior depends on the characteristics of the recipient and found that experimental participants are more altruistic, on average, toward a "deserving" recipient (a poor person) than toward an unknown individual. The question is whether "deservingness" is the only feature that distinguishes a poor person as a recipient from an unknown subject or, more generally, if poverty invokes different perceptions and attitudes from different participants. Therefore, one should be careful about the actual implementation of an experiment and the possible measurement errors.

Finally, perhaps the most important assumption is that the counterfactual approach provides "unbiased" estimates of the treatment effect. However, such unbiased estimates are not necessarily "precise." In Deaton's and Cartwright's (2018, 3) words, "Unbiasedness means being right on average, where the average is taken over an infinite number of repetitions using the same set of subjects in the trial, but with no limits on how far any one estimate is from the truth, while precision means being close to the truth on average; an estimator that is far from the truth in one direction half of the time and equally far from the truth in the other direction half of the time is unbiased, but it is imprecise."

A common solution for the potential lack of precision of a single experimental result is "scientific replication." Replicating a result once and again is the cornerstone of scientific advancement and knowledge accumulation (Freese & Peterson 2017). Replication involves either reproducing the exact experimental settings of the original trial or testing the same knowledge claim using a different experimental mode.

4.4 EXPERIMENTS, CAUSALITY, AND THEORY

Randomized experiments offer a powerful tool to address causal claims, but they might not be enough for, at least, the three issues raised earlier. What else do we need to address causality? The answer to this question is "theory." As Breen (2022, 284) has recently suggested, in sociology, "causal claims derived from observational data, rather than being cleanly and definitively proved, are most likely to be credible if they are established through evidence gathered and analyzed in multiple ways." A thorough understanding of a causal process via experiments is only possible through the lens of an appropriate theory. The goal of experimental research in sociology is often associated with "causation as consequential manipulation," that is, with manipulating one or more "known" causes and establishing the effects of such causes (Rubin 1974; Holland 1986; Goldthorpe 2001). Randomized controlled trials (RCTs) are typically of this nature and have been criticized for the lack of theory (Blossfeld 2017a; Deaton & Cartwright 2018).[6] Although experimental interventions might be theoretically informed, it has been argued that no theoretical assumptions or knowledge of causal mechanisms are needed (Holland 1988). However, in line with Weber's (1978 [1921/22]) description of sociology as a science that aims to understand social action through causal explanations of its course and consequences, we advocate and embrace the concept of "causation as generative process" (Goldthorpe 2001). "The causation as generative process approach has the comparative advantage that it focuses our thoughtful consideration on the theoretical and statistical elaboration of an underlying, generative causal process, existing in time and space, including also actors who make decisions within changing social contexts" (Blossfeld 2017b, 12).

A more detailed description of "causation as generative process" is provided by Goldthorpe (2001) and Blossfeld (2017b). We will summarize here its core argument and relate it to experimental research. Causation as a generative process includes three steps: "(i) establishing the phenomena that form the *explananda*; (ii) hypothesizing generative processes at the level of social action; and (iii) testing the hypothesis" (Goldthorpe 2001, 10). The first step involves exploratory research, where observational data have proven to be very valuable. However, experimental research can also contribute to our knowledge of the *explananda*. The type of experiments that search for empirical regularities (i.e., *explananda*) and investigate phenomena that cannot be explained by existing theories are typically known as empirically driven experiments (Willer & Walker 2007; Jackson & Cox 2013; Gërxhani & Miller 2022). Based on both observational and experimental knowledge of "what is happening" out there[7], an experimentalist

---

[6] See Chapter 5 for a detailed discussion on various design types in experimental sociology based on the relationship between theory and experimental design.

[7] Note, however, that "observation is not a necessary prerequisite. The research issue could be suggested by elaborations of other theories or by purely deductive implications of a formal system" (Webster & Sell 2014b, 13).

can move to the second step of the theoretical rationale for why it is happening. As Elster (2007, 21) put it, "...to cite the cause is not enough: the causal mechanism must also be provided, or at least suggested." In pursuing this step, an experiment would start by proposing an action-based sociological explanation that clearly lays out the generative processes through which the theoretically causal link between the *explanans* and the *explananda* is established. Put differently, this process involves providing mechanism-based explanations, which is the type of causality advocated by rigorous and mechanism-based sociology (Hedström & Swedberg 1998; Hedström & Bearman 2009; Gërxhani, de Graaf, & Raub 2022). The resulting testable hypotheses are then operationalized and tested experimentally. This is known as theory-driven experiments (Willer & Walker 2007; Jackson & Cox 2013; Gërxhani & Miller 2022). See Chapter 5 for a more detailed discussion of this distinction between theory-driven and empirically driven experiments.

Think, for instance, of a situation where you are experiencing some form of offense in your neighborhood, you disapprove of it and want it to go away, but you rather wait for others to intervene. This is known as the volunteer's dilemma (Diekmann 1985), where a collective good (a trustworthy and calm neighborhood) is desirable to all (members of the community), but because volunteering to contribute is costly (one risks being scolded or even beaten up), one prefers others to volunteer (bring an end to it and show the neighborhood's high community spirit). For experimental research based on "causation as generative process," first empirical knowledge on this phenomenon happening regularly is needed. When this *explanandum* is established, an experimentalist can turn to, for instance, bounded rational choice theory to specify the reasons why individuals act in the way they do, to make explicit the assumptions on the micro and macro conditions under which the action holds, and to formulate testable hypotheses. This is precisely what Diekmann and his colleagues have done by using game theoretical models to provide causal explanations of the volunteer's dilemma and by testing their theoretically formulated hypotheses via laboratory experiments (Diekmann 1985; Diekmann & Przepiorka 2016).

Experiments focusing on "causation as generative process" provide a feedback loop from empirics to theory and back. Without previously accumulated knowledge on the matter, a single experiment may offer a very imprecise estimation of a causal effect, as Deaton and Cartwright (2018) argued. Theories are needed to draw mechanism-based explanations of the causes of effects and derive hypotheses that can be tested using new experimental data. This theoretical basis ensures that the experimental conclusions are internally valid (Loewenstein 1999), and by way of examining the underlying mechanisms, it also increases their generalizability beyond the original experimental setup (Gerring 2001). Theory typically establishes the scope conditions of an experiment and serves as a benchmark to compare the experimental results with. Every new piece of evidence is contrasted against the theory, which is modified accordingly. Ultimately, causality is not a technical matter but a matter of credibility in the explanatory power of sociological theory. Theory construction, theory testing and refining through complementary research designs (Jackson & Cox 2013; Barrera Busken & Raub 2015; Baldassarri & Abascal 2017; Gërxhani & Miller 2022), and theory-guided meta-analyses[8] all contribute to increase the credibility of a causal sociological claim.

---

[8] Theory-guided meta-analysis uses data from previous experiments to study whether methods, populations, and experimental settings affect findings.

5 Experimental Designs and Typologies

5.1 THEORY AND EXPERIMENTAL DESIGN

The discussion of the relationship between theory and experiments introduced in the previous chapter is common across social sciences. Several handbooks distinguish between deductive experiments designed to test theories and inductive experiments based on intuitions, often leading to the discovery of new phenomena (e.g., Morton & Williams 2010). In experimental economics, where experimentation is traditionally linked to formal modeling, Niederle (2015) described "treatment-driven" experiments, that is, experiments in which the main hypothesis is *not* grounded in a formal model. In the preceding chapter of this volume, we introduced causality, distinguishing between experiments that test hypotheses derived from theoretical models and experiments that aim at establishing empirical regularities.

Arguing that empirically driven experiments are essentially tools for discovering new phenomena, Willer and Walker (2007) suggest that theory plays no role in the design of such experiments. Probably related to this argument, experimental sociology is criticized for a lack of theoretical foundations (Blossfeld 2017a). However, besides the fact that it is open to discussion whether such empirically driven experiments do not, in fact, rely on some basic theoretical reasoning, many experimental sociologists share a view of sociology as a theory-guided discipline where theories consist of explicit assumptions and testable implications carefully derived from those assumptions (Gërxhani, de Graaf, & Raub 2022). Depending on the relationship between theory and experimental design, experimental sociology comprises a wide variety of design types. We propose to examine this variation, not as a dichotomy, but – as shown in Figure 5.1 – as a continuum composed of abstract types that lie at the two extremes of the continuum.

At the deductive end of the continuum, we find experiments based on formal models that provide point predictions on the actors' behavior or at

Experimental Designs and Typologies

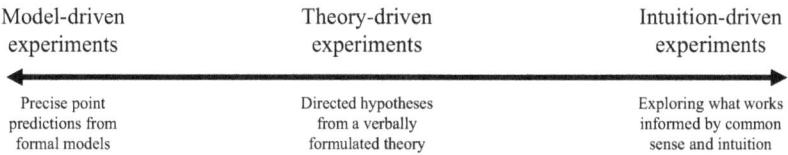

Figure 5.1 The role of theory in experimental sociology.

the aggregate level. Such model-driven experiments are a special case of theory-driven experiments since they rely on a formalized theory. Proposing a similar classification for experiments in economics, Roth (1995) referred to this category as "speaking to theorists" experiments. Sociological examples of this type include experiments on network exchange theory (Willer 1999; Corra & Willer 2002) as well as tests of game-theoretical models. With this type of theoretical model in mind, Willer and Walker (2007) argued that the design of a theory-driven experiment consists of building a replica of the model and then comparing the behavior of the experimental subjects directly with the model's predictions. This definition seems to imply that in an ideal type of model-driven experiment, manipulation may even become superfluous. In fact, if a model gives point predictions for behavior in a given interaction, thereby providing a clear benchmark against which actual behavior can be compared, behavioral data gathered in one condition mirroring the model assumptions could directly support or reject the model's predictions. Although designs of laboratory experiments without manipulation are actually very rare and most experimenters in the social sciences would not even consider them "true experiments," in some instances, a single condition may, in principle, suffice to provide a rigorous test of a formal model.

Foundational experiments in behavioral game theory can serve to illustrate this point. Simple two-player games – such as prisoner's dilemma, trust or investment game, dictator game, and ultimatum game – typically have a clear predicted outcome under the standard assumptions of a rational choice model. Many experiments, especially in the early days of behavioral game theory, collected systematic evidence of cooperative behavior in settings where the models predicted otherwise. For example, in Berg, Dickhaut, and McCabe (1995), the experiment had two conditions. However, the hypotheses were not about differences between the conditions: The first condition was a replica of the investment game model, while the second condition was a replication of the first condition. In the second condition, the researchers provided participants with additional information concerning the results of the first condition to see whether the additional information may push behavior toward the theoretical prediction of the standard model. It is precisely by observing behavioral deviations from standard models' predictions over many such model-driven experiments that the scientific community gained much knowledge and understanding of human rationality, social preferences, and cognitive biases in decision-making. One prominent example of a simple model-driven design without treatment manipulation can be found in Henrich et al. (2004) series of cross-cultural investigations. Henrich and colleagues used simple games to investigate cultural variations in altruism and cooperative behavior. As culture was the independent variable in these studies, every experiment consisted of a single condition without any manipulation. Henrich and colleagues measured human behavior and compared it across sites in terms of the magnitude of behavioral deviations from the normative predictions of the theoretical model underlying each of the games.

More commonly, formal theoretical models provide predictions that depend on critical thresholds of some parameters of the model. For example, Przepiorka and Diekmann (2013) discuss a model of a trust game in which the trustor's decision to place trust depends crucially on the probability to meet a "long-term" trustee, that is, a trustee who expects long-term repeated interactions (rather than a trustee who expects one-shot interactions). In such cases, the model guides the design of the experiment defining conditions under which different predictions hold. In their experiment, Przepiorka and Diekmann (2013) compared a condition in which the probability of meeting a long-term trustee was low (well below the threshold) with a condition in which that probability was high (well above the threshold) and tested the hypothesis that trustors place more often trust in the latter than in the former condition. Thus, even when formal models allow for point predictions, experiments test hypotheses concerning the "direction" of effects of the experimental manipulations in terms of comparative statics (see Buskens & Raub 2013 for a similar discussion and other examples). In a similar fashion, it is also possible to design a single experiment testing hypotheses derived from theoretical models based on different assumptions. For example, Barrera and Buskens (2007) designed an experiment in which participants played a repeated trust game and manipulated the exchange of information among the trustors. The experiment allowed testing for the effects of learning and control behavior. Learning effects are related to the trustor's information on the past behavior of the trustee. Control effects are related to the trustor's opportunities for sanctioning a trustee in future interactions. The hypotheses on learning and control are based, respectively, on backward-looking and forward-looking models of strategic behavior (Buskens & Raub 2002).

Similarly, experiments can be designed to test the implications or assumptions of agent-based models. Agent-based models are theoretical tools used to study interaction models, especially when the interaction is too complex to be analyzed using mathematical equations only. Then, the researcher builds a replica of the interaction model into a simulation program and analyzes the simulation results to derive testable hypotheses that follow from the assumptions upon which the model was specified. For example, Willer, Kuwabara, and Macy (2009) designed a series of experiments testing hypotheses related to the "false enforcement" of unpopular norms. The mechanism of false enforcement indicates compliance to a norm based on the false premise that others uphold the norm. In their experiment, Willer and colleagues (2009) empirically tested the implications of an agent-based simulation model designed to account for the mechanism of false enforcement (Centola, Willer, & Macy 2005).

In model-driven experiments, indeed, the experiment provides a replica of a formal model (here, including both mathematically formalized models and agent-based simulation models) because, generally, both the theory and the design of the experiment are built upon one classical model of interaction. Over time, specialists from various fields conducted a large number of studies using a set of common interaction models. Guala (2006, 659) termed such interaction models "prototypes," which have been widely used for many years in experimental research. For some of these models of interactions, cumulative evidence of studies using variations of the same experimental designs allowed for extensive reviews and meta-analyses (Spadaro et al. 2022b). In social psychology, models of strategic interactions inspired by game theory, whereby the strategy that maximizes the individual payoff leads to a collectively deficient outcome, are generally called "social dilemmas" (e.g., van Lange et al. 2013). Other popular game-theoretical models of interactions that do not concern social dilemmas include the dictator game, ultimatum game, and third-party punishment game.

At the inductive end of the continuum, we find empirically driven experiments based on controlled manipulation that are not testing implications of explicitly formulated theoretical models but are informed by intuition and common sense. Roth (1995) referred to this type of experiments as "searching for facts." Yet, we would not say that sociological experiments of this type do not test theory, as argued by Willer and Walker (2007, 31), since they usually involve some kind of implicit theoretical argument. "Pure" intuition-driven experiments aiming at the discovery and exploration of new phenomena have played an important role in major breakthroughs in science but are more common in other disciplines, such as economic psychology and market research, than in experimental sociology. For example, Kahneman (2011) described many brilliant experiments that typically originate from a simple intuition and indeed often result in the discovery of new phenomena, such as the "endowment effect," that is, the tendency for people to attach a higher value to an object when they own it compared to the same object when they do not own it.

However, sociology's main interest arguably lies in the explanation of macro-level phenomena and macro-level outcomes, often through theoretical accounts that include explicit assumptions concerning the behavior of individual actors. Experiments in sociology test assumptions on micro-level regularities of behavior that produce those macro-level phenomena and are hard to observe or control in settings outside a laboratory (Gërxhani, de Graaf, & Raub 2022). Accordingly, most sociological experiments that use controlled manipulation typically test implications of verbally formulated assumptions that are consistent with a theory of action and apt to produce testable predictions in the context of the experiment. These are the theory-driven experiments, as indicated in Figure 5.1. For example, Keizer, Lindenberg, and Steg (2008) and Keuschnigg and Wolbring (2015b) tested the theoretical proposition from the influential "broken windows theory" (Wilson & Kelling 1982) that signs of disorder such as garbage on the ground and illegal graffiti on the wall lead to further violations of the same and different norms. In their concealed field experiments, they found evidence that signs of disorder indeed trigger deviant behavior such as littering, jaywalking, and stealing (for details, see Chapter 7).

Sociological experiments like these are informed by verbally formulated theories that allow testing hypotheses about the "direction" of effects but do not make predictions about exact effect sizes or critical thresholds. Experiments guided by verbally formulated theories are located in between the two extremes of model-driven and intuition-driven experiments. In the design of such a theory-driven experiment, the researcher chooses the key explanatory factor that differentiates the experimental conditions with the explicit aim of (i) testing one of the assumptions upon which the theory of action holds or (ii) testing one of the implications derived from the theory of action or logically consistent with it. The distinction introduced in this section serves as an analytical tool to link experimental design and theory. As argued here, model-driven and intuition-driven experiments should be seen as analytical categories of a continuum along which experiments can be classified.

5.2 FEATURES OF EXPERIMENTAL DESIGNS

In the previous chapter on causality, we introduced the fundamental problem of causal inference, that is, the impossibility of creating a situation in which the same individual is, at the same time, exposed and not exposed to the experimental treatment. Then, we presented two solutions by which the fundamental problem of causal inference can be addressed using a

Experimental Designs and Typologies

counterfactual approach: (i) comparing two experimental conditions – with and without experimental manipulation – implemented on groups of different individuals at the same time; or (ii) comparing the same individuals in two experimental conditions but in different times. In the former, the experimental effects are estimated "between subjects"; in the latter, the experimental effects are estimated "within subjects."

The most typical between-subjects experimental design is a design with one treatment and one control group (Campbell & Stanley 1966; Shadish, Cook, & Campbell 2002):

$$R \rightarrow T_1 \rightarrow Y_1$$
$$R \rightarrow \rightarrow Y_0$$

where R indicates that subjects are randomly assigned to either the treatment (T_1) or the control condition (absence of T_1). Thus, in principle, the control condition corresponds to a situation in which nothing happens. For example, some laboratory experiments provide additional information about interaction partners (e.g., their gender or ethnicity) as a treatment while withholding this information in the control condition. Similarly, it is common in field experiments to manipulate some features of the original setting in the treatment condition while not interfering with the field in the control condition.

However, in other instances, relying on a control condition in which nothing happens is not recommended. For example, by not receiving a treatment, subjects can become aware of the assigned condition, which, in turn, might affect their behavior. Hence, similar to receiving a placebo in medicine, subjects in the control condition of a sociological lab experiment often perform a task similar to the treatment condition except for a crucial difference, that is, the actual treatment variable. Such a randomized design, comparing two treatments, can be represented as follows:

$$R \rightarrow T_1 \rightarrow Y_1$$
$$R \rightarrow T_0 \rightarrow Y_0$$

For example, the actual treatment of interest T_1 can be some kind of task. When the control condition does not require a task matching the treatment condition, researchers sometimes use a filler task, that is, an irrelevant task that is only intended to fill time and conceal the assignment to the control condition, while subjects in the treatment condition perform the treatment task. Often, in model-driven experiments that are based on a standard model of interaction, the control condition corresponds to a standard version of the game or interaction model. Then, the control condition is sometimes called the "baseline" condition and the treatment condition is a version of the same interaction model in which the researcher modifies one of the key features or adds a new feature to the standard model. The simple example illustrated earlier has only two conditions. The same design can be applied with more than two conditions, for example, when the factor manipulated has more than two possible states. In this basic randomized design, the treatment effect is generally estimated by comparing group means, following Eq. (4.3) (in Chapter 4).

Social psychologists highly recommend using the basic randomized design with pretest, whenever possible (Shadish, Cook, & Campbell. 2002, 261). The pretest measurement can occur before or – more commonly – after random assignment:

$$R \rightarrow Y_1^{t0} \rightarrow T_1 \rightarrow Y_1^{t1}$$
$$R \rightarrow Y_0^{t0} \rightarrow T_0 \rightarrow Y_0^{t1}$$

If randomization worked, the mean pretest measurement should be equal in the two conditions, that is, Y_0^{t0} should be equal to Y_1^{t0}. Thus, using a pretest allows evaluating the independence assumption by checking the balance of the distribution of covariates and outcome measures across groups before the treatment (randomization test). This is particularly helpful in settings with limited control over the assignment mechanism and subjects' compliance with it. For example, pretest measurements are common in field studies evaluating the efficacy of policy interventions, especially in research on education when random assignment of subjects to conditions is not possible or when randomization takes place at the group level (Bloom, Bos, & Lee 1999). In addition, using pretests allows for statistical analyses that increase the statistical power to reject the null hypothesis (Maxwell & Delaney 1990) because the treatment effect can be measured by comparing the means of the within-subjects change scores across conditions, as in Eq. (9).

$$ATE = E(\tau) = E(Y_1^{t1} - Y_1^{t0}) - E(Y_0^{t1} - Y_0^{t0}) \tag{9}$$

Using pretest measurement is problematic when the pretest is likely to influence the posttest measurement producing sensitization effects or when it can increase the risk of selective dropout (e.g., in field and online experiments). Both situations can occur in sociological experiments, which is why researchers should carefully consider the pros and cons of pretesting (see Chapter 11 on incentives).

A similar line of reasoning applies to within-subjects designs. As argued earlier, pure within-subjects designs without a control group apply the scientific solution to the fundamental problem of causal inference (Holland 1986). Thus, a pure within-subjects design can consist of a single condition in which the subjects experience sequentially both the presence and absence of the experimental manipulation. A version of this design was relatively common in the behaviorist tradition, where it was also known as ABA design (Meeker & Leik 2007). In the ABA design, participants started in the control condition where the experimental manipulation was absent. Then the manipulation was introduced in the second stage and removed again in the third stage.

$$X_0^{t0} \rightarrow Y_0^{t0} \rightarrow T_1^{t1} \rightarrow Y_1^{t1} \rightarrow T_0^{t2} \rightarrow Y_0^{t2}$$

In sociology, pure within-subjects designs are hardly ever possible because the assumption of causal transience is generally difficult to maintain. The measurement of the dependent variable in the control condition at time t_0 is likely to influence subsequent measurements of the same variable after subjects have experienced the experimental manipulation, thereby producing "carryover effects."[1] In addition, the sequence in which participants experience variations in the experimental environment also matters and can produce "order effects." Carryover effects refer to effects produced by a measurement procedure on subsequent measurements of the same variable. Order effects imply that the measurement produced on subjects experiencing first T_0 then T_1 differs from the measurement obtained when subjects experience first T_1 then T_0. Within-subjects designs are used in sociology only when it is plausible to expect no carryover effects and when a procedure that allows controlling for order effects is considered. The procedure used to control for order effects is called "counterbalancing." A counterbalanced (within-subjects) design is as follows:

$$R \rightarrow T_0^{t0} \rightarrow Y_0^{t0} \rightarrow T_1^{t1} \rightarrow Y_1^{t1}$$
$$R \rightarrow T_1^{t0} \rightarrow Y_1^{t0} \rightarrow T_0^{t1} \rightarrow Y_0^{t1}$$

In a counterbalanced design, the sample is divided into two groups differing with respect to the order in which participants experience the experimental manipulation; participants are randomly assigned to one of the two groups. For example, Fehr and Gächter (2002) applied such a design in their highly cited study on altruistic punishment. In one condition, subjects played a regular public goods game over six rounds (T_0^{t0}), and then they played another sequence of six rounds in which they had the

---

[1] Carryover effects generally indicate measurement biases that can occur in within-subjects designs when one treatment produces persistent effects that carry over to the subsequent treatment(s) (Charness, Gneezy, & Kuhn 2012). Other mechanisms, which may produce similar biases in within-subjects designs, as well as in experiments using repeated measures, include fatigue, sensitization, and practice. In classical methodological texts, all these biases are labeled context effects (Greenwald 1976).

opportunity to sanction other participants for lack of cooperation (T_1^{t1}). In the other condition, the basic setup was identical, except for the order of T_0^{t0} and T_1^{t1}, which was reversed. The results revealed remarkably similar patterns in both conditions, more specifically low and declining cooperation rates in the rounds without punishment and much higher cooperation rates increasing over time in the rounds with punishment.

When an experiment requires manipulation of two or more independent variables, the researcher uses a full factorial design. An experiment with two factors and with two levels each produces a full factorial design with $2 \times 2 = 4$ experimental conditions:

$R \rightarrow T_0 Z_0 \rightarrow Y_{00}$
$R \rightarrow T_1 Z_0 \rightarrow Y_{10}$
$R \rightarrow T_0 Z_1 \rightarrow Y_{01}$
$R \rightarrow T_1 Z_1 \rightarrow Y_{11}$

For example, Vogt et al. (2016) used movies as treatments in field experiments in Sudan to change cultural attitudes toward female genital cutting – a still widespread practice in this area with severe negative consequences in affected females. Guided by theoretical considerations and empirical evidence on major obstacles in overcoming this dysfunctional practice, Vogt et al. varied two factors with two levels each in a full factorial design. They did so by adding subplots to the main plot in a movie describing a family in rural Sudan. The first subplot (factor T_1) addressed concerns "related to health, purity, and perceived religious obligations," while the second subplot (factor Z_1) focused on parents' beliefs that abstaining from cutting has detrimental effects on "the future marriage prospects of their daughter" (Vogt et al. 2016, 506). In one experiment, the researchers combined the full factorial approach with a pretest–posttest measurement collecting additional baseline measures of attitudes toward female cutting. As compared to the control condition, which consisted of a movie with the main plot only ($T_0 Z_0$), the combined treatment ($T_1 Z_1$) significantly improved attitudes towards uncut girls.

The scheme for the full factorial design applies to the simplest case of two factors with two levels each, but the same logic and the same notation could be applied to experiments with more than two factors and factors with more than two levels. If we add a third factor with two levels, we have a $2 \times 2 \times 2$ factorial design with eight conditions. If the third factor had three levels, we would have a $2 \times 2 \times 3$ factorial design with 12 conditions. Factorial designs have three advantages: first, holding statistical power constant, they require smaller sample sizes compared to running two separate studies with a basic randomized design. Second, they allow observing the cumulative effect of the two factors manipulated. Third, they allow for statistical tests of possible interaction effects between the factors (Shadish, Cook, & Campbell. 2002).

Factorial designs can also be applied to experiments that use a mix of between- and within-subjects manipulations. Here, we illustrate an example of a 2 × 2 counterbalanced factorial design where one factor (T) is manipulated between subjects and the other (Z) within subjects. When order effects can be excluded, such an experiment would require only two conditions without counterbalancing (first and third rows, or second and fourth rows, below). If order effects are plausible, it is necessary to have designs with all four possible combinations for counterbalancing.

$$
\begin{array}{ccccccccc}
R & \to & T_0 Z_0^{t0} & \to & Y_{00}^{t0} & \to & T_0 Z_1^{t1} & \to & Y_{01}^{t1} \\
R & \to & T_0 Z_1^{t0} & \to & Y_{01}^{t0} & \to & T_0 Z_0^{t1} & \to & Y_{00}^{t1} \\
R & \to & T_1 Z_0^{t0} & \to & Y_{10}^{t0} & \to & T_1 Z_1^{t1} & \to & Y_{11}^{t1} \\
R & \to & T_1 Z_1^{t0} & \to & Y_{11}^{t0} & \to & T_1 Z_0^{t1} & \to & Y_{10}^{t1} \\
\end{array}
$$

For instance, Przepiorka and Diekmann (2013) used such a counterbalanced factorial design to examine the effects of temporal embeddedness and signals of trustworthiness on levels of trust in laboratory experiments in the United Kingdom, Russia, and Switzerland. Temporal embeddedness – operationalized as the likelihood of short-term (T_0) versus long-term interactions (T_1) between the trustor and the trustee – was manipulated between subjects, while signaling opportunities – in the form of giving up a part of the endowment to send a card to the trustor – were part of the within-subjects design and were provided ($Z_0^{t0}; Z_1^{t1}$) or removed over time ($Z_1^{t0}; Z_0^{t1}$). Consistent across all three countries and in line with theory, temporal embeddedness increased trust levels in the trust game. However, introducing a signaling opportunity, surprisingly, did not increase overall levels of trust and sometimes had even adverse effects.

5.3 PRACTICAL LIMITS TO RANDOMIZATION

By randomly assigning subjects to treatments, experimentalists ensure that statistical measures which summarize traits of treatment groups, such as the mean or the variance, are identical in expectation. Randomness here means that every participating subject has the same chance to be assigned to any treatment. It does not imply that these subjects are representative of some population and that the results can be generalized to that population, which is less relevant for the internal validity of experiments that test general theories (see Chapter 9).

If the number of subjects per treatment is sufficiently large, experimentalists invoke the central limit theorem to statistically compare treatment outcomes. The number of observations required for a valid test of treatment effects depends on the type of variable that is considered and the type of test required for that variable. For example, for binomial tests of binary variables and homogeneous units of analysis, which are independently and identically distributed (iid), it can be shown that summary statistics converge sufficiently to put trust in the comparison of treatment effects when about 25–30 units are observed per treatment. The problem, however, is that we have argued in the introduction of this book that the iid condition may be difficult to invoke for the analysis of human behavior. Given the many dimensions along which humans may differ, even complete randomization across treatments may not provide a balance for every relevant human characteristic for the traditional number of observations. Hence, from a statistical point of view, sociological experimentalists may need considerably larger numbers of subjects per treatment than this rule of thumb. It is, therefore, rapidly becoming good practice to use power analysis to explore the statistical properties of treatment comparisons. To conduct a power analysis, the researcher needs to specify (1) the statistical test that will be used in the analyses, (2) the level of confidence required to reject the null hypothesis (type I error, conventionally $p < 0.05$), (3) the minimum effect size that the statistical test should be able to detect, and (4) the required statistical power, that is, the level of confidence required for the risk of type II error.[2] Using this information, power analysis determines the sample size needed for statistical inference at a given level of confidence (for details, see Cohen 1988; Barker Bausell & Li 2002).

Further complexity is introduced by the fact that multiple experimental sessions are typically administered at different points in time for the simple reason that laboratories for social scientific experiments are limited in size. The term *session* is generally used to indicate the experimental unit consisting of a group of experimental subjects who participated in one experiment at the same time in the same place. A popular size for a laboratory is 24 seats because this number can be divided in many ways, thus offering various opportunities to run several treatments or multiple groups during the same session. But given that external factors, such as natural phenomena, societal developments, or political events, may potentially influence behavior in the

---

[2] Type I error occurs when the researcher concludes that there is a statistically significant treatment effect when there is no such effect in the population. Conversely, type II error consists of incorrectly concluding that there is no effect, when in fact an effect is present in the population. A sample size that is too small does not typically lead to type I error. Instead, a low sample size increases the likelihood of type II error.

laboratory, the data must be considered as consisting of a multilevel structure with individuals clustered in sessions.

In sociological experiments, which are often interested in group-level effects of treatment conditions, the number of individuals per treatment is not the only relevant parameter for the central limit theorem to hold. Groups develop dynamics of their own, which critically depend on a group's composition of individuals. Hence, on top of individuals, the group becomes a unit of observation of its own. As a consequence, the data have an even more complex multilevel structure, consisting of individuals in groups, which, in turn, are situated in laboratory sessions. As a result of random allocations of individuals to treatments, one could argue that, in expectation, groups are randomly formed well. But small groups may vary considerably in the composition of individuals, and to the extent that composition matters, outcomes may also exhibit large variation. Hence, the actually observed summary statistic of a specific group may be far off the expected value. This heterogeneity in the group composition comes on top of the heterogeneity of the individuals in the group. Therefore, though differences between groups may seem to be the same as differences between individuals, there is good reason to believe that group heterogeneity is larger. In order to rely on the group-internal summary statistics for comparisons across groups, one would thus need to generate conditions for the central limit theorem to hold at the group level, which is, given the random allocation of individuals to treatments and groups, simply a sufficiently large number of groups and sessions.

Hence, one would expect groups to be subject to potential biases from insufficient randomization. However, in practice, constellations of individual characteristics are not uniformly distributed, and just a handful of trait combinations are empirically relevant. Nevertheless, this formal exercise shows that some caution is in order, and care must be taken to elaborate the theoretical argument in sufficient detail to decide which aspects of personality are relevant. Another example is social values (Messick & McClintock 1968). While in theory, social values may take on any angle on a circle defined by positive and negative attitudes to self and others (Murphy, Ackermann, & Handgraaf 2011), only a small range between competitive and prosocial orientations is actually empirically relevant. Thus, unless the group composition is the focus of interest, the random allocation of subjects to treatments may generate sufficient randomness in the group composition to attribute average group differences to the treatment.

The statistical standards presented here are extremely high. In practice, experimental research in the social sciences hardly ever reaches these standards. One important exogenous limit is posed by the size of the pool of available experimental subjects. Generally, all experimental labs maintain a *subject pool*, the "population" from which subjects are drawn to be invited to a particular session. Such pools typically consist of students periodically recruited from the population of students enrolled at the university where the lab is located. The funding available for experiments poses additional limits to the statistical demands. Experimentalists must be aware that their designs often do not meet the statistical criteria underlying their inferences from data analysis, and the issue remains a potential concern for robustness checks. Importantly, however, replication of experimental results is becoming increasingly compelling. It has always been the case that important results are replicated as part of a project that extends previous research (e.g., replicating a result to serve as a benchmark), but the need for exact replication is now widely recognized (Camerer et al. 2016; Auspurg & Brüderl 2022). It is through replication that experimental results become recognized as "established." As part of this process, it is important that both replications – those that support and those that contradict a previous finding – are published. This includes statistically insignificant and null results because each replication adds to the number of observations on which a theory has been tested.

5.4 EXPERIMENTS IN DIFFERENT SETTINGS

In this chapter, we have explained the role of theoretical considerations in guiding the design of experiments and have introduced some common experimental techniques, such as within- and between-subjects designs and counterbalancing. These techniques can be leveraged for running experiments in different settings. The most common types of experiments in different settings are laboratory, field, factorial survey, and natural experiments. In this section, we shortly introduce each of them and give a first impression of the strengths and weaknesses of each approach. In the second part of this volume, we will then introduce principles of experimentation for each type of experiment in more detail and will elaborate on practical aspects of planning and conducting these types of experiments.

"Laboratory experiments" are maybe the best-known type of experiment (Falk & Heckman 2009; Webster & Sell 2014a). Laboratory experiments contain the three design elements common to all experiments – manipulation, group comparison, and randomization – and take place in the rather artificial, anonymous, and controlled setting of a laboratory. A laboratory is a research environment that is purposefully designed for conducting experiments while controlling for external nuisances (confounders). The laboratory environment thus provides not only the advantage of good replicability but gives researchers strict control over the setting, treatment manipulation, and measurement of independent and dependent variables. Because of this high degree of replicability and control, the laboratory is the prototypical location for conducting experiments and is thus especially well-suited for testing theoretical mechanisms. While optimal for causal inference in theory, many social scientists are skeptical about the possibility to generalize results generated in a laboratory experiment to real-world situations (external validity). This critique especially concerns the artificiality of the laboratory setting and the standard approach of sampling students generally from Western countries for testing general theories about human behavior (Henrich, Heine, & Norenzayan 2010).

A second important group of experiments are "field experiments" (see Harrison & List 2004; Gerber & Green 2012; Baldassari & Abascal 2017). Field experiments are staged in a "natural" research setting where individuals usually interact in everyday life and regularly complete the task under investigation. The implementation in the field is the core feature distinguishing the approach from experiments in other settings. It is also one of the main reasons why researchers use field experiments: They allow incorporating social context, investigating subjects under "natural" conditions, and collecting unobtrusive measures of behavior. When conducting a concealed field experiment, subjects may not realize that they are part of an experiment, which substantially reduces one major threat to internal validity: reactivity. However, these advantages of field experiments come at the price of reduced field control (Shadish, Cook, & Campbell. 2002; Teele 2014). In contrast to the controlled setting of the laboratory, in the field, many factors that are not under the control of the experimenter and are often hard to measure can influence the outcome. Deviations from random assignment, spillover effects, treatment refusal, and attrition of subjects are more likely to occur due to the lack of field control (see Chapter 7 for more details). Moreover, ethical, political, and practical restrictions (e.g., a lack of field access, concerns about the treatment, or its randomization) can cause severe challenges for the actual implementation in the field. Irrespective of these limitations and challenges, field experiments often allow for rigorous causal inference due to the implementation of an experimental design in a natural setting.

A third type of experiments are "multifactorial survey experiments" such as vignette studies, choice experiments, and conjoint analysis (Mutz 2011; Auspurg & Hinz 2015b; Liebe & Meyerhoff 2021). In survey experiments, respondents are confronted with hypothetical situations or choices and are asked, usually in a between-subject design, to rate different scenarios or to choose between different alternatives. Each scenario or alternative contains one or several factors that systematically vary across the study and is randomly assigned to survey participants. Multifactorial survey experiments thus combine the methodological rigor of an experimental design with the advantages of survey research. Compared to laboratory experiments, in multifactorial survey experiments, it is much easier and cheaper to collect large-scale data necessary for complex factorial designs with many treatments. Including an experimental module in the survey also allows researchers to conduct population-based survey experiments, promising broader generalizability than selective subject pools. Since treatment manipulation happens just for hypothetical scenarios, the infeasibility of randomized trials in the laboratory and in the field due to ethical concerns, practical restrictions, and lacking manipulability of the treatment of interest is usually no issue in factorial survey experiments. The approach can thus even offer insights into hypothetical worlds and can inform policy about potential interventions currently discussed in the public discourse without taking the risk and covering the costs of actual implementation in the field. At the same time, the multifactorial survey experiments' reliance on self-reported attitudes and intended choices has its caveats. Social desirability and reactivity might be at work in treatments that are too obvious. Furthermore, it remains unclear to what degree self-reported behavioral intentions in a hypothetical situation correspond with real-world behavior.

Finally, instead of actively manipulating a treatment, researchers can also rely on some naturally occurring variation to get some traction on the causal effect of a treatment in so-called natural experiments (Dunning 2012). Sources of exogenous variation can be some quasi-randomly distributed effects of natural events (such as the devastating but hard-to-predict route of a hurricane) or of human decision-making (such as the conquest of territories or a terrorist attack). While natural experiments are actually no real experiments since the researcher neither has control over the manipulation of the treatment nor its assignment, the methodological foundations of natural experiments with the assumption of an as-if random assignment of the treatment are closely related to experiments with active intervention and randomization. At the same time, the assumption of as-if random assignment is one of the most critical points of natural experiments. Although techniques exist to foster the plausibility of this core assumption (e.g., by increasing the comparability of subjects in the treatment and in the control group), one can only indirectly check its validity using statistical tests and qualitative evidence. However, identification still rests on a rather strong assumption that cannot be proven and thus becomes a question of credibility. Furthermore, while natural experiments are a great way to examine causal effects, their potential to test sociological theories is limited due to the lack of active intervention from the researcher. This certainly does not mean that natural experiments cannot contribute to building and testing theories, but it is a matter of chance to have the right natural experiment at hand to examine a certain theoretical mechanism. By contrast, laboratory, field, and factorial survey experiments provide more direct and rigorous ways to advance sociological theorizing by establishing a setup that closely fits the scope conditions of a theory and varying one factor at a time in a controlled and systematic manner.

PART II

The Practice of Experimentation in Sociology

6 Laboratory Experiments

6.1 INTRODUCTION

Laboratory experiments are the closest approximation in social sciences to the imagination of experimental work among lay people. These experiments typically take place in a room equipped with computerized workspaces that are carefully separated in order to prevent participants from observing what happens on others' computer screens and communicating outside of the channels provided in the experimental design.[1] Some laboratories use closed cubicles to ensure these conditions.

This setting allows researchers to consider subjects as "atomistic" decision-makers in the sense of not being directly influenced by others in their decisions.[2] From this starting point, the experimenter can build social situations by matching subjects into pairs or groups and generating communication channels or spaces that operationalize the social structure to be examined. In this way, interactions between subjects are shielded from outside influences, ensuring that the assumptions underlying the theory to be tested are met, apart from any predisposition and condition that participants bring into the laboratory (for more details, see Chapter 11). Most importantly, it can reasonably be assumed that no uncontrolled exogenous factors interfere with participants' behavior during the laboratory session. This is why laboratory experiments are considered the type of experiment that provides the highest degree of control, which, in turn, makes them particularly valuable in testing and appraising sociological theories. "When the purpose

---

[1] Laboratory experiments can also take place in a noncomputerized room where participants are asked to make their decisions manually, also known as "the paper and pencil" approach. This approach can be useful when the experiment needs to be conducted in different locations where computer facilities are not easy to arrange. For an example, see Gërxhani and Schram (2006).

[2] Note that it is impossible, even in a laboratory experiment, to isolate individuals from society in a strict sense because participants cannot separate themselves from their experiences, attitudes, and values.

of an empirical study is to test theories, the possibility that laboratory experiments offer to isolate the causal processes deemed important by the theory from those deemed irrelevant is crucial" (Gërxhani & Miller 2022, 314).

A laboratory experiment is an artificially built social situation in which participants are well aware that they are involved in an experiment since they have voluntarily registered to this experiment and, in many cases, to the subject pool of the experimental laboratory. Subjects receive written instructions in which the situation, the upcoming process, and the decisions to be made are described. Next to the issue of nonrepresentativeness of a country's population (see Chapter 10), this artificiality may be experienced by some as a special situation unrelated to natural settings, a feature that has given rise to much hesitation among the larger population of social scientists to accept laboratory experimental findings as relevant. Yet, artificiality introduces the unique advantage of tailoring the interaction form exactly to the conditions that are needed to test a theory (Schram 2006). This capacity makes laboratory experiments specifically attractive to test rigorous theoretical models (Zelditch 2014b; Gërxhani, de Graaf & Raub 2022). In the next section, we describe a leading example to illustrate when laboratory experiments are used as well as their strengths and weaknesses.

6.2 LEADING EXAMPLE: LABORATORY EXPERIMENTS ON THE VOLUNTEER'S DILEMMA

One of the most fundamental questions of sociology is the emergence of social norms. Norms are social in the sense of being external to the individual, who is confronted with their existence as a "social fact" (Durkheim 1982 [1895]). However, they are also rooted in the individual because they can only exist through individual behavior. Individuals form expectations about each other's behavior by referring to a relevant social norm, and they reinstate a social norm by sanctioning each other's nonconformity to the norm.[3] Social norms are difficult to observe in everyday life because as long as people behave in line with their mutual normative expectations, the norm is not made explicit. Since we cannot observe a norm independently from behavior and there are more fundamental motives of behavior, such as self-regarding and other-regarding preferences, identifying norms as a cause of

---

[3] See Eriksson et al. (2021) for a large comparative study focusing on meta-norms, that is, social norms regulating the behavioral response to the violation of a social norm.

behavior is a serious challenge. Because of the possibility to design and systematically vary the interaction conditions, laboratory experiments have been and are regarded as a highly promising tool for studying social norms. For this reason, they have become a focal interest of experimental sociologists since the early days of the development of the field.

As a leading example, we use a laboratory experimental study by Diekmann and Przepiorka (2016) that exhibits the specific perspective of sociologists on the study of social norms. To study the emergence of latent norms, the authors use the volunteer's dilemma (Diekmann 1985, 1993), a variant of the public goods game in which one cooperator suffices to produce the collective good. Latent norms are "expectations concerning behavioral regularities emerging in the course of repeated interactions," which can be regarded as "precursors of social norms" (Diekmann & Przepiorka 2016, 1310).

More specifically, Diekmann and Przepiorka (2016, 1311) are interested in examining the "structural conditions under which behavioral regularities and latent norms can emerge." To do so, they focus on a cooperation dilemma, in which they contrast a symmetric with an asymmetric interaction situation, that is, homogeneous vs. heterogeneous payoff expectations. They also explore the effect of repeated interactions as compared to one-shot games. Using a game-theoretic representation of the volunteer's dilemma, the authors first establish theoretical predictions that a mixed-strategy equilibrium would solve the game under symmetric conditions but that this equilibrium generates implausible predictions in the asymmetric case. Their testable hypotheses are that (1) in the symmetric condition, a latent norm of turn-taking will emerge, whereas (2) in the asymmetric condition, subjects will coordinate on the norm that the actor incurring the lowest cost (i.e., the strong actor) volunteers to contribute. They also predict that (3) the focal subject will volunteer, while the other subjects will defect.

In the laboratory experiment, the participants play a volunteer's dilemma in groups of three. In each round of the game, they can either defect (not volunteer, thus not incurring the cost of providing the public good) or cooperate (volunteer, thus incurring the cost). The earnings are realized if at least one subject volunteers. The authors examine the structural conditions under which behavioral regularities and latent norms can emerge by implementing specific constellations in their experimental treatments. For instance, in the symmetric treatment, all subjects incur the same cost from cooperating. In the two asymmetric treatments, one subject has a lower cost than the other two: In one treatment, this cost is slightly less (asymmetric 1 treatment), while in the other, the cost is much less (asymmetric 2 treatment). A fourth treatment is identical to the symmetric treatment, except that one subject is made focal by being highlighted in a different color.

In an experimental session, participants go through three consecutive parts, which consist of a fixed number of rounds. At the beginning of each part, subjects are randomly allocated into groups and remain in the group for all rounds of that part (partner matching). They also keep their role throughout the part. After each part, subjects are randomly rematched into new groups of three, thereby ascertaining that no one encounters the same subjects again (perfect stranger matching). The emergence of latent norms is measured by the length of interaction sequences in which either one actor volunteers uninterruptedly to cooperate, while the others defect or two or three actors take turns in cooperating. Doing so generates the public good at maximum efficiency while spreading the costs equally.

In line with the hypotheses, the authors find a volunteering rate of 33 percent in the symmetric condition, while in 50 percent of the rounds, all three subjects take turns. In the asymmetric condition, only the subjects that incur the lowest cost volunteer in 58 and 77 percent of rounds. Because these strong subjects volunteer at lower rates in the asymmetric 1 treatment than in the asymmetric 2 treatment, the authors additionally hypothesize that the subjects who incur the lowest costs "were often reluctant to tacitly agree on them cooperating throughout because this would also lead to them earning less than the other group members" (Diekmann & Przepiorka 2016, 1322). In order to test this conjecture, the authors devised a second experiment in which subjects are randomly rematched into new groups in every round (stranger matching), and in the asymmetric treatments, the strong actor is also randomly determined in every round. Thus, subjects have no possibility to reciprocate, and the expected payoff is equal for all. The authors find no coordination in the symmetric treatment and almost immediate coordination on the strong actor being the one to volunteer to provide the public good in both asymmetric treatments.

Diekmann and Przepiorka conclude that the differences between treatments in the emergence of latent norms result (1) from the interplay of the structure of the volunteers' dilemma game, (2) from whether subjects interact repeatedly, and (3) from inequity aversion. The structure of the game induces the development of a latent norm of either turn-taking or coordinating on the strong actor to volunteer. Repeated interaction allows for the norm to establish itself. Inequity aversion undermines efforts to coordinate on the efficient solution either due to the volunteering of a weak actor that incurs the highest costs, thus raising total costs, or due to the defecting of a strong actor that incurs the lowest costs. In the latter case, the strong actor has to expect a cumulation of lower payoffs as a result of always volunteering, thus reducing total payoffs.

6.3 PRINCIPLES OF LABORATORY RESEARCH

This leading example contains many elements that characterize a laboratory experiment. The *first* element is theory testing. The study relates to an important theoretical puzzle: the free-rider problem in collective action theory. More specifically, it focuses on a specific situation within the broader theoretical discussion, namely, the volunteer's dilemma, in which one cooperator suffices for the collective good to be provided to all. It then addresses two dimensions of the social structure and discusses how individual behavior responds to variations in these dimensions, thereby using a formal model that captures the essential elements of the theory.[4] Laboratory experiments are well-suited for testing this kind of theory because they can be easily adapted to the conditions specified by the theory. By sequentially manipulating the parameters of the model, the researcher can make precise predictions about the outcome while holding all other potentially intervening factors constant.

In recent years, partly as a consequence of the "replication crisis" that spread from social psychology to the other social sciences (Open Science Collaboration 2015; Duvendack, Palmer-Jones, & Reed 2017), a new trend has emerged. The theoretical hypotheses to be tested with experimental data are increasingly expected to be preregistered (see Chapter 12 for a discussion). As a result, a number of tools and platforms have been developed to facilitate this new standard that is gradually developing into a condition for publication in high-ranking journals (Nosek & Lakens 2014).

The *second* element of our leading example that characterizes a laboratory experiment is the way in which the theoretical predictions are translated into the experimental design. Variations in two dimensions, symmetry and repeated interactions, define the treatments in the two reported experiments. The first experiment holds the repeated interaction constant and implements (1) a baseline treatment, which is symmetric in the sense of equal costs for all subjects; (2) two asymmetric treatments – motivated by a game-theoretic solution concept – where the difference in the cost of volunteering is either small or large; and (3) one treatment – motivated by an alternative solution concept – where one player is highlighted. The second experiment compares repeated interactions with one-shot interactions by repeating the first three treatments of the first experiment under the condition that players interact only once. This setup ensures that reciprocity can

---

[4] In fact, Diekmann and Przepiorka (2016) discuss a third dimension as well, namely, the nature of the dilemma. This can be a dilemma of cooperation or coordination, but in the experimental design, they only implement a cooperation game.

be ruled out as a motivation for behavior. Jointly, the two experiments yield a 2 × 3 design (partner vs. stranger matching; symmetric, asymmetric 1, asymmetric 2) with an extension in the partner matching experiment for the test of an alternative explanation.

More generally, the laboratory experiment of the leading example illustrates the flexibility of laboratory research in responding to research outcomes. The ultimate 2 × 3 design resulted after reflecting upon the outcome of the first experiment. By implementing a simple change to the experimental protocol, which is most easily implemented in a laboratory experiment, the researchers were able to better test the theory.

A *third* element is how social interactions can be arranged in a laboratory setting. The researcher can determine the type of communication possible, ranging from computer-generated messages about other subjects' decisions via binary codes or numbers, to sets of predefined messages, and to free-form text that can be entered by the subjects in chat windows. The researcher can determine who can see and respond to a message, thus generating different subgroups or implementing a particular network structure. While computer-generated messages restrict the choice set to the options provided on the computer screen and thus maximize control of the social interaction, free-form messages approximate communication in natural settings at the cost of minimal control. Our leading example employs a computer-generated message system. Subjects have a binary choice between (1) contributing, that is, yielding a payoff of the earnings minus the cost of contributing, and (2) defecting, that is, leading to full earnings if at least one other subject contributes and to null earnings if no other subject contributes. After each round, subjects are informed about the others' decisions and the outcome. In the partner treatment, they learn to respond to each other's past behavior and thus coordinate on a specific pattern, but they cannot explicitly negotiate that pattern. This rather restricted form of communication minimizes potential interferences and uncontrolled social dynamics, which may occur in more extensive forms of communication. In the stranger treatment, this tacit form of coordination is precluded. Sometimes, a communication network can be created in a laboratory experiment simply by providing participants with information about the behavior of other participants in similar interactions. For example, this type of information exchange was implemented to investigate whether subjects use this information to learn about their future interaction partners (Buskens, Raub, & van der Veer 2010) and whether subjects imitate the behavior of other participants in similar conditions (Barrera & Buskens 2009).

At the other end of the communication continuum, subjects can freely discuss and deliberate. While this setting substantively reduces the control that the researcher has over the treatment, this disadvantage is compensated by a core advantage of the laboratory setting, which offers the possibility to control and manipulate the context in which the social interaction occurs. Since many sociological research questions focus on the relational level of interaction between individuals and less on individual behavior per se, the unit of analysis is often the group, not the individual. Thus, the researcher can study the effect of different institutional or structural conditions, such as decision rules or power relations, on group-level variables. Examples are the ways in which subjects negotiate about, for example, coordinating on efficient voting behavior (Kalwitzki et al. 2015) or the distribution of a resource (Neuhofer 2021). The software used in laboratory experiments automatically records metadata of every message sent via the chat function. This information can be used to produce an exact and complete transcript of the deliberations. The latter is then the basis for the analysis of individual strategies and group-level processes (Kalwitzki, Luhan & Kittel 2012). Given that the chat function is the only means of communication, differently from the complexity of social interactions in natural settings, the social processes that result in the collective decision in the laboratory are fully transparent to the researcher.

A *fourth* element relates to the type of people who typically participate in a laboratory experiment. Most laboratories are situated at universities, and all or the majority of participants are undergraduate students. This setting allows for relatively easy access to data collection, but not without concerns about the generalizability of findings. Most notably, students have been considered to be unrepresentative of the general population, and thus, research has been accused of producing biased findings that cannot be generalized to the population of interest. Moreover, findings based on the behavior of students living in Western, educated, industrialized, and rich democracies ("WEIRD" countries, Henrich, Heine, & Norenzayan 2010) have been said to be invalid for humankind as a whole. These concerns have been extensively studied in other social sciences, most notably experimental economics, and their results may give some guidance for the interpretation of sociological experiments as long as the latter use similar designs. Overall, the results of comparisons of student samples with samples from other professional groups suggest that there are minor differences in intercepts and effect sizes, which do not, however, change the interpretation of the direction of effects (Fréchette 2015). A similar result from a comparison of behavior in standard ultimatum game experiments across societies that are rather different from the Western world suggests that findings on the direction of effects seem to hold for diverse social groups and can be explained by contextual factors (Henrich et al. 2004). A more detailed discussion can be found in Chapter 10.

A *fifth* element is incentivization. Monetary incentives are offered to participants in laboratory experiments in order to override other motives that might affect behavior in the laboratory (Bowles & Polanía-Reyes 2012). By making the amount earned dependent on the individual outcome – which depends on the behavior of the subject i and the behaviors of the other subjects $j, k, \ldots$ with whom i interacts in the experiment – experimentalists attempt to raise the salience of decisions to participants in the experiment. The assumption underlying this setup, which is standard in experimental economics, is the principle of non-satiation (Smith 1976, 275), positing that subjects strictly prefer earning more to earning less money in the laboratory. The subjects' preference orders are thus induced by the experimenter (see Chapter 11).

Because sociological experiments often have a broader scope, they may also encompass intrinsic motivations, in particular in those research areas that have some overlap with social psychology. In such studies, inducing preferences by means of monetary rewards would interact with the focus of interest. Intrinsic motivations may, for example, be based on personality traits or socialization. They affect behavior independently of the specific social and institutional context and are part of the conditions that subjects bring into the laboratory. Although the experimenter does not control these conditions in the same way as treatment manipulations, they can often be measured, and these measures can be part of the experimental study. A more detailed discussion on incentives can be found in Chapter 11.

A sixth element is *randomization*. Due to their highest degree of control – compared to other types of experiments – laboratory experiments are expected to ensure that every participating subject has the same chance to be assigned to any treatment. To achieve such a random assignment to treatments, a three-step procedure can be followed. First, treatments are allocated to time slots in a way that ensures a cross-treatment balance in both the time of day of sessions and the day of the week. Whenever possible, registration in the experiment is controlled over time (only random subsets of the subject pool are invited to register in certain time periods). Second, whenever possible, multiple treatments are held within any single session. Third, allocation to seats and experimental roles within a session is done randomly.

Given the limits on the number of observations that can be generated in a single experiment due to budget restrictions and the size of the pool of potential participants, the random allocation of participants to treatments may not perfectly cancel out potential interfering factors in practice. For this reason, it is recommended to collect data on sociodemographic variables as well as variables that, for theoretical reasons, may affect the causal relationships tested in the experiment and to include these as control variables in the statistical models used to test the hypotheses. These variables are either contained in the subject pool information or can be added to a questionnaire that is administered before the treatments or at the end of a session. Including such questions after the treatment is often preferable to ensure that exposure to the questions does not bias behavior in the experiment.

6.4 ESTABLISHING EMPIRICAL REGULARITIES

Although laboratory experiments are well-suited to test existing theories, they can also be applied to establish empirical regularities and to advise policymaking (Roth 1995; Willer & Walker 2007). The goal of establishing empirical regularities is typically pursued when existing theories cannot explain the phenomenon in question or when puzzling results arise after testing existing theories. Establishing empirical regularities can, in turn, contribute to theory development. A very well-known example of the latter is the study by Güth, Schmittberger, and Schwarze (1982). They conducted a laboratory experiment to study people's strategic interactions and found that, contrary to an important assumption of modern economic theory – that individuals are selfish and rational – most individuals act prosocially in strategic interactions. A vast number of laboratory experiments, conducted across different contexts and countries, further established the regularity of such an empirical finding, which ultimately contributed to the development of the so-called social preference theories (e.g., Fehr & Schmidt 1999; Bolton & Ockenfels 2000; Charness & Rabin 2002).

A more recent example relates to the gender and competition literature. There is by now abundant experimental evidence that, by and large, women "shy away" from and underperform when competing for resources (e.g., Gneezy, Niederle, & Rustichini 2003; Niederle & Vesterlund 2007). Inspired by social expectation and status characteristics theories (Berger, Connor, & Fişek 1974; Correll & Ridgeway 2006), a series of laboratory experiments recognizes another important dimension of competition – social-status ranking[5] – and tries to find out whether (and why) gender differences in performance are also observed when people compete for status. In the first study, Schram, Brandts, and Gërxhani (2019) conduct a laboratory experiment to isolate the effects of social-status ranking by eliminating the rivalry dimension of competition in the experimental design.

---

[5] Competition leads to a ranking of the competitors, and such ranking determines one's status, that is, one's "individual's standing in the hierarchy of a group based on the prestige, honor, and deference accorded her by other members" (Lovaglia, Lucas, & Thye 1998, 202).

They find no gender differences when there is no competition (neither social-status ranking nor rivalry for resources) and strong gender differences when participants know they will be compared to others (social-status ranking, but no rivalry for resources): Women underperform compared to men. A replication of this design across different cultural settings, namely, Italy, the Netherlands, and Spain, supports the original findings of no gender differences under no competition and of women doing worse than men under social-status ranking competition in more competitive and masculine environments such as Italy and Spain (Gërxhani 2020). A follow-up study (Gërxhani, Brandts, & Schram 2023) makes the step toward theory development by conducting a number of additional laboratory experiments. The first experiment considers both rivalry for resources and social-status ranking and again finds that, in the absence of any of these competitive dimensions, there are no gender differences in performance. As soon as either dimension is introduced, women underperform compared to men, which shows that the two dimensions of competition act as substitutes in having this gender effect on performance. The rest of their experiments examines theoretical mechanisms that could explain the processes that lead to such gender inequalities under competition. The main finding is that, in the presence of both dimensions of competition, men believe that they are better than women, which stimulates them to excel. In contrast, women seem to adhere to a "prescribed stereotype" that stipulates that they should not harm others, which makes them underperform.

The basic principles and methodologies based on model- and theory-driven experiments discussed so far generally carry over to experiments that aim at establishing empirical regularities. There is one exception. While all types of laboratory experiments ensure internally valid findings, they may differ in the extent to which the results can be generalized outside the laboratory. In the case of model- and theory-driven experiments, it is not a particular empirical finding that is to be generalized but a "theoretical construct" (Deaton & Cartwright 2018). In the case of experiments that aim at establishing empirical regularities, even when theoretically informed, the generalizability of an empirical regularity requires "some confidence that what happens in the environment of the laboratory is a reasonable representation of what happens in the real world" (Jackson & Cox 2013, 38). One solution to the issue of generalizability, as already successfully applied (e.g., Correll, Benard, & Paik 2007), is to incorporate as many key features as possible of contexts outside of the laboratory that are of relevance to one's research question. Another solution is to consider running field experiments, which will be the focus of the next chapter. In Chapter 10, we provide a more extensive discussion on the "trade-off" between the internal and the external validity of different types of experimental designs.

6.5 THE ANALYSIS OF LABORATORY DATA

In order to legitimately invoke the central limit theorem for significance testing with laboratory data, one ought to assume that the data points are independently and identically distributed. Put otherwise, a researcher assumes that the participants are randomly selected from a homogeneous population of unrelated individuals. These two properties warrant that the findings can be generalized and replicated. Contrary to many natural sciences, where these conditions are easily met by including arbitrary specimens in the sample, these properties are violated in various ways in experiments involving humans. Most importantly, one has to consider session effects and repetition effects, which result from laboratory data being structured into several layers.

The data points are typically decisions. These decisions are taken by individuals embedded in groups or networks, as is typical of sociological research questions. We speak of groups if communication between group members is unrestricted, and of networks if the experimental design structures communication channels such that some edges of the network are open and others closed. Moreover, individuals participate in one specific session of an experiment. The implication of this structure is that the assumption that the data points are independent may be violated in several ways.

Session effects are defined as "within-session correlation in the variable of interest (or the residual) once the relevant factors are controlled for" (Fréchette 2012, 487). This happens because sessions take place in a specific place at a specific time, which means that the behavior of participants may be influenced by some exogenous factor that differentiates decisions in one session from decisions in other sessions. These exogenous factors may be events that happen before one session but not others, or they may be related to participant properties. For example, a specific session may be scheduled when sociology students have a course and cannot participate, whereas another session conflicts with a course taken by economics students. To the extent that sociology and economics students systematically differ in their prosociality (Frank, Gilovich, & Regan 1993) and to the extent that the composition of the sessions is affected by the availability of students of these disciplines, any experiment that involves this property will produce session effects. In the presence of session effects, estimated coefficients may be inconsistent and biased, and the variance will be incorrect, implying potentially false hypothesis tests.

Individual decisions are also affected by the group level. Even if participants are randomly assigned to groups or networks and, thus, the composition of groups is expected to be identical, any particular group will be composed of a specific set of individuals. Using the same example as before, some groups may have a majority of prosocials, while others may be dominated by self-regarding people. To the extent that the experimental protocol involves interactions within the group, group-level properties such as the share of prosocials will affect individual behavior (Luhan, Kocher, & Sutter 2009).

Furthermore, many experiments involve repeated observations of the participants in a session (within-subjects design). This design produces two potential causes of dependence between decisions. First, if the same participant is asked to make the same decision repeatedly, the outcome of earlier decisions will affect behavior in later decisions. Second, if the same participants are asked to interact repeatedly, group-level phenomena such as reciprocity and conditional cooperation may emerge. In order to answer research questions that relate to such phenomena, these designs may be the most adequate way to analyze them. However, such designs imply that the assumption of independent decisions is violated and that the lowest level of *independent* observation is the group and not the individual.

The upshot of this discussion is that there exist many situations in which laboratory experiments produce a multilevel data structure. Decisions are nested in individuals, which are nested in groups, which, in turn, are nested in sessions. As we have seen in Chapter 3, sociological research questions often involve phenomena that emerge at the group level. Depending on the exact situation, the number of independent observations may be reduced to the number of participants, groups, or sessions, which may severely reduce the power of statistical tests and raise the costs of the experiment. In such situations, one can adjust for group and session fixed effects using dummy variables or use multilevel models, as also suggested by Shikano, Bräuninger, and Stoffel (2012).

7 Field Experiments

7.1 INTRODUCTION

Field experiments rely on the three design elements common to all experiments – manipulation, group comparison, and randomization – and, therefore, share well-known strengths regarding causal inference with other experimental designs. In addition, field experiments are staged in a "natural" research setting where individuals usually interact in everyday life and regularly complete the task under investigation. This feature of "naturalness" is the core feature distinguishing field experiments from experiments in other settings. It is also one of the major reasons why researchers use field experiments: They allow the investigation of behavior under "natural" conditions. Hence, by bringing a realistic social context into experiments, field experiments are a valuable complement to other types of experiments.

Another major appeal of field experiments is the possibility to observe subjects without their knowledge of participating in an experiment (see Webb et al. 2000[1965]). While not all field experiments can rely on unobtrusive measures for ethical, practical, or political reasons, field experiments relying on this unobtrusive approach have the potential to provide convincing empirical evidence on the effects of an intervention because they rule out one major source of potential bias that can occur when individuals are aware that they are participating in an experiment. For example, in the so-called audit studies (for an overview, see Gaddis 2018), researchers send fake applications to employers, systematically varying the characteristics of the applicant. Since employers do not know that they are part of an experiment, such an approach is well-suited to study discrimination against certain social groups, which employers might otherwise not admit. Thus, using unobtrusive measures, such as concealed observation or behavioral traces, helps avoid reactivity and social desirability bias that can occur in both observational and other experimental studies.

In this chapter, we take a closer look at when and how to conduct field experiments. We start by introducing two field experiments on the broken windows theory. Based on those studies, we then discuss the strengths and challenges of field experiments. We then conclude with a summary of a relatively recent trend, namely, "digital field experiments."

7.2 LEADING EXAMPLE: FIELD EXPERIMENTS ON THE BROKEN WINDOWS THEORY

In this section, we introduce a leading example of experiments in the field. The studies discussed here examine the broken windows theory and are typical examples of concealed field experiments staged in people's everyday life. Originally proposed by Wilson and Kelling in 1982, the broken windows theory states that physical and social disarray, such as garbage on the streets, broken windows, and drunken homeless people, fosters additional norm violations and, therefore, the spreading of disorder. Put into practice, the broken windows theory advocates the removal of signs of disorderliness and incivility as well as the severe sanctioning of minor offenses in order to curb crime. Picked up by policymakers, the approach had a significant impact on policing and inspired a zero-tolerance policy in New York in the 1990s that spread around the world in the following decades. However, empirical evidence on the effectiveness of this approach was far from clear at that time (e.g., Kelling & Sousa, 2001; Corman & Mocan, 2005; Harcourt & Ludwig, 2006). Since most studies were based on observational data, they did not allow decisive conclusions about the causal effect of a zero-tolerance policy on crime (e.g., Levitt, 2004; Braga & Bond, 2008).

Against that background, Keizer, Lindenberg, and Steg (2008) revived the discussion on the broken windows theory with a highly influential empirical contribution focusing on the consequences of disorder for minor norm violations. In a series of field experiments, they showed that physical disorder (e.g., litter, graffiti, and the sound of firecrackers) encourages further norm violations by others (littering, nonconformity to trespassing, and stealing). The basic setup of the experiments was somewhat similar across the different studies and involved the active manipulation of physical or social disorder and the concealed observations of subjects' decisions regarding norm compliance or deviations.

We illustrate their experimental approach based on the "lost letter experiment" in Groningen, the Netherlands. An envelope that clearly contained a faked €5 bill was placed in a mailbox in such a way that the envelope was still sticking out. As a consequence, the envelope and the €5 bill were visible to everyone walking by, and each passerby – the uninformed subjects in the experiment – could either ignore the envelope, push it into the mailbox, or steal the envelope. Only subjects who walked by the mailbox alone were considered subjects in the experiment. In the baseline condition with 71 subjects, the mailbox and its physical environment were clean, whereas graffiti was sprayed on the mailbox in one experimental condition, and litter was placed around the mailbox in another experimental condition (each with $N = 60$). All experimental sessions took place in the early afternoon and under similar weather conditions. While 13 percent of the subjects stole the envelope in the baseline condition, 27 percent and 25 percent did so in the graffiti and litter conditions. The experimental results by Keizer, Lindenberg, and Steg (2008), therefore, provided clear empirical support for one core mechanism formulated in the broken windows theory, namely, that visible signs of minor norm violations trigger a further erosion of the same and other norms.

Given the high practical relevance of these findings, Keuschnigg and Wolbring (2015b) tested the robustness of the findings in a replication of the "lost" letter experiment by Keizer, Lindenberg, and Steg (2008). While aiming for high comparability in the design, they conducted the field experiment in a different context and introduced further variations regarding the outcome measure, the incentives to steal, and the characteristics of the neighborhood. The replication study was staged in the city of Munich, Germany, at public mailboxes with a sufficient number of passers-by during the daytime. In the control condition, the areas surrounding both mailboxes were kept clean. In the treatment condition, two heavily wrecked bicycles were attached to a railing next to the mailboxes. Control and treatment conditions were alternated twice, starting with a clean surrounding.

Going beyond Keizer, Lindenberg, and Steg (2008), Keuschnigg and Wolbring incentivized norm violations in two experimental conditions not just with a faked €5 bill but with a faked €10 bill or €100 bill since it remained unclear from the original study, whether people are also willing to steal envelopes containing larger amounts of money. From a rational choice perspective, one would expect a larger extent of stealing due to a stronger monetary incentive. However, people might also steal less because they perceive stealing a €100 bill as a more severe norm violation. In addition, they did not place the envelope in the mailbox in such a way that the envelope was still sticking but placed it on the ground in front of the mailbox. Based on that setup, they could distinguish three different outcomes: ignoring the letter, stealing it, or helping by putting it in the mailbox. The rationale for this modification was to isolate the effects on stealing and omitted help that the original design could not disentangle. However, different mechanisms might drive both behaviors since stealing is an offense, while not helping – though maybe socially disapproved – is not a violation of a legal norm in that context. Furthermore, Keuschnigg and Wolbring (2015b) staged the experiment in one rather "good" and one rather "bad" urban district in Munich, expecting stronger broken windows effects in the former than in the latter neighborhoods.

The first important result of this follow-up study was that the original results could be successfully replicated both in direction and effect size, despite the different context and the modifications of the experimental design, in particular the exact experimental stimulus and decision situation. However, while the overall rate of stealing was higher in rather "bad" than in rather "good" neighborhoods, the extent of disorder mattered less in the former than in the latter context. Such replications testing the robustness of results are important because what works in one local context does not necessarily work in another local context. The transportability of field experimental results across contexts is a widely debated topic in the field of randomized controlled trials (see Deaton & Cartwright 2018). Therefore, replicating results in different contexts or with different populations increases the confidence that results are, at least to some degree, generalizable since a more general mechanism is at work (for more details, see Chapter 10).

Moreover, replications can also contribute to cumulative progress and further theory development by extensions of the original design. For example, in addition to showing that physical disorder fosters stealing, the study by Keuschnigg and Wolbring (2015b) reports that physical disorder reduces the likelihood of helping (i.e., putting the letter back in the mailbox). This suggests that the broken windows mechanism not only fosters norm violations but also discourages prosocial behavior. Furthermore, the study revealed important variations of the broken windows effect by the amount of money and neighborhood. Compared to the condition with a €5 bill, the disorder effect became weaker for envelopes with a €10 bill and disappeared completely for envelopes with a €100 bill. This result raises questions about whether a zero-tolerance policy ultimately prevents serious crimes in "bad" neighborhoods.

7.3 POTENTIALS AND CHALLENGES OF EXPERIMENTING IN THE FIELD

The previous section illustrated that field experiments are an important source to expand our knowledge about the social world as well as to advance social theory and inform policy. Using designs tailored to the specific research questions, Keizer, Lindenberg, and Steg (2008) and Keuschnigg and Wolbring (2015b) could test core mechanisms of social dynamics in real life. At the same time, both studies had to address certain challenges when designing and doing their experiments. Taking a closer look at those strengths and challenges and how they have been addressed in applied research is instructive for designing one's own field experiment. One common issue of experimenting in the field is that researchers have less control over the research environment than in a laboratory experiment. Different caveats can arise from this reduced degree of field control. In this subsection, we focus on the recruitment of subjects, the assignment of treatments, interference between experimental units, and, finally, reactivity and the measurement of core variables.

7.3.1 Subject Recruitment and Study Participation

One advantage of experimenting in the field is that it is usually easier to observe nonstudent subjects than in laboratory experiments. Field experiments can thus be a valuable complement to laboratory experiments, if concerns exist that students might behave differently than other parts of the population. While field experiments can be useful to test the robustness of results across different populations and to study effect heterogeneity, they share with other types of experiments the challenge of nonrandomness of sampling and participation in the experiment. As became clear, both these studies did not rely on random population samples but on convenience samples: Subjects were pedestrians walking by certain mailboxes at certain times. Like laboratory experiments, the broken windows experiments were thus certainly not based on a representative population sample but on a selective subgroup of people. However, nonrandom sampling is not a problem if experiments serve the purpose of testing social theories and if one is willing to assume that human behavior follows certain general regularities, which can be sufficiently approximated by examining students or other subgroups. Concerning the broken windows theory, there are no strong reasons to assume otherwise.

Furthermore, it is a major advantage that field experiments can often be designed in such a way that potential subjects actually do not make an active decision about whether to participate in an experiment or not. For example, in the broken windows experiments, passersby were unaware of the fact that they participated in the study. This makes it unlikely that refusal to participate adds another layer of selectivity. Other field experiments which ask individuals for participation and consent, however, can suffer from such problems. For example, in the well-known Moving to Opportunity experiments (for sociological contributions see Clampet-Lundquist & Massey 2008; Sampson 2008; De Souza Briggs, Popkin, & Goering 2010), randomly selected families in high-poverty housing projects in the United States received the opportunity to move to less-poor neighborhoods, but not all of them actually decided to use the offered monetary support for relocation. Especially if the experiment requires subjects' informed consent about the treatment and if the study deals with a sensitive, controversial, or high-cost topic (see Chapter 12), potential subjects might refuse to participate. If participation is correlated with the outcome of interest, this leads to selection bias. For example, subjects could have a special motivation to participate in the study, such as being in special needs or expecting the intervention to be particularly effective.

Related to the previous context, not only refusal to participate but also repeated participation can be a challenge in field experiments. While repeated participation can also occur in other types of experiments, field experiments are particularly prone to this potential threat to validity due to the lower control over the experimental setting in the field. In the leading example, subjects could and possibly did (un)intentionally participate more than once in the experiment when walking by the mailbox at different times and days of the experiment. Even though the researchers tried to minimize the risk of repeated participation and removed problematic observations when detected, finding doublets is tedious, and some margin of error always remains, given that researchers did not have a prior list of participants. In the two studies discussed previously, this should not pose a serious problem since subjects did not have a strong incentive for repeated participation due to the use of fake money. However, in other field experiments, repeated participation can lead to serious biases, especially when repeated participation is driven by monetary incentives or intrinsic motivations. For example, subjects might try to participate more than once in order to influence the results of a policy-relevance study in a certain direction. The latter type of field studies are known as social experiments (see Heckman & Smith 1995; Campbell & Russo 1999; Greenberg & Shroder 2004).

7.3.2 Treatment Assignment and Compliance

A second challenge resulting from a lack of field control can be about successfully randomizing the treatment assignment. Field experiments are more prone to such randomization failure than laboratory or vignette experiments. For example, the broken windows experiments had to rely on a rather small number of subjects per experimental condition. In order to rule out the risk of systematic group differences, Keizer, Lindenberg, and Steg (2008) and Keuschnigg and Wolbring (2015b) had to take a closer look at the distribution of covariates across experimental conditions. Furthermore, in these field experiments, it was not possible to randomly assign participants to conditions while maintaining the main advantage of unobtrusive observation. Instead, the researchers conducted the different experimental sessions at comparable time slots and under comparable weather conditions to ensure that treatment assignment became as good as random. However, doing research in the field involves caveats that might undermine the comparability of experimental groups. For example, Wicherts and Bakker (2014) argue in a critique of Keizer et al.'s broken windows experiments that one of the experimental locations was close to a food market that took place on certain weekdays. This and other uncontrolled events might lead to differences in the sampling population across experimental conditions with respect to relevant variables such as their attitude toward littering.

There are other reasons that can also result in deviations from a random treatment assignment: Experimental units might refuse to participate in one specific experimental group, might not comply with the treatment assignment, or might drop out of the study in the course of time. While these reasons were not present in the broken windows experiments due to the unobtrusive measurement approach, they can occur in field experiments requiring informed consent. For example, in the Moving to Opportunity experiment, households in the treatment group received a voucher offering financial support for moving, while households in the control group did not. As expected, despite the additional incentive, not every household in the treatment group actually moved, while not all households in the control group stayed. In the terminology of causal inference, some households complied with the assignment, while others did not, in this voucher-based "encouragement" design of the Moving to Opportunity experiment.

As depicted in Table 7.1, the literature distinguishes different types of subjects' compliance and noncompliance (Angrist, Imbens, & Rubin 1996). While compliers always follow the intended assignment and hence are no cause for trouble, defiers always do exactly the opposite of the intended assignment and are, hence, a notorious source of methodological concern. In contrast to that, always-takers and never-takers are subjects with one-sided noncompliance because they comply with one type of assignment but not with the other: Always-takers join the treatment group even if they are

Table 7.1 Different types of subjects' compliance/noncompliance

Researcher	Subjects			
Intended		One-sided noncompliers		
Assignment	Compliers	Always-takers	Never-takers	Defiers
Treatment group	✓	✓	✗	✗
Control group	✓	✗	✓	✗

Note: ✓ indicates that subjects comply with the assignment intended by the researcher; ✗ indicates that they do not comply.

assigned to the control group. For example, some households in the Moving to Opportunity experiments moved, even though they received no financial voucher that encouraged them to do so (control group). On the other hand, never-takers enter the control group, regardless of their assignment and are never treated. For example, some households in the Moving to Opportunity experiments did not move, even though moving was incentivized by a voucher. Such one-sided noncompliance is suboptimal for a study, but this is unfortunately not that rare in field experiments. For example, subjects might refuse to be assigned to the treatment group if the treatment is potentially harmful or if it is at least perceived by the subjects to be so. On the other hand, subjects might want to be part of the treatment group if they think that the intervention withheld in the control group is beneficial to them.

Luckily, some statistical tools exist that help extract relevant information from an experiment with one-sided noncompliance. One well-established statistical approach to deal with always-takers and never-takers (but not defiers) is the so-called intention-to-treat (ITT) analysis. The basic idea of the ITT is to use the intended, instead of the actual, assignment for the group comparison. The ITT effect is not identical to the average treatment effect in case of systematic noncompliance, but it is still informative under certain assumptions: It measures the effect of intended treatment assignment and of treatment if taken up by the subjects.[1]

Nonetheless, it is best if one tries to avoid noncompliance by design instead of applying statistical ex post fixes. Convincing subjects about the importance of participating in the study according to the experimental instructions, providing incentives to comply with the assignment, and conducting concealed field experiments are three measures to minimize noncompliance. The latter approach was taken in the leading example. Not informing subjects about their participation in the experiment and using unobtrusive behavioral measures, such as concealed observation, makes it highly unlikely that noncompliance played a major role in those field experiments.

As mentioned earlier, however, deviations from random treatment assignment can also occur in field experiments. It is, therefore, advisable to explore whether assignment is compromised by conducting randomization checks (see Chapter 5). These randomization tests rely on the idea that

---

[1] Some designs – so-called encouragement designs – anticipate and exploit the fact that only some experimental units pick up the treatment and deliberately rely for practical or ethical reasons on an ITT analysis to derive conclusions. The Moving to Opportunity experiments is an example of such an encouragement design. For further details, see Gerber and Green (2012, chapters 5 & 6).

the distribution of key variables in the different experimental groups is expected to be balanced if randomization works. However, if the number of observations per group is small, the covariate distributions between the groups can also differ simply by chance. A blocked or stratified randomized design can help here to secure a comparable distribution of covariates across experimental groups (covariate balance) (for more details, see Alferes 2012).

7.3.3 Interference between Experimental Units

Another issue in field experiments can be interference between experimental units and resulting spillover effects between treatment and control groups. Even if random assignment to the experimental conditions was successful, such interference could undermine the experiment. Due to limited field control, researchers need to be particularly attentive to prevent research units belonging to different experimental groups from coming in contact with and influencing each other.[2] In the course of such interactions, knowledge can spill over, social contagion can be at work, and positive or negative externalities of the treatment can affect the control group. For example, in the case of a vaccination program, those not receiving the treatment might profit from a reduced risk of being infected due to a general equilibrium effect (positive externalities). In contrast, participation in a job training program might give applicants for a new job a head start over other unemployed not receiving the intervention, resulting in a crowding out of the controls by the treated (negative externalities). Finally, subjects in the control group might become aware of the experimental intervention and search for alternative ways to get treated, fully undermining the comparison between experimental groups.

Technically speaking, interference between experimental groups leads to a violation of the stable unit treatment value assumption (SUTVA, see Chapter 4). Social interactions between experimental groups cannot be completely ruled out in the field experiments on the broken windows theory. For example, a person in the baseline condition might influence a future participant in the treatment condition by telling her about this extraordinary experience and the decision to put the letter in the postbox. While such instances are probably rare in the respective field experiments,

---

[2] Unless contact between experimental groups is part of the study. For example, Sherif et al. (1961) assigned boys at a summer camp to two different experimental groups, allowed the two groups to interact, and studied their intergroup conflict.

researchers should always be aware of possible interference between experimental units since it can severely bias experimental results.

Researchers can prevent some of these social processes leading to violations of the SUTVA by choosing smart experimental designs. For example, they might choose experimental locations for the treated and control with sufficient geographical and social distance so that social interactions between units from different experimental groups become unlikely. In the broken windows experiment, that would require giving up the goal of running conditions on the same spot, the same weekday, the same time, and the same weather condition. Because doing so potentially undermines comparability across experimental conditions, a change in location for the sake of securing the SUTVA would come at the price of losing control over potentially confounding factors.

Another way to avoid spillover effects and knowledge diffusion can be confidentiality requirements for the experimental subject. If interference is unavoidable, one can either design an experiment that relaxes the SUTVA assumption or one can try to directly model spillover processes and adjust for resulting biases in causal inference (for details, see Gerber & Green 2012, chapter 7). In both cases, the study becomes more complicated and requires substantive knowledge about the social processes that cause biases. In addition, researchers need to be aware of the presence of interference in the first place for them to take such measures. It is thus important to keep a watchful eye on potential interactions across experimental groups during the field phase of the experiment.

7.3.4 Reactivity, the Measurement of Core Variables, and Studying Long-Term Effects

As mentioned in the Introduction of this chapter, subjects' knowledge of being part of the study can cause unwanted behavioral changes in the field experiment. Such reactivity might be erroneously attributed to treatment and can lead to biased estimates of the treatment effect. While it is essential for a high treatment validity that the dimension experimentally varied is salient in subjects' minds, it is a thin line between securing sufficient salience and causing unwanted reactivity. For example, the physical disorder in the broken windows experiments needed to be large enough and clearly visible to the subjects in order to allow for an effect on their behavior. At the same time, this intervention must not raise suspicion since, similar to the laboratory, reactivity can occur in field experiments when experimental units accidentally become aware of the experiment or are actually informed about the study and its topic. That is why, as a rule of thumb, experimental units of all types of experiments should not be informed about the research question, hypotheses, and treatment designs (see Chapter 12). The reason is that otherwise, subjects might start to behave in a socially desirable way, might try to prove or disprove the (actual or expected) research hypothesis, or might try to generate an outcome that supports a certain policy. A famous example is the Hawthorne effect (Roethlisberger & Dickson 1939; Gillespie 1991): The productivity of industrial working groups at Western Electric's factory at Hawthorne appeared to be substantially increased merely because workers became aware that scientists conducted a study with them. While the results of the study have been the topic of much debate (e.g., Jones 1992; Levitt and List 2011), it has become an emblem of the risk of reactivity. The presence of reactivity causes serious problems because both the external and the internal validity of the experimental results can be limited.

In the field experiments on the broken windows theory, reactivity is unlikely to be an issue. The reason is that both studies relied on concealed experiments in combination with unobtrusive measures of behavior. In the experiment on the broken windows theory, pedestrians walked a street in Groningen or Munich and saw an envelope that accidentally was not completely pushed into the mailbox. The experimenters needed to ascertain that nobody detected them observing the subjects' behavior, which can sometimes be challenging.

At the same time, concealed experimentation comes at a price because the measurement of core variables can become difficult. Since subjects were not aware of participating in the two broken windows studies, participants could not be surveyed about their socioeconomic background, their attitudes, or their perception of the decision situation. As a consequence, except for some rather easily observable characteristics such as presumed gender or age, not many covariates could be taken into account in the field experiments on the broken windows theory. While this is not a major issue for causal identification, it restricts the opportunities to conduct subgroup analyses, explore causal effect heterogeneity, and get more insights into the underlying mechanisms. In principle, one could contact subjects after the experiment and try to survey them, but revealing the previously concealed experimental design may induce, especially those who broke the norm, to demand that their data are deleted from the study, thereby undermining the results (see Chapter 12). In addition, participation in such a follow-up survey might be selective and might be driven by the behavior in the experiment, causing endogeneity problems. For example, if Keizer, Lindenberg, and Steg (2008) had contacted the subjects right after stealing the envelope, some of them might have been embarrassed or just refused to answer any questions in order to stay out of any further trouble.

This discussion brings us to two final challenges for many field experiments: the identification of long-term effects of an intervention and the scalability of estimated treatment effects. While politicians are often short-term-oriented, wanting quick results on the effectiveness of a social program from a small-scale study, it can take years and can be very costly for field experiments to provide answers about the scalability and long-term effects of social interventions. Identifying such effects can require a larger-scale implementation of treatments, long observation windows and repeated measurement of the same units over time. In addition, it may be necessary to uphold the treatment for a long period of time. For example, the experiments by Keizer, Lindenberg, and Steg (2008) advanced knowledge in important ways by showing that physical and social disorder trigger further violations of the same and other norms. However, for practical and also ethical considerations, they could only provide suggestive evidence on the scalability of these effects and the longer-term social dynamics of disarray, which are central to the practical implications of the broken windows theory.

Furthermore, experimental subjects might drop out of the study due to death, might be untraceable due to moves, or might refuse to participate in further stages of data collection. As is well-known from methodological research on panel data (e.g., Lynn 2009), these different types of attrition can introduce systematic bias. Attrition can also undermine random assignment if units in the treatment or the control group differ in their propensity to drop out of the study. Establishing a good tracking system of subjects and providing incentives to participate further in the experiment are effective measures to minimize attrition. In addition, researchers can try to correct for related bias by means of multiple imputation and weighting (for introductions, see Allison 2001; Little and Rubin 2002; Enders 2022) based on information on these subjects from previous years. Although those corrections on statistical grounds are not free of assumptions about the sources of dropout, they can help to address the problem and allow quantifying the degree of uncertainty introduced into the estimation of treatment effects by missing data.

To conclude, despite the challenges and potential pitfalls in conducting field experiments, their relevance is undeniable. As Keizer, Lindenberg, and Steg (2014, 404) put it, "Somebody once compared doing field experiments to washing dishes. Even though the water is somewhat murky, dishes come out cleaner."

7.4 DIGITAL FIELD EXPERIMENTS

A specific type of field experiment, namely, digital field experiments has gained prominence with the rise of the World Wide Web and social media and offers exciting new ways to study social behavior. Most people in industrialized countries have internet access, use smartphones, and are active on social media. All these trends provide new opportunities to conduct experiments (Golder & Macy 2014; Salganik 2018, chapter 4). Digital field experiments share key features with other types of experiments, such as active intervention in a standardized setting. At the same time, they allow collecting large-scale data from a much more diverse population than students recruited in university-based laboratories, with fine-grained and unobtrusive behavioral measures (e.g., geo-codes and time stamps). Another advantage of digital field experiments is the relatively low costs. While the fixed cost to implement an online experiment (e.g., for setting up a webpage) may often be larger than that for a similar analog experiment, the variable costs of a digital field experiment are often much lower and approach zero if humans participate without a monetary incentive (Salganik 2018, 190ff.).

A well-known example of an early digital field experiment is the study by Salganik, Dodds, and Watts (2006). To examine how social influence affects product success and inequality in cultural markets such as those for songs, books, and movies, they created an artificial "music lab" on a website containing 48 songs of unknown bands. By advertising the music lab with banners on a different, well-established website, Salganik et al. could recruit over 7.000 teens and young adults from the United States for the study. Importantly, participants did not know that they are part of a large online experiment leading to unobtrusive behavioral measures. Once the experiment, including the web infrastructure, was set up (fixed costs), there were no additional variable costs for collecting these large-scale data.

Participants entering the music lab were randomly assigned to different "worlds." In the baseline condition (with 20 percent assignment probability), subjects could listen to songs that were listed in a random order, were asked to rate songs they played on a five-point scale, and could download them. In this "world" without social influence, subjects did not receive any information on the behavior of other participants. In contrast to the baseline condition, the list of songs shown to the subjects in the treatment condition was sorted according to the download history, and the accumulated download numbers were additionally provided. For this treatment condition, eight different "worlds" (each with 10 percent assignment probability) were implemented to allow for independent social dynamics and to compare them with each other and with the baseline condition.

The empirical results of this digital field experiment showed that social influence increases both the inequality in success in terms of listening choices and downloads as well as the unpredictability of product success as compared to the baseline condition. While the quality of a song – measured based on the subjective song ratings – had a positive effect on product success, the exact outcome was far from clear and could be very different in the eight social influence conditions.

In digital field experiments like this, the typically large number of observations makes it possible (i) to apply more complex factorial designs with numerous treatments, (ii) to identify even small effects with sufficient statistical power, and (iii) to explore interaction effects for subgroups. All three features help advance knowledge about underlying mechanisms because they allow researchers to examine how different versions of treatments or treatment combinations work and whether certain subgroups react differently to the stimulus than others. Digital field experiments also allow scholars to answer research questions about group processes and emergent phenomena at the aggregate level, which are otherwise hard to study with observational or experimental data. For example, van de Rijt et al. (2014) conducted a series of digital field experiments on success-breeds-success dynamics. They actively intervened in existing online systems such as a crowdfunding platform and a petition website by providing support for randomly selected cases (e.g., crowdfunding projects or petitions). Then, they observed social dynamics on a daily basis over several weeks and examined whether the treated cases were more successful (e.g., in terms of funding or signatures) than the control group. The treatment group turned out to be substantially more successful over time than the control group, highlighting the role of small initial advantages in explaining inequalities in the success of qualitatively similar products, projects, petitions, etc.

Furthermore, as the study by van de Rijt et al. (2014) illustrates, digital traces offer particularly good opportunities for unobtrusive measurement. Being staged in the participants' "natural" environment of the web, digital field experiments are thus well-suited to study human behavior in a nonreactive way and under less abstract and artificial conditions than in the laboratory. However, actively intervening in the lives of people who have not given informed consent also raises important ethical and legal issues. Combined with the large-scale nature of such digital field experiments and the potential amplification of treatment effects via social dynamics, such concerns deserve particular attention. Likewise, treatment implementation and data access can require working with private companies. This can offer interesting new perspectives and opportunities, but such cooperation might also limit the questions researchers can ask, restrict the design of experiments, and raise questions about potential conflicts of interest. Moreover, due to legal or reputational concerns, companies might not be enthusiastic about sharing data with the scientific community, thereby creating tensions with the current push in academia toward open and reproducible research. While there has been an explosion of digital field experiments (e.g., Centola 2010; Bond et al. 2012; Munger 2016; Álvarez-Benjumea & Winter 2018), this area of research is still nascent and not all of these questions are solved yet. Nonetheless, the digital age offers exciting new opportunities to conduct field experiments and advance sociological theories.

8 Vignette Experiments

8.1 INTRODUCTION

The vignette or factorial survey experiment is a technique developed by Peter Rossi in the 1970s that subsequently evolved into a means to implement experiments on stated preferences within survey research. The main aim of vignette experiments is the study of normative judgments and choice behavior by "uncovering the underlying collective preference schedules concerning some domain of objects or actions" (Rossi 1979, 177). In a nutshell, vignettes are brief descriptions of social objects, including a list of characteristics that researchers deem to be relevant – based on some theory – for the choice or judgment at stake. In a vignette study, those characteristics represent predictors that vary systematically across vignettes and are used to explain respondents' choices.

Although it was initially devised for the study of social status,[1] this method is applicable to any research problem that can be reduced to persons making evaluations or choices concerning complex objects (Wallander 2009). For example, vignette experiments have been used to study justice evaluations of earned income (Jasso & Rossi 1977), attitudes toward a no-smoking norm (Opp 2002), hiring intentions of employers (Di Stasio & Gërxhani 2015), and migration decisions in partnerships (Abraham, Auspurg, & Hinz 2010). A similar technique, known as conjoint analysis, was developed in marketing research and later applied in political science (Green & Rao 1971; Hainmueller, Hopkins, & Yamamoto 2014). Conjoint analysis differs from vignette analysis in terms of presentation style, sampling design of the vignettes, and commonly used statistical analysis, but the

---

[1] Rossi (1979) developed the vignette technique to obtain ratings of various combinations of family characteristics (occupation, ethnicity, place of residence, educational attainment, etc.) that could be used to understand the principles underlying social status judgments.

basic idea is essentially the same. We elaborate on these differences in Section 8.3, where we describe these design characteristics.

Regardless of the specific nature of the object to be evaluated, human choices and judgments typically depend on many factors that differentiate the objects of judgment. In a traditional survey approach, researchers would investigate individual preferences by asking direct questions. However, this approach is problematic for two reasons. First, the direct measurement of judgments is subject to cognitive biases and limitations of the respondents (Krosnick, Judd, & Wittenbrink 2014). Second, isolating and measuring the importance of a single characteristic of a given social object is problematic because the characteristics that are most relevant for the evaluation are often correlated with each other in real life. Assuming that individual judgments possess an underlying ordered structure upon which individuals make choices carefully weighing all relevant factors, Rossi developed vignette analysis as an instrument to solve the collinearity problem and single out the effect of every factor on the judgment.

According to Jasso (2006), the choices that are suitable to be investigated using a vignette experiment can be classified into two types: positive beliefs and normative judgments. When the respondents' judgment concerns a positive belief, the evaluation of the vignette demands an answer about the nature of the situation according to the respondent. For example, Reilly et al. (1982) used a vignette study to investigate the perception of what constitutes sexual harassment on campus. On the other hand, normative judgments refer to those applications in which respondents provide a normative statement about the situation or the consequences that the situation should have, in their opinion. For example, Denk et al. (1997) asked participants to judge whether an expensive medical treatment administered to a terminally ill person was to be continued depending on various characteristics of the patient. In a review of vignette studies in sociology, Wallander (2009) identified a third type of judgment that is commonly elicited using vignette studies: own intentions or actions. In these studies, participants are asked what they would do if they were to make the decision that is presented in the vignette. For example, in an experimental study focusing on trust, Buskens and Weesie (2000) drew vignettes presenting car sellers with different characteristics and asked the participants to choose a car seller from whom they would buy a second-hand car.

8.2 TWO EXAMPLES OF VIGNETTE EXPERIMENTS

In this section, we describe two studies that will serve as references in the following section to illustrate the main design features of vignette experiments. We chose two examples that are rather different, both in terms of the design and the topic they address. The reason for doing so is that such flexibility is arguably one of the main advantages of this experimental technique.

8.2.1 Why Should Women Get Less?

The persistence and ubiquity of the gender pay gap suggest that, at least to a certain degree, both female and male workers consider the difference in wages for otherwise comparable male and female employees to be fair. Auspurg, Hinz, and Sauer (2017) conducted a large vignette study to investigate this puzzle in Germany. The German labor market is rather gender-segregated and characterized by high gender inequality. Furthermore, Germany has generous welfare provisions for parents who are likely to reinforce traditional work arrangements that generally benefit especially the male "breadwinner." In the literature on the gender pay gap, two alternative explanations for its persistence have been proposed. According to same-gender referent theory, women tend to compare themselves with other women or employees working in "feminine" occupations where they typically earn a lower salary than in more "masculine" occupations. According to social expectations theory, women's work is perceived to be less valuable than men's work because gender is a status characteristic: Men are generally assumed to have higher status and higher competence and, therefore, they are entitled to earn more. The existing empirical evidence is consistent with both explanations. Using a vignette experiment, Auspurg, Hinz, and Sauer (2017) investigated the perception of fairness in a setting in which the theories gave different predictions.

In this study, respondents were asked to evaluate the fairness of wages of fictitious employees described in the vignettes. The authors manipulated (between subjects) the amount of information provided to the respondents, creating three different versions of the vignettes containing five, eight, or twelve characteristics (i.e., predictors). Box 8.1 presents an example of a vignette with eight characteristics: age (four levels), gender (binary), vocational degree (three levels), occupation (ten levels), gross earnings per month (ten levels), experience (binary), job tenure (binary), and number of children (five levels). The gender of the vignette person provides a test for the hypothesis based on social expectation theory, that is, ceteris paribus, female workers are expected to earn less than male workers. Conversely, the gender of the respondent operationalizes the same-gender referent theory, that is, female respondents are expected to have lower reference standards. All other variables manipulated in the vignettes are standard control variables. In addition, in order to check for the effects of fatigue in larger vignette sets, the authors randomly assigned 10, 20, or 30 vignettes to each respondent. Instead of sampling from the whole vignette universe

> **Box 8.1** Why should women get less? (Auspurg, Hinz, & Sauer 2017) (italics added)
>
> A *50-year-old woman with no vocational training has two children.* She works as *a clerk* and has *a lot of job experience.* She *has worked for the organization for a long time.* Her monthly gross earnings total *1,200 euro* (before taxes and extra charges).
>   Are the monthly gross earnings of this person fair, or are they, from your point of view, unfairly high or low?
>
> | Unfairly low | | | | | Fair | | | | | Unfairly high |
> |---|---|---|---|---|---|---|---|---|---|---|
> | -5 | -4 | -3 | -2 | -1 | 0 | +1 | +2 | +3 | +4 | +5 |
> | ☐ | ☐ | ☐ | ☐ | ☐ | ☐ | ☐ | ☐ | ☐ | ☐ | ☐ |

(consisting of 48,000 unique vignettes in the version with eight characteristics), the authors created a subset of 240 vignettes using a quota design that maximizes the variance of vignette levels while minimizing the correlation between the characteristics. The study was administered to a random sample of the adult population in Germany in 2009. Overall, 1,604 respondents evaluated 26,207 vignettes.

The results of the study indicate that – consistent with social expectation theory – the gender of the fictitious employee significantly affects the perception of fairness: On average, women are perceived as overpaid and men as underpaid. Contrary to the prediction of same-gender referent theory, the results also show that the gender of the respondent does not influence the perception of fairness.

8.2.2 Trust Problems in the Purchase of a Second-Hand Car

The second study that we discuss is completely different from the first, not only for the obvious reason that it addresses a completely different research question but also because it focuses on own intentions or actions, rather than beliefs or judgments (see Jasso 2006 and Wallander 2009). The hypotheses are based on formal theoretical modeling, it uses a convenience sample, and it also differs on several design features. The vignette described above focuses on a normative judgment (Jasso 2006), while trust problems – the topic of this study – are typically analyzed as discrete choices, are often modeled using game-theoretical tools (e.g., Buskens & Raub 2013), and are generally studied through laboratory experiments (e.g., Yamagishi, Cook, & Watabe 1998). In these models, one actor (the trustor) faces a dilemma because (s)he has the opportunity to place trust in a second actor but fears that the trustee may behave opportunistically. These models postulate effects of dyadic

Box 8.2 Buying a Used Car (Buskens & Weesie 2000)

1	2
- You can buy a car for about $4000. - You bought a car from The Autoshop before and you were satisfied. - You do not expect to move out of town soon. - The Autoshop is a well-known garage and has many customers in your neighborhood. - As far as you know, none of your friends have bought a car from The Autoshop before. - You do not have a close social link with the owner of The Autoshop.	- You can buy a car for about $4000. - You never bought a car from The Autoshop before. - You will move to the other side of the country in a few weeks. - The Autoshop is a well-known garage and has many customers in your neighborhood. - You have friends who bought a car from The Autoshop before and they were satisfied. - The owner of the garage and you are members of the same football team.

2

If you prefer situation 1, press \1".
If you prefer situation 2, press \2".
If your preference for situation X is far from clear, press \1".
If your preference for situation X is rather clear, press \2".
If your preference for situation X is clear, press \3".
If your preference for situation X is very clear, press \4".

control, dyadic learning, network control, and network learning (Buskens & Raub 2013). Dyadic control refers to potential opportunities for the trustor to sanction the trustee in future interactions in case trust is abused. Dyadic learning refers to the possibility of learning about the trustworthiness of the trustee from past interactions. Network control and learning represent the same mechanism operating indirectly through social networks that can provide the trustor with opportunities to learn from others (network learning) or to sanction the trustee damaging his or her reputation through the network (network control). Buskens and Weesie (2000) devised a vignette experiment where these mechanisms were tested using a scenario in which the trustor is a customer who needs to select a seller from whom to purchase a second-hand car. An example of a vignette is presented in Box 8.2.

In these vignettes, six characteristics of the scenario vary, and each of them has two levels. From top to bottom, these variables represent (1) the magnitude of the stake (small vs. high), (2) opportunity for dyadic learning yes/no), (3) opportunity for dyadic control (yes/no), (4) opportunity for both network control and learning provided by a dense network (yes/no), (5) opportunity for network learning (yes/no), and (6) opportunity for network control (yes/no). As shown in Box 8.2, the authors presented the vignettes in pairs and asked the respondents to make a discrete choice, indicating the preferred scenario for buying a used car. This design consisted of 64 unique vignettes, forming 2016 different unordered pairs of vignettes. However, the authors reduced the vignette universe to 992 unordered pairs by eliminating pairs that would present the respondent with a trivial choice, that is, pairs in which one vignette had a larger number of characteristics facilitating trust. Each respondent evaluated ten vignettes, and pairs were generated randomly but with some constraints on the number of differing characteristics within pairs. The study was conducted in three sessions, and participants were undergraduate students from the University of Chicago (40) and from the University of Utrecht (72), as well as researchers participating at a conference on game theory held in Tilburg (13). The results supported the hypotheses; all characteristics representing opportunities for control and learning significantly increased the probability that a seller of a second-hand car was chosen.

8.3 DESIGN CHARACTERISTICS

The basic idea of a vignette study is to implement a factorial design, which is typical of laboratory and field experiments, into a survey. For this reason, vignette studies are also called factorial surveys. As illustrated by both the examples discussed earlier, the characteristics that are used as *factors* in the vignettes are usually either dummy variables – as in Buskens and Weesie (2000) – or ordinal variables – as in Auspurg, Hinz, and Sauer (2017). Once the researcher has chosen the factors that are theoretically relevant for the judgment (e.g., gender) and has determined the number of levels per each factor (e.g., male vs. female), a computer program generates vignettes randomly. Depending on the number of factors and levels of each factor, the size of the universe of unique vignettes covering all possible combinations can be easily computed as a Cartesian product. In an ideal textbook example of a vignette design, the universe of vignettes would be small enough that every respondent can judge all combinations (full factorial). As stated in the Introduction, one of the main reasons for conducting vignette studies is that they allow the researcher to disentangle the effects of factors that typically happen to correlate in real-life settings. For example, while the gender pay gap is largely prevalent in real-life settings, Auspurg, Hinz, and Sauer (2017) created a vignette sample in which the gender of the fictitious employees was not correlated with their gross wage. Similarly, the effects of network learning and control are difficult to test using survey data because

Vignette Experiments

they depend on the same network features (e.g., network density) and are thus usually highly collinear (Buskens & Weesie 2000).

8.3.1 Vignette Selection

In a setting where every respondent judges all existing unique vignettes, orthogonality among factors would be guaranteed. In reality, however, this is hardly ever possible because it would severely limit the number of factors and levels that researchers can include in the design. Therefore, in vignette studies, respondents judge only a subset of the vignette universe. Two main methods to select the vignette subset from the universe of possible combinations exist: random designs and quota designs (Dülmer 2007). Next to the use of full factorial designs, random designs are most common in sociological vignette studies (see Treischl & Wolbring 2022). By contrast, conjoint analysis generally adopts quota designs. Random designs consist of extracting independent samples (most often random without replacement) from the vignette universe. Then, the correlations between factors will obviously not be zero in all samples, but they will be very small in most samples. For example, Buskens and Weesie (2000) used a random design after excluding vignettes that implied trivial choices. An alternative solution is to use a clustered random design, that is, draw a limited number of samples and administer each sample to multiple respondents. This solution allow the researcher to investigate the effects of a single vignette on multiple respondents (Beck and Opp 2001).

Quota designs are strategies to identify a relatively small subset of the vignette universe that preserves the property of orthogonality among all factors and interactions between the factors. One way to achieve this is by using fractionalized factorial designs. Sometimes it is possible to obtain a fractionalized factorial design where factors are orthogonal, and all levels occur with the same frequency (orthogonal and balanced design). However, often generating a subset of the vignette universe that retains orthogonality between the factors is only possible if not all factor levels occur with the same frequency. In this case, orthogonality can be preserved only among the main effects of the factors. This solution is acceptable when it is theoretically plausible to assume no interaction effects between the factors (Dülmer 2007). An alternative strategy is to use D-efficient designs. D-efficient designs are a type of quota designs that relax the requirement of perfect orthogonality. As it is sometimes not possible to define a vignette sample that retains both orthogonality and balance, fractionalized factorial designs sacrifice balance to preserve orthogonality. By contrast, D-efficient designs use algorithms that aim at finding an optimal solution in which deviations from perfect balance and orthogonality are minimized. For example,

Auspurg, Hinz, and Sauer (2017) generated their vignette sample using a (nonorthogonal) D-efficient design that minimized correlations between the factors and still allowed them to estimate interaction effects between the factors. Kuhfeld, Tobias, and Garrat (1994) proposed D-efficiency as a measure of goodness of a design based on orthogonality and balance. If all variables included in the vignettes are standardized orthogonally coded, D-efficiency ranges between zero and 100, whereby 100 would be the score of a balanced orthogonal design (i.e., a vignette selection in which all factors' levels occur with same frequency and all correlations between the factors are zero). In most cases, a balanced orthogonal design is unattainable. Yet, the score of 100 provides a benchmark against which the D-efficiency obtained for a given design can be straightforwardly compared. When not all variables are standardized orthogonally coded, 100 is no longer the maximum value for D-efficiency, but the relative efficiency of alternative candidate designs can still be compared (Kuhfeld, Tobias, & Garrat 1994; Dülmer 2007). Efficient vignettes subsets are chosen using computer programs implementing search algorithms that use D-efficiency as an optimization criterion (see Dülmer 2007 for more details).

8.3.2 Type of Dependent Variables

In principle, the respondents' judgment on a topic (i.e., dependent variable) can have different measurement levels. The most common way of expressing judgments is by using ratings (e.g., Horne 2003; Auspurg, Hinz, & Sauer 2017). However, the outcome can also be a ranking task (e.g., Denk et al. 1997; Boots, Cochran, & Heide 2003), a binary choice (e.g., Buskens & Weesie 2000; Barrera & Buskens 2007), or both (Hainmueller, Hopkins, & Yamamoto 2014). A possible limitation of rating tasks is that they can produce ceiling effects, thereby reducing the statistical power to detect the effects of the vignette's characteristics. An alternative possibility is to use open scales (i.e., scales for which the minimum and maximum values are open, not predefined by the researchers, see Jasso 2006). However, a study comparing a classical rating with an open-scale rating found more measurement problems and missing values associated with the open scale (Sauer, Auspurg, & Hinz 2020). Ranking tasks are more common in market research and conjoint analysis, where researchers are often interested in the consumers' rankings of preferences for alternative products, while sociologists generally prefer ratings. As a consequence, conjoint analysis and vignettes often differ in terms of statistical analysis because rankings require nonlinear models, while ratings are often treated as metric and analyzed using linear models (Dülmer 2007). A binary choice task may be more realistic for the respondents when the judgment concerns their own actions or intentions (Barrera & Buskens 2007), while a rating task works best with normative judgments. This is because, in real life, actions typically consist of black-and-white (i.e., yes/no) decisions, whereas normative judgments are more likely to look like shades-of-gray decisions (e.g., the grade we give to a movie in a review).

8.3.3 Presentation Style

In most studies, the vignette looks like a short story and includes irrelevant details that only serve the purpose of enhancing realism. For example, Boots, Cochran, and Heide (2003) used vignettes depicting two murder scenarios. The description included the perpetrator's name, race, and gender; some details of the crime scene; and the weapon used. All vignette characteristics that are included in order to increase realism are held constant across vignettes. Therefore, they should not have any effect on the judgment. However, irrelevant pieces of information could obfuscate the main factors, leading the respondent to focus on the wrong details. Thus, often the vignette text description only lists the factors that are actually manipulated, as in Auspurg, Hinz, and Sauer (2017) (see Box 8.1). An alternative approach is to drastically reduce the vignette description and present only a table with the vignette factors and levels, as in Buskens and Weesie (2000) (see Box 8.2). This type of presentation is common in conjoint analysis, and its main advantage is that it makes it possible to also randomize the order of factors within the vignette (Sauer, Auspurg, & Hinz 2020). Hainmueller, Hangartner, and Yamamoto (2015) compared vignettes described in the form of an extensive text with vignettes described in a parsimonious way, via a tabular format without irrelevant details, with corresponding behavioral data from a natural experiment in Switzerland and found higher external validity in the data obtained from the tabular format. However, the tabular format may not be suitable for all research problems (Shamon, Dülmer, & Giza 2022). By making relevant information more salient, the tabular presentation could induce an acquiescence bias in the respondents (Sauer, Auspurg, & Hinz 2020). Shamon et al. (2019) and Sauer, Auspurg, and Hinz (2020) also compared text vignettes with tabular format vignettes focusing on measurement quality. The former study found more missing values in the text vignette version, while the latter found no significant differences between the two presentation formats. Regardless of the presentation format, the information provided to the respondents sometimes can confound the effect of the treatment because information on one attribute may induce respondents to update their beliefs on other attributes as well as, for example, attributes that, in real life, tend to be correlated with the attribute displayed in the vignette (Dafoe, Zhang, & Caughey 2018).

As a consequence, causal attribution of the effect observed to the factors manipulated could be problematic. To minimize this problem, one should carefully consider if it is plausible to assume that the information included in the different vignette versions presented to the respondents is equivalent with respect to the background features of the scenario (Dafoe, Zhang, & Caughey 2018). As possible countermeasures, Dafoe, Zhang, and Caughey (2018) recommend increasing the amount of fixed background information provided to the respondents in order to control for possible covariates or presenting the vignette as an "embedded natural experiment, that is, describing the assignment of the causal factor in the vignette as the result of a lottery, or of some other random process."

8.3.4 Respondents Sample

Another important difference between various vignette studies is the type of respondents' sample. One of the main advantages of vignette studies is the possibility to embed them in a regular survey and administer the study to a random sample of the general population (e.g., Hainmueller, Hopkins, & Yamamoto 2014; Auspurg, Hinz, & Sauer 2017). Nevertheless, as the factorial approach is a core component in the design of vignette experiments, this technique has been particularly popular among experimental researchers. Sometimes, vignette studies have been conducted by recruiting participants from the same subject pool used for laboratory experiments (e.g., Buskens & Weesie 2000; Barrera & Buskens 2007). The choice of the most appropriate respondent sample is often discussed in relation to external validity. As discussed in more detail in Chapter 10, students or convenience samples are considered valid as long as they can corroborate theoretical mechanisms that are difficult to observe with other methods, while the extent to which data obtained from these samples can be generalized to the general population is considered limited. Sometimes the research topic and setting require that the sample consists of experts because data on choices made by a random sample of a large population would not be very useful if the individuals making that very decision belonged to a specific group of experts. For example, to study juries' decisions to recommend a death sentence, a sample of members of a jury would certainly be preferable to a random sample of the general population (Boots, Cochran, & Heide 2003).

In the last decade, the availability of tools and platforms to recruit survey participants at a faster pace and with low costs has greatly increased. Therefore, the use of online panels has become more popular. In addition, more recently, crowdsource-labor sites such as Amazon Mechanical Turk, Prolific, or Qualtrics have also become popular. Thus, researchers are now using both population-based representative online samples and self-selected crowdsource-recruited samples to conduct surveys, online experiments, and vignette studies. In particular, the diffusion of "experimental rats," that is, semiprofessional participants in online studies, raises some concern about the external validity of results obtained with such nonrandom samples (e.g., Chmielewski & Kucker 2019; Kennedy et al. 2020). However, one study comparing three vignette experiments conducted using an online random sample and a crowdsource-recruited sample found very similar results, even though the two samples were quite different in terms of demographics (Weinberg, Freese, & McElhattan 2014). In a similar vein, Coppock (2018) and Mullinix et al. (2016) found that results obtained from online convenience samples like Amazon Mechanical Turk are similar to those obtained from national samples. Coppock, Leeper, and Mullinix (2018) showed that the correspondence between studies conducted with convenience and representative samples results from treatment homogeneity across subgroups in the experiments.

9 Natural Experiments and Quasi-experiments

9.1 INTRODUCTION

There are occasions in which conducting a randomized experiment might not be possible for legal, ethical, or practical reasons. For example, a policy intervention may require that all potential participants receive the same treatment, preventing the possibility of assigning participants to treatment and control randomly. Another example is the analysis of policy or other past changes that may have affected some outcome variables of interest. In this case, the researcher cannot, obviously, assign the units to treatment randomly. However, in these examples, researchers may still be interested in the causal effect of the policy or intervention. An alternative to randomized experiments in these cases are the so-called natural or quasi-experiments. In this chapter, we address these designs that, although not based on experimental data, share many features with experimental designs.

9.2 NATURAL EXPERIMENTS

Hurricane Katrina was one of the most powerful Atlantic storms on record, reaching category 4 on the commonly used Saffir–Simpson hurricane scale. It caused catastrophic damages in the city of New Orleans in the summer of 2005. More than one million people left before the storm, but tens of thousands remained in a city that, by the end of August, was mostly underwater. One of the major and long-lasting effects of this hurricane was that the city had lost almost 30 percent of its population by 2011, and by 2020, it still remained 20 percent below its level in 2000.

A large number of social science papers explore the social, economic, and political consequences of the dramatic and unexpected shock caused by Hurricane Katrina. Just to name a few, De Silva et al. (2010) estimate the effect of immigration on workers' earnings taking advantage of the displacement of the population to new areas produced by the hurricane; Phan and Airoldi (2015) investigate social network formation, friendship, and social dynamics using data from the student population affected by the hurricane; and Kirk (2009, 2015) studies the effect of relocation of ex-prisoners to different geographic areas due to the hurricane. All these examples have one thing in common: They claim that they use a *natural experiment*. They are not unique in this; a simple online search returns several hundred papers that do the same after that hurricane happened. Other natural disasters have been likewise used to understand social dynamics and human behavior. For example, Hikichi et al. (2017) exploit the 2011 Great East Japan earthquake and tsunami to understand changes in social capital in Japan.

To comprehend the logic of a natural experiment, we will first focus on Kirk's (2015) study due to its sociological significance. The study departs from a well-established social regularity in the United States: Approximately one-half of released prisoners return to prison within three years of release. The question is what causes this high level of recidivism? As in many sociological examples, one can think of (1) individual characteristics of the offenders that make them more prone to re-offend or (2) structural features like social conditions (poverty) or established criminal networks in certain neighborhoods. In Chapter 4, we have called the first explanation *selection* of individuals into some behaviors (crime), and the second would be the treatment effect of returning to certain neighborhoods on recidivism. With observational data, where a researcher can observe that prisoners go back to their neighborhood after prison, these two explanations cannot be separated: It is the same individual going back to the same type of neighborhood. However, using a natural disaster like the Katrina shock, Kirk builds two comparison groups: those who went back to their original geographic area and those who were relocated to other areas due to the hurricane. He finds that those sent to neighborhoods with a lower rate of ex-prisoners diminish their reincarceration rate.

The idea of natural experiments goes well beyond natural disasters. A second area populated by natural experiments, and perhaps the one that has popularized them most, is institutional or policy changes. A classic example on the effect of changing a key labor institution – the minimum wage – on employment levels deserved a Nobel Prize in 2021. Card and Krueger (1994) exploited the fact that in 1992, the hourly minimum wage was increased in New Jersey but remained unchanged in the comparable area of eastern Pennsylvania. The treatment was the minimum wage increase, the treatment group fast-food restaurants in New Jersey, and the control group fast-food restaurants in Pennsylvania. Note that the two groups are restricted to fast-food restaurants since they are affected by minimum wage regulations. Also, these two states have a border in common and are expected to be affected by similar macroeconomic shocks. All these research decisions are taken to guarantee that the two groups are comparable, which is crucial for natural experiments, as we will argue later. The outcome variable was full-time employment, measured before and after the increase of the minimum salary in New Jersey, and the main conclusion of the study was that this increase did not reduce full-time employment in the treatment group as predicted by economic theory.

This design has inspired hundreds of studies using policy changes as natural experiments, especially in the fields of labor market, population studies, and education. Lefebvre and Merrigan (2008) exploited the introduction of a new childcare policy in Canada to estimate the effect on the labor supply of mothers with young children; González (2013) studied the temporary introduction of a universal child benefit in Spain on conceptions, abortions, and maternal labor supply; Gërxhani and Kosyakova (2022) relied on national dispersal policies that determine the residential allocation of refugees in Germany to study the effect of co-ethnic social capital on immigrants' labor market integration; and Azmat and Iriberri (2010) took advantage of the fact that for one year only, a cohort of students received information about their relative performance in class to explore the effect of this information on their subsequent performance. Note that this last example uses real data that mimic a situation commonly explored in the laboratory: the provision of feedback on relative performance in social, mostly competitive interactions.

Natural disasters and policy changes share the fact that they are *unexpected* for the subject population. Also, they cannot be manipulated by this population. This is obvious for natural disasters, and it is thought to be so for policy changes. When events are unexpected and cannot be manipulated, we commonly say they are exogenous to the involved population. It is precisely this *exogeneity* that natural experiments leverage for causal identification. However, if manipulability was one of the defining characteristics of experiments, why do we call a situation that, by definition, cannot be manipulated an experiment? A simple answer is that natural experiments are not experiments in a strict sense but a highly appreciated subset of nonexperimental – observational – methods that try to mimic an actual experimental design (Titiunik 2021). The latter implies that natural experiments follow a counterfactual logic, where natural disasters or policy changes exogenously create two comparable conditions, thereby mimicking manipulation.

A second characteristic that is typically associated with natural experiments is *randomness*. A classic example was the study of the effects of the Vietnam draft lottery on a number of variables in the United States, including payoffs to schooling (Angrist & Krueger 1992), political attitudes (Erikson & Stoker 2011), and mortality rates (Conley & Heerwig 2012). All these cases rely on the fact that a physical device (a lottery) was used to assign groups of men to a treatment (drafted to war) or a control (undrafted) group. Again, the idea is that the assignment to the treatment groups cannot be manipulated by the researcher, guaranteeing the exogeneity of the treatment assignment. The use of an actual device that secures randomness ex ante helps the research design fulfill the requirements of causal identification described in Chapter 4 of this book: The treatment assignment is unbiased.

However, sometimes the exogeneity of the so-called natural experiment is not as crystal clear as in a natural disaster or in an unexpected policy change. Take, for instance, the study of Legewie (2013), exploiting the fact that the terror attack in Bali on October 2002 occurred during the fieldwork period of the European Social Survey to study the causal effect of terrorist events on attitudes toward immigrants. Balcells and Torrats-Espinosa (2018) also focus on several terrorist attacks in Spain that coincided with the fieldwork of nationally representative surveys. Researchers observed subject responses before and after the attacks and estimated the effect of this unexpected event on attitudes. A similar example is described in Muñoz, Falcó-Gimeno, and Hernández (2020), in which the authors exploit the Charlie Hebdo terrorist attacks in 2015 in Paris as a shock to study French citizens' satisfaction with their national government and their attitudes toward immigration. A terrorist attack is certainly unexpected, but one could argue that it is not completely exogenous, especially on public opinion, something that terrorists are arguably intending to influence. In this sense, exogeneity does not seem to be the crucial characteristic defining a natural experiment in these cases. Similarly, Brugarolas and Miller (2021) claim they use a natural experiment in a clearly not exogenous situation. As in the previous examples, they exploit a shock during the fieldwork of a survey, in this case, the release of the most important election forecast during the fieldwork of a large-scale poll in Spain. But the release of the forecast by the poll institute and even the decision to call elections are hardly exogenous. The Spanish President has the right to arbitrarily decide when to call elections, and this decision is definitely influenced by polls.

In summary, we have reviewed studies claiming to exploit a natural experiment that are based on an undoubtedly exogenous event (a natural disaster), randomness (a lottery draft), or situations that are hardly exogenous or random (shocks during the fieldwork of surveys). What does then define a natural experiment? We argue that a natural experiment is simply defined by the fact that an *external force* assigns the treatment of interest. Why is then a natural experiment commonly considered a privileged method of causal identification? Because it helps the researcher to use observational data while clearly identifying the control and treatment groups and study the intervening variables that may confound the causal identification. A natural experiment is an *as-if* experiment, a situation that is not experimental by definition but that mimics an experiment. It is not experimental because there is no experimenter's intervention and manipulation, but it resembles an experiment in that the experimental groups are comparable as if they were produced by the intervention and manipulation of the researcher. Guaranteeing the comparability of the experimental groups created by the external force constitutes the cornerstone of natural experiments.

9.3 QUASI-EXPERIMENTS

In sociology, there is a long tradition of *quasi-experiments*, defined as experiments in which units are not assigned to conditions randomly (Shadish, Cook, & Campbell 2002). They share with natural experiments the fact that they are not randomized trials, but they differ in that natural experiments are the outcome of an external force and quasi-experiments require intervention and manipulation. On close inspection, this distinction is not as important in practical terms as one could expect. In both cases, the problem is how to estimate causal effects using nonrandomized data. Moreover, and more importantly, here we argue that the main answers to the problem of the nonrandom assignment are the same in both cases.

Consider the logic of many social and policy interventions in which randomization is not possible for legal, political, or ethical reasons. A prototypical example is a training program to help unemployed people to find a new job. How do we assess the effect of the program? Typically, we cannot rely on a randomized experiment since the intervention only targets those who need it and we face a problem of self-selection or selection into treatment. At best, we can work on a quasi-experimental design in which we compare the mean outcome (finding a job) between those who took part in the program and a comparable group in terms of observable characteristics of unemployed people. In this case, we clearly need to resort to balance tests of predetermined covariates and placebo tests, as advocated earlier.

This is also true for the classic ex post facto experiment (Chapin 1936; Greenwood 1945), in which the researcher cannot manipulate ex ante the treatment of interest. This design has been referred to as a quasi-experiment. However, it is closer to the types of natural experiments discussed in this chapter, and in most cases, it fits the definition proposed earlier. This classic account of Thistlewaite and Campbell (1960, 309) serves the purpose:

"[the ex post facto design] has come to indicate more specifically the mode of analysis in which two groups – an experimental and a control group – are selected through matching to yield a quasi-experimental comparison. In such studies, the groups are presumed, as a result of matching, to have been equivalent prior to the exposure of the experimental group to some potentially change-inducing event (the "experimental treatment"). If the groups differ on subsequent measures and if there are no plausible rival hypotheses which might account for the differences, it is inferred that the experimental treatment has caused the observed differences."

Romanò and Barrera (2021) used a similar approach to investigate the effects of a set of market-oriented reforms on inequality in Cuba. These reforms led to the introduction of a dual-currency system that benefited especially those workers who had legitimate access to exchanges in hard currency (tied to the US dollar). The authors selected two (treated) groups of workers with legitimate access to exchanges in hard currency – small entrepreneurs and employees of state-owned enterprises operating in the touristic sector – and a comparable (control) sample of workers from the general population, who did not have legitimate access to exchanges in hard currency. Their results showed that not only the entrepreneurs but also the state employees operating in the touristic sector had accumulated more wealth than the workers in the control group.

Regardless of whether we call this approach a natural experiment or a quasi-experiment, the instruments for analyzing it are the same. The three steps introduced next to define and analyze observational data as if it were experimental apply to both natural experiments and quasi-experiments.

9.4 NATURAL EXPERIMENTS AND QUASI-EXPERIMENTS AS AS-IF EXPERIMENTS

The analysis of natural experiments[1] involves a three-step process: (1) identifying the external force causing the treatment assignment; (2) testing and showing that the treatment groups are similar in all relevant characteristics but the treatment, as if they were assigned randomly; and (3) estimating the treatment effect in the same way one would do it in a randomized experiment. In this section, we will review these three steps paying special attention to the crucial step 2.

9.4.1 Identifying the External Force Defining the Natural Experiment

The first step is not technical but relies on sociological imagination. Researchers must find a situation in which two groups can be clearly

---

[1] For the sake of simplicity, from now on, we will only write natural experiments when referring to both natural experiments and quasi-experiments.

separated using the independent variable of interest. This variable is the shock (natural experiment) or the nonrandom assignment mechanism (quasi-experiments), for example, Hurricane Katrina causing a shock to the reallocation of ex-prisoners to different areas or the increase of the minimum income causing a shock in the fast-food industry's labor conditions. The dependent variable should then be easy to measure, like recidivism or employment levels in these cases. Note that natural, economic, political, or social shocks and interventions may offer ideal conditions for the treatment groups to be easily identified and compared. However, there are no special features of the situation that guarantee *per se* the ideal conditions of a natural experiment. Whether these conditions are met or not is the task of step 2 of the process.

9.4.2 Constructing the Treatment Groups

The goal of step 2 is to construct, using nonrandomized observational data, a situation in which the treatment groups are as similar as if they were the result of a randomization process. Then, the first task is to test whether the treatment groups differ in relevant predetermined covariates. However, determining which covariates are relevant is not obvious. An example may illustrate the case.

Brugarolas and Miller (2021) exploit a shock – the release of the most important election forecast during the fieldwork of a representative survey – to study changes in voter turnout. To do so, they test whether the groups of survey respondents before and after the shock are sufficiently similar. The problem is that the survey contains dozens of variables, and it would be unpractical to test the differences between the two groups for each potential variable. What they do, and this may apply to much sociological survey-based research, is starting from the set of predetermined covariates used by the poll institute to define its random sample of the Spanish population and assess whether their data can be treated as if the treatment was randomized. They work with a random sample that is representative of the Spanish population and was generated through randomly chosen sampling points (random routes) and gender, age, and town size quotas. They use these three predetermined covariates as the basis for their comparison tests. Their control and treatment groups are, therefore, subgroups of a random sample of a large population, which are balanced in terms of this selection of predetermined covariates. This is becoming standard in the analysis of natural experiments: Find a data-generating process (e.g., the fieldwork of a survey) that is affected by an external force that generates groups as in a purposely designed randomized intervention. How is this done in the complex social world?

A way to find naturally occurring as-if experimental groups is to exploit time and space discontinuities. Brugarolas and Miller (2021) knew the exact hour in which the interview was taken and used this information to compare groups of respondents who took the interview just before and just after the release of the forecast. This allows the researchers to work with such a small time window that nothing else but the treatment was expected to happen. However, this also offers the possibility to use larger time windows and test whether the selected time period matters. In fact, they replicate their effect using thirteen time windows of different sizes and show that their main result is robust to different window specifications. Finally, they used all the information contained in the survey to perform placebo tests and check whether the release of the forecast affected any other variable. Other researchers use geographic discontinuities in which a geographic or administrative boundary splits the sample of units into treated and control areas in an assumed as-if random fashion (Keele & Titiunik 2015).

A widely used instrument to construct as-if random groups in political science is the results of close elections. A prominent example is the study of incumbent advantage. The idea is that if close elections are partly determined by chance, the effect of winning an election can be considered an external force that affects the results of the subsequent election. The effect of this external force may vary across studies, however. Klasnja and Titiunik (2017) study all Brazilian mayoral elections between 1996 and 2012 and show that becoming the incumbent party results in large subsequent electoral losses. Hainmueller, Hangartner, and Pietrantuono (2017) also utilize a close result to analyze a sociologically relevant problem: the effect of naturalization on the integration of immigrants in Switzerland. They exploit referendums on naturalization across Swiss states and compare immigrants residing in states where laws promoting naturalization won the referendum by a narrow margin and residents of states where these laws lost by a narrow margin. In this way, they can compare immigrants that are otherwise similar and estimate the causal effect of naturalization.

All previous examples are examples of the so-called *regression discontinuity design* (RDD).[2] In RDDs, researchers exploit sudden jumps in time, space, or other variables – referendum results, date of birth, etc. – to construct groups of individuals or units that are similar on everything but the treatment. RDDs are then paradigmatic examples of natural experiments. Still, even in the best-case scenario of as-if random assignment,

---

[2] For recent reviews of the methodology of RDDs, see Cattaneo, Idrobo, & Titiunik (2020).

RDDs are not actual randomized experiments, and small differences between the treatment and control groups may persist and affect the experiment's outcome. If this is the case, researchers may use additional techniques to guarantee that the two groups are comparable. One of these techniques is *matching*. The idea of matching is to find, for every treated unit, one or more nontreated units with similar observable characteristics. In general, the idea is to construct comparison groups ex post that mimic a randomized experiment. Once this as-if experiment is constructed, the same statistical techniques typically employed to analyze randomized experiments are used.

There are other research designs that exploit naturally occurring phenomena to construct natural experiments and quasi-experiments. Besides RDDs, another prominent example is the difference-in-difference (DID) technique. DID employs longitudinal data from treatment and control groups to create a counterfactual to estimate a causal effect. A typical example is the effect of a specific intervention or treatment (such as a passage of a law or a large-scale program implementation) by comparing the changes in outcomes over time between a population that is enrolled in a program (the intervention group) and a population that is not (the control group).[3] We now turn to step 3 of the analysis of natural experiments.

9.4.3 Analyzing Natural Experiments

When analyzing natural experiments, two important features have to be considered. First, one can never be completely sure that there is no unobserved characteristic that is driving the difference between treatment and control. In other words, in natural experiments, one should assume a larger degree of unobserved heterogeneity across groups than in randomized experiments. Second, regression discontinuity designs, matching methods, and other instruments for causal identification may reduce the sample size substantially since, many times, the analysis only focuses on small groups of individuals or units around a specific cutoff point. This has implications for the type of statistical analysis used. The recommendation is to use a number of techniques that may reduce the uncertainty around the reported treatment effect. Three common techniques are the analysis of predetermined covariates before estimating the treatment effect, the use of inference methods for small samples when estimating the treatment effect, and the implementation of placebo tests after estimating the treatment effect.

---

[3] For an extended treatment of DID techniques, see Angrist and Pischke (2009); for an application to policy and program evaluation, see Gertler et al. (2011).

Balance tests on the relevant predetermined covariates are not unique to natural experiments; they are also highly recommended for randomized, especially field, experiments. The idea is to balance those covariates not affected by their treatment status. Ideally, one wants to select two groups in which all relevant covariates are balanced. In many of the aforementioned examples, researchers typically compare small groups of individuals or units just above (before) and below (after) a cutoff point, for example, the dates of the hurricane in the prisoners' example or the days of the terrorist attacks in the survey example. Once these groups are selected, one performs falsification tests on the relevant covariates to rule out the possibility of imbalances between the groups. These falsification tests are similar to the tests that are later used to estimate the treatment effect, and the falsification logic is the same.[4]

Once one is satisfied with the balance between the treatment groups, the treatment effect is estimated as in a randomized experiment. To avoid problems associated with small sample comparisons and the assumptions of most parametric tests, Imbens and Rubin (2015) recommend using randomization tests that involve shuffling the data before computing values (e.g., mean and median differences) and then comparing the results after shuffling to the original data.

However, one is never completely sure about the results in the analysis of natural experiments, and a third technique involves the so-called placebo tests. The principle underlying the implementation of placebo tests is the same as the one for falsification tests or for predetermined outcomes. One should analyze the placebo in the same way as the outcome of interest. Examples of placebo tests include testing the purported treatment effect in a time window not containing the natural shock, testing outcomes that are not assumed to be affected by the shock, or doing so on a population that could not be affected because, for instance, they are in a geographically separated area where the shock did not possibly produce remarkable consequences. Again, here the researcher is trying to find a null effect, and higher p-values are recommended. One aspect that is often problematic in natural experiments is the violation of the SUTVA due to the fact that the treatment of one group also affects the control group (see Chapters 4 & 7). For example, introducing fees for universities in one state might lead students to study in another state.

---

[4] Note that here one is looking for a null effect, so to be on the conservative side, one should rely on higher statistical p-values. Cattaneo, Idrobo, and Titiunik (2020) recommend using p-values above 0.2 to reject the hypothesis of significant differences in relevant covariates between the control and treatment groups.

PART III
Methodological Challenges of Experimentation in Sociology

10 Validity

10.1 INTRODUCTION

The issue of validity in empirical research refers to the robustness and replicability of what we learn from the data beyond the case under investigation. Therefore, validity refers to the approximate truth of an inference or a knowledge claim. In simple terms, validity asks whether the conclusions drawn from a research study are justified.[1] In sociology, most researchers continue to use the distinction between internal and external validity introduced by Donald Campbell and his collaborators more than 60 years ago (Campbell, 1957; Campbell & Stanley 1966; Cook & Campbell 1979). In their original contributions, internal validity "refers to the approximate validity with which we infer that a relationship between two variables is *causal* or that the absence of a relationship implies the absence of *cause*" (Cook & Campbell 1979, 37) (italics added). External validity, on the other hand, "refers to the approximate validity with which we can infer that the presumed causal relationship can be *generalized* to and across alternate measures of the cause and effect and across different types of persons, settings, and times" (italics added). In short, internal validity relates to causality – inferences "in" or "within" the experiment ensured by experimental control – and external validity relates to generalizability – inferences "beyond" or "outside" the experiment.

The sustained popularity of this classic internal/external validity contraposition is surprising. In the mid-eighties, Campbell (1986, 68) himself proposed abandoning this terminology, referring to misunderstandings that had arisen caused by the idea of equating internal validity to "pure" (laboratory) treatments and external validity to "representativeness."

---

[1] An alternative use of the concept of validity can be found in the literature on "nonrandom measurement error." In this literature, validity does not refer to the truth of scientific inferences, but to the quality of measurement instruments. For a recent discussion of measurement error, see Gallop and Weschle (2019).

Instead of internal validity, he proposed a new concept of "local molar validity" to stress the fact that (i) a single experimental result can only be interpreted locally and (ii) any experimental treatment comprises a complex combination (or "whole molar package") of many components, which are all tested simultaneously within the treatment condition. As an alternative to external validity, Campbell (1986) suggested the idea of "proximal similarity." In doing so, he recognizes that no two environments are precisely equal. Nevertheless, one would like to use experimental results to draw conclusions about situations that are sufficiently similar to the experimental treatment setup. In this way, proximal similarity emphasizes the need for generalizability more than representativeness.

These new concepts enjoyed little fortune. In fact, Campbell and associates themselves abandoned them and returned to the internal/external distinction. In doing so, they did add two other concepts: construct validity and statistical conclusion validity.[2] The latter refers to the size and significance level of an experimental result. Construct validity is a more involved concept; it "concerns how to go from the particular units, treatments, observations, and settings on which data are collected to the higher order constructs these instances represent" (Shadish, Cook, & Campbell 2002, 20). In other words, construct validity involves the extent to which a measure summarizing data assesses the theoretical construct it intends to describe. For example, if one runs an experiment using a social value orientation test to measure the theoretical construct "social value orientations," then construct validity concerns the extent to which the outcomes of this test – applied in the particular way as determined by one's experimental design – accurately describe social value orientations. Note that construct validity also represents a kind of generalization, but it is not a substitute for external validity (Morton & Williams 2010).

Statistical conclusion validity and construct validity are concerned with the extent to which one can logically draw conclusions from an experimental analysis. With these two concepts, Shadish, Cook, and Campbell (2002) extend the notion of internal validity beyond the question of causality alone. They also extend the notion of external validity beyond the concept of generalization by introducing the notions of ecological validity and population validity. The former is related to whether the methods, materials, and settings of the research are similar to a given target

---

[2] The idea of construct validity was not new. In the context of measurement theory, Cronbach and Meehl (1955) are argued to be the first to propose it. Construct validity is used in the context of assessing the validity of a measurement by means of comparison with some theoretical implications when an objective term of comparison for the measurement (i.e., a criterion) is not available.

Figure 10.1 Types of validity.

environment, for example, whether an experiment about hiring is similar to a corresponding setting in the labor market. Population validity refers to the extent to which the sample is representative of the target population about which the researcher wishes to make inferences, that is, representative of employers' hiring behavior. Thus, this type of external validity refers to the generalizability of the subject pool.

All these concepts can be represented in a continuum going from causal identification to generalization (see Figure 10.1) without implying that the two extreme poles are mutually exclusive. Still, as we have discussed in previous chapters – most notably in Chapter 4 on causality – every concept in this continuum has received several interpretations in sociology and the whole social sciences.

In assessing the validity of experimental research, the first problem one faces is selecting a conceptual framework. This is not trivial since using one framework or another gives rise to several conceptual ambiguities. The case of external validity is especially troublesome because it has been related to very different concepts, including generalizability (of the treatment effect), generality, relevance (for policy), representativeness, extrapolation (to a population or to a target), realism, and similarity. The goal here is not to discuss the meaning of all of these concepts but to show the multiplicity of ideas associated to external validity in the different social science literatures.

A second concern refers to the logical relationship between internal and external validity. Social psychology textbooks (e.g., Brehm, Kassin, & Fein 1990; Smith & Mackie 1999) commonly refer to a tension between internal and external validity. This implies a trade-off between causality through control (internal validity) and generalizability (external validity) of experimental results (Jimenez-Buedo & Miller 2010). On the one hand, internal validity requires shielding the experiment against extraneous influences that could interfere with the experimental treatment. On the other hand, this shielding against external factors could reduce the extent to which one can "transport" the results to other contexts and populations. In contrast, an experiment that is designed to "realistically" represent the world outside the laboratory may increase external validity, but it limits control over all potential intervening factors that may interact with the treatment, and therefore, it may reduce the possibilities for causal inference.

Although the trade-off between internal and external validity is intuitive, the idea has been widely contested (Thye 2000; Hogarth 2005).

One important reason why the trade-off is no longer generally accepted stems from the realization that internal validity is a prerequisite of external validity. Here, the argument is that it is difficult to see how causal inferences from an experimental study that is not internally valid could be generalizable. Interestingly, Campbell and Stanley (1963, 5) were the first to state this argument when they argued that "While internal validity is the *sine qua non*, and while the question of external validity, like the question of inductive inference, is *never completely answerable*, the selection of designs strong in both types of validity is obviously our ideal" (emphasis added).

Because the trade-off is no longer central to the debate, we will not structure our analysis of validity in this chapter around the internal versus external validity discussion.[3] Instead, we will focus on a slightly different and more recent debate that can be best summarized as relating to empirical and theoretical approaches to validity. In a nutshell, the empirical approach to validity proposes that there are empirical methods (e.g., field experiments) that are as good as other methods (e.g., laboratory experiments) in attaining internal validity but superior in achieving external validity. This approach assumes there is a "gold standard" for valid experimental research. In contrast, the theoretical approach to validity argues that there is no methodological gold standard and that external validity can only be achieved through theory. What is generalized is a theoretical mechanism and not a single empirical finding.

The rest of the chapter will describe these two approaches to validity in more detail. We can anticipate that the reader will not find a definitive answer to the validity issue, but we do aspire to provide a better understanding of the assumptions underlying each approach. Given that causality through control (internal validity) has been extensively addressed in Chapter 4, in the following, we will mostly focus on the concept of validity as generalizability.

10.2 THE EMPIRICAL APPROACH TO VALIDITY

We start with the empirical approach to validity (EAV, hereafter) because it is the validity concept in the minds of most social scientists. The EAV refers to the concepts of "realism," "similarity," and "representativeness." The

---

[3] The reader can find good summaries of this debate in widely employed handbooks in sociology (Willer & Walker 2007; Webster & Sell 2014a), political science (Morton & Williams 2010), and economics (Guala 2005; Bardsley et al. 2010).

basic requirement here is that research constructs are as similar or as representative as possible to "reality." For this reason, EAV favors experiments that are performed on relevant samples and in natural conditions. As a consequence, field experiments and randomized trials are typically considered the gold standards under this framework.

The EAV approach has been strongly endorsed by the so-called randomistas.[4] These are primarily economists, and among them, John List and several of his coauthors (Levitt & List 2009; Al-Ubaydli & List 2015) have been prominent in arguing that due to their occurrence in natural settings, field experiments are superior to laboratory experiments with regard to external validity. Al-Ubaydli and List (2015) present an ad hoc model in which they show that this superiority of field experiments holds regardless of whether the results of a particular experiment can be generalized globally (to any other empirical instance), locally (to similar settings), or not at all (to no other case). They argue that if any result is, by definition, generalizable, "neither field nor laboratory experiments are demonstrably superior to the other" (433), but if results can only be generalized locally (to neighboring cases), "field experiments are more useful than laboratory experiments" (434). Field experiments are argued to be more useful because of being conducted in a natural setting. This last statement is a good summary of the position of many social scientists who, assuming the empirical uncertainty or even the practical impossibility of extrapolation, claim that only research conducted in "relevant" settings is (externally) valid (see Jackson & Cox 2013 and Baldassarri & Abascal 2017 for extensive discussions). If results are strongly dependent on specific settings like social context or population, then no experiment can be generalized beyond the context in which it was run. One may believe that the context of a field experiment is more relevant for other field applications than for the social environment of a laboratory, but in the current state of the field, the verdict is still out (see the Discussion).

Al-Ubaydli and List (2015) go even further in their defense of the superiority of field experiments and claim that this type of experiment is also as strong as laboratory experiments in internal validity. Their argument is that both laboratory and field experiments can be similarly affected by extraneous factors that can confound the experimental treatment. The researcher needs to control these factors in the laboratory as well as in the field. Such claims have led to an ongoing debate between laboratory and field experimentalists, which has contributed to the development of

---

[4] In recent years and due to its popularity, researchers who use randomized control trials have been called *randomistas*. This group includes prominent researchers such as the 2019 Nobel prize laureates in economics –Abhijit Banerjee, Esther Duflo, and Michael Kremer.

experimental methodology in the social sciences, on the one hand, but it has led to persistent stereotypes of laboratory experiments, on the other hand. This latter view is discussed in various studies, such as Schram (2005), Falk and Heckman (2009), and Camerer (2015).

In an influential paper, trying to address precisely the criticism of List and his associates on laboratory experiments, Camerer (2015, 253) argues that "the idea that concerns about generalizability are not special to lab experiments, [which is] in fact, found in Levitt and List [2007] too, at the end of their paper: the sharp dichotomy sometimes drawn between lab experiments and data generated in natural settings is a false one. The same concerns arise in both settings regarding the interpretation of estimates and their generalizability outside of the immediate application, circumstances, and treated population." The main argument of this camp in the laboratory–field controversy is that since the main goal of experimentation is to isolate a causal effect on a variable of interest, the research question is ultimately what determines the best method to be applied (Falk & Heckman 2009). Like with any other empirical method, the answer to the research question will tell us more about how our explanatory variables will affect our outcome variable(s). Because of their tight(er) control on the explanatory variables, laboratory experiments are often the more appropriate method to apply if the goal is to examine "pure" treatment effects. Because field experiments can offer more potentially relevant variation in explanatory variables, they can be applied to complement laboratory experiments in providing quantitative results on a targeted population or context.

In the end, the question of generalizability is an empirical one. Indeed, numerous empirical studies have been conducted to substantiate claims made by both camps of the laboratory–field debate. These studies have primarily appeared in the economics literature since this debate is most prominent in experimental economics (e.g., Camerer 2015; Snowberg & Yariv 2021). To date, little to no evidence has been found in support of the idea that field experiments in economics have higher generalizability than laboratory experiments, especially if one is interested in the direction of treatment effects (e.g., whether a change in an independent variable has a positive or a negative effect on a dependent variable). In sociology, the proponents of the empirical approach to validity, by and large, share the intuition that field experiments are stronger in external validity and, therefore, more relevant to the study of sociological phenomena (Franzen & Pointner 2013). Their concerns are concentrated around three main topics of the debate, namely, (1) the use of student samples, (2) selection into the laboratory, and (3) artificiality of laboratory experiments, which is why we offer a glimpse of the debate around these topics here.

The use of student samples has been a continuous line of attack against laboratory experiments. Those raising this concern question whether we can learn anything about the "real world" by studying such a population.[5] They draw on empirical studies where students appear to behave differently; for instance, students are less prosocial than nonstudent samples in experimental situations involving the distribution of unearned resources (Carpenter, Burks, & Verhoogen 2005; Carpenter, Connolly, & Myers 2008; Anderson et al. 2013; Falk, Meier, & Zehnder 2013; Belot, Duch, & Miller 2015). In sociology, Bader et al. (2021) conclude that quantitative behavioral data obtained from standard student samples differ significantly from data obtained from the broader population, although qualitative treatment differences remain stable across samples. Likewise, combining an original study and a meta-analysis of previous studies, Galizzi and Navarro-Martinez (2018) present results suggesting that behavior in experimental laboratory games predicts very poorly current and past behavior in the field. On the other hand, Reindl, Hoffmann, and Kittel (2019) find that student behavior in the laboratory predicts their cooperation in classroom tasks very well. The main counter-argument to the concerns underlying these studies is that the key goal of laboratory experiments is not to predict everyday behavior but to measure treatment effects of a causal relationship (i.e., comparative statics) (Schram 2005; Falk & Heckman 2009; Camerer 2015). Moreover, these scholars refer to other empirical studies that do show consistent results between student and nonstudent samples (Bellemare, Kröger, & van Soest 2008; Dohmen et al. 2011). For instance, in an overview of thirteen studies in experimental economics that compared student subject pools to "professionals," Fréchette (2015) found little evidence of any important difference. Similar outcomes are also found in a recent study by Snowberg and Yariv (2021), which aims precisely to address concerns about the external validity of experiments with student samples. They compare behavior between an almost entire population of undergraduate students in an American university, an MTurk convenience sample of US participants, and a representative sample of the US population. Based on their findings, they conclude that "experiments utilizing undergraduate students, in or outside the lab, allow generalizable inferences about behavior. This is despite undergraduates differing in important ways from other populations." (p. 688).

---

5 Note that this is not an objection against laboratory experiments per se, only against the way they are predominantly organized. One could, of course, run laboratory experiments with other subject pools than students.

Critics of laboratory experiments argue that part of the potential biases introduced by the use of student samples might come from the fact that they tend to be self-selected; that is, they are a sample of volunteer participants that may be especially predisposed to participate in experimental studies for reasons unknown to the experimental researcher. Yet, empirical evidence does not seem to support such a concern. For instance, Exadaktylos, Espín, and Brañas-Garza (2013); Cleave, Nikiforakis, and Slonim (2013); Falk, Meier, and Zehnder (2013); and Snowberg and Yariv (2021) empirically study whether there are differences between the student population that self-selects into participating in a laboratory experiment and the overall student population. All these studies report no such differences. More generally, the argument is that selection issues hold for all types of experiments and not only those conducted in the laboratory. A case in point are the nonresponse and attrition biases that are quite frequent in field experiments (see Chapter 7).

Another important criticism to laboratory experiments is artificiality. Artificiality occurs whenever a researcher creates an experimental frame that is artificial with reference to the naturally occurring phenomenon of interest. Artificiality is indeed a feature of laboratory experiments, in which the situation has been completely constructed by the experimenter, but it is also a feature of field and survey experiments (Jackson & Cox 2013). One problem of artificiality is intrinsically connected to the problem of awareness, the fact that in an artificial experiment, participants are aware that they are taking part in an experiment. This can give rise to demand effects (see Chapter 7). However, some argue that (1) because laboratory (economic-based) experiments are incentivized and participants' behavior is typically utility-driven, they are less prone to demand effects than other types of experiments (Jackson & Cox 2013; Camerer 2015); (2) although there is not much empirical evidence of such effects, laboratory experiments can, in fact, be used to isolate such effects and study whether they matter (Falk & Heckman 2009); and (3) it is precisely this artificiality that makes laboratory experiments an ideal tool for replication (Camerer 2015). Beyond the laboratory, Mummolo and Peterson (2019) find little evidence for demand effects in survey experiments, even under the most favorable conditions for these effects to occur.

All in all, it is not that obvious that empirically constructing an experiment as representative or similar as possible to "reality" ensures its generalizability. Moreover, the verdict is still out on whether field experiments and randomized control trials are the gold standards of validity and, thus, more relevant to study sociological phenomena, as advocated by the proponents of the empirical approach to validity.

10.3 THE THEORETICAL APPROACH TO VALIDITY

The main assumption underlying the theoretical approach to validity (TAV) is that no single result can be directly generalized to other populations, contexts, experimental settings, and times. The word directly here is crucial since generalization might be possible indirectly through theory. With reference to experiments in the social sciences, Deaton and Cartwright (2018, 12) wrote that "Establishing causality does nothing in and of itself to guarantee that the causal relation will hold in some new case, let alone in general." Bardsley et al. (2010, 51) argue in a similar manner: "strictly, all that happens in a particular laboratory experiment is what happens in it." The proponents of TAV contend that what one then generalizes is not a particular experimental result but a theoretical construct (Schram 2005; Willer & Walker 2007; Jackson & Cox 2013; Camerer 2015). Nonetheless, they do emphasize that experimentally testing a theoretical construct is typically done under ceteris paribus conditions. The experimental result is thus generalizable if it can be shown that such conditions do not affect the result (Zelditch 2014c). This is where stress testing, that is, testing a theory under varying conditions, can be useful. "Stress tests in the laboratory are a way to explore the applicability of a theory while relaxing some of the assumptions in a controlled way." (Schram 2005, 232). An experiment is thus just one instantiation of a theoretical construct, and if a new experiment offers confirmatory evidence supporting the theoretical construct, we can say that the external validity of the theoretical construct has increased.

Under the TAV, there is no privileged type of experiment to achieve external validity. Every single piece of empirical evidence obtained in the laboratory or in the field contributes to reducing the uncertainty around a theoretical proposition. Thus, what matters is empirical accumulation supporting, contradicting, or refining a particular theory (Schram 2005; Jackson & Cox 2013). Figure 10.2 offers a schematic representation of this process. Generalizability is understood not as a binary concept (something is representative or not) but as a continuum showing the degree of confidence we have in a specific theoretical proposition. The larger the amount of evidence in line with a theory, the more generalizable it is. Note that there are no lines that horizontally connect the different pieces of evidence. The connection is always between these empirical instances and the theory. It is the theory that is being generalized, not a particular result. Moreover, there is never definitive proof of the generality of an empirical claim. The process of evidence accumulation is potentially infinite. However, increases in external validity beyond a certain point could only be gained if key variables of the experiment (e.g., sampled population, main manipulations, measure of

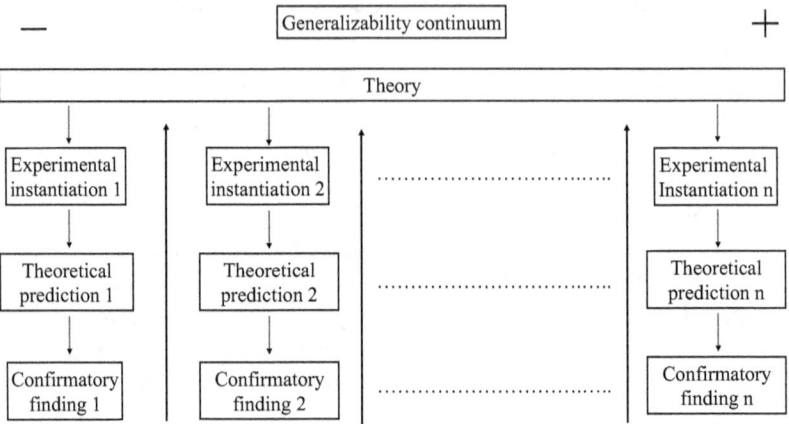

Figure 10.2 Generalizability continuum.

the dependent variable, and experimental context) are changed and the experiment is rerun. Theory-guided replication involves a thoughtful process of introducing small variations in the experiment to understand the effect of single features. Note that this is precisely the goal of stress testing, as described earlier.

In sum, the main proposition of the TAV is that something more general than an experimental result is necessary to transport this result to other situations. This more general thing can be called "knowledge claim", "statement about the world," or "theory." The idea is that experimental results speak to that more general "claim" and not directly to other experimental results. Under this approach, results obtained in a single experiment are not directly transportable to other empirical situations. This means that, for instance, the results of an experimental policy evaluation conducted under ideal conditions in India cannot be straightforwardly used as evidence for a policy intervention in other countries (e.g., Colombia). At best, these results would offer evidence supporting a theory that would eventually inform new interventions.

10.4 GENERALIZABILITY AS SCIENTIFIC REPLICATION: AN EXAMPLE

Although for different reasons, both the proponents of the EAV and those of the TAV recommend empirical replication as a path to generalizability. In the former case, it is considered a way to study the generalizability of an empirical finding; in the latter, it is considered as a provisional proof of the validity of a theory. In any case, evidence of external validity must, by definition, be empirical (Morton & Williams 2011), and most discussions on the generalizability of experimental results recommend scientific replication as the cornerstone of scientific advancement and knowledge accumulation (Falk & Heckman 2009; Jackson & Cox 2013). There are, however, two very different ways of replicating an inference or knowledge claim: (1) by directly replicating the exact experimental settings of the original trial and (2) by testing the same knowledge claim using a different experimental method or design (i.e., stress-testing). Focusing on this second definition of replication, two methods emerge as the ideal candidates for increasing the generalizability of a theoretical construct: theory-guided meta-analysis and cross-validation or empirical cross-checking. The former uses data from previously conducted experiments to study whether methods, populations, and experimental settings affect findings (e.g., Kalkhoff & Thye 2006; Balliet et al. 2011; Spadaro et al. 2022a). The latter compares experiments involving different methods to test the same theoretical constructs.

Common examples of empirical cross-validation or cross-checking in experimental social science involve the comparison of laboratory, field, and survey experimental results on the same theoretical construct (Guala 2005, chapter 9; Barabas & Jerit 2010; Bardsley et al. 2010, chapter 5; Mitchell 2012; Buskens & Raub 2013; Coppock & Green 2015; Snowberg & Yariv 2021). In the empirical approach to validity, correspondence between the results from these different types of experiments is typically interpreted as evidence of external validity. In the theoretical approach to validity, replication of results between experimental modes would increase the generalizability of their theoretical claim. Take, for instance, the example of a few recent papers across the social sciences that study the correspondence between behavioral and survey results measuring similar theoretical propositions. Falk et al. (2018) present a dataset containing experimentally validated survey measures of five individual preferences and behavioral tendencies much studied by experimental social scientists. Chen and Tam (2020) correlate three measures of inequality preferences captured in behavioral games, vignette studies, and conventional attitudinal survey items. Eifler (2010), Eifler and Petzold (2019), and Petzold and Wolbring (2019) discuss the validity of survey experiments more generally by looking at the correspondence between behavioral intentions reported in survey experiments and actual behavior in the field. They find similarities between the two experimental modes, especially regarding treatment effects, but also quantitative deviations between the two.

To illustrate in more detail how empirical cross-validation can be conducted, we focus on a study by Barr, Miller, and Ubeda (2023). They present the results of a cross-validation exercise to test the generalizability of a widely studied theoretical prediction, showing that earned entitlement is acknowledged. First proposed by Homans (1961), this principle implies that justice is served when the benefit received by a group member is proportional to her investments. Over the last 60 years, a large number of experimental studies have been conducted in sociology, economics, psychology, political science, and philosophy on the empirical validity of the equity (a.k.a. proportionality) principle (e.g., Cook & Hegtvedt 1983; Wagstaff, Huggins, & Perfect 1993; Scott et al. 2001; Konow 2003). One of the main conclusions of these studies was anticipated by Homans (1961, 246) when he claimed that people "differ in their ideas of what legitimately constitutes investment, reward, and cost, and how these things are to be ranked."

Barr, Miller, and Ubeda (2023) test whether the acknowledgment of earned entitlement effect is robust across experimental conditions and populations. To do so, they perform a cross-validation exercise that involves survey and laboratory experiments with heterogeneous samples. At the core of this strategy is an experimental paradigm that has been extensively used in social sciences and has been previously called a distributive justice experiment (Barr, Miller, & Ubeda 2016). A distributive justice experiment typically entails two consecutive phases. In the production phase, people undertake an individual or group task. This phase might be hypothetical (a vignette or story created by the researchers) or real (actual participants in the experiment undertake the task). In the distribution phase, (other) participants are asked to distribute the surplus created in the production phase. Again, this can be done hypothetically, that is, participants subjectively rate the fairness or social appropriateness of various proposed distributions, or it can be real, that is, participants actually (re)distribute monetary or nonmonetary rewards. The main experimental manipulation involves informing participants in the distribution phase about the source of the surplus that is to be distributed. In "Earned" treatments, participants are informed at the start of the distribution phase about the contribution or performance of individual subjects in the production phase. In "Random" or "Luck" treatments, participants are informed at the start of the distribution phase that the initial distribution was generated randomly, by chance, or by some other arbitrary mechanism. The main theoretical prediction is that, on average, across methods, settings, and populations, inequality is deemed more acceptable if one's result from the production phase is earned than if it is determined randomly.

Barr, Miller, and Ubeda (2023) report three sets of results. The first is derived from a between-subject analysis of two independent, but comparable samples of nonstudent adults. One sample participated in a standard, incentivized behavioral experiment and was recruited following a number of strategies, including making use of mailing lists of public institutions, employment centers, and local companies. The other sample was part of an ongoing program evaluation and participated in a survey experiment during the first day of the program. Despite the many differences between the behavioral and survey experimental designs, they both showed similar treatment effects, consistent with the theoretical prediction of an acknowledgment of earned entitlement. The second set of results relates to a sample of students drawn from a laboratory pool of registered subjects. They participated in both the laboratory and the survey experiment. Barr, Miller, and Ubeda (2023) perform a between-subject comparison of the two treatment-elicitation methods but, this time, focusing on the same sample of subjects. Again, the treatment effects are very similar, supporting the prediction of earned entitlement being acknowledged. Finally, using the data from the student-sample experiment, within-subjects comparisons show some consistency between the decisions and responses made under the two experimental modes – incentivized laboratory and unincentivized survey. These results from a broad spectrum of experimental methods all point to the robustness of the theoretical prediction on the importance of entitlement for the acceptability of inequality.

Other studies have also addressed the sensitivity of laboratory findings to changes in experimental samples and settings. In the case of prosocial behavior, Bader et al. (2021) find that treatment effects vary significantly in absolute quantitative terms across conditions, while qualitative treatment effects are mostly consistent. The different approaches to cross-validation between Barr, Miller, and Ubeda (2023) and Bader et al. (2021) tell us something important about empirical tests of validity. The two papers are complementary in that they assess the generalizability of laboratory results in two different types of study: Bader et al. (2021) focus on preferences and behavioral tendencies that map directly onto choices, whereas Barr, Miller, and Ubeda (2023) focus on preferences that map onto differences in choices across contexts, that is, that map onto treatment effects rather than choices. Typically, replication and cross-validation exercises adopt one of these two strategies: focusing on the quantitative (point predictions) or on the qualitative (treatment effect) nature of the results. The latter is particularly useful for theory advancement.

11 Incentives

11.1 INTRODUCTION

In an experiment, researchers have to face two distinct challenges concerning incentives. The first task is to motivate invited subjects to participate in the experiment and the second is to provide incentives in the decision task under investigation. Concerning the former task, it is a common practice in laboratory experiments to offer participants a so-called show-up fee. This is a lump-sum payment that every participant receives for showing up, irrespective of their behavior or performance in the experiment. The amount of this show-up fee is usually based on the opportunity costs of participating in the experiment. These include the effort required to travel to the experimental laboratory and the potential forgone earnings by participating in the experiment (Traub et al. 2023). There also exist alternative ways of incentivizing participation. For example, in concealed field experiments, subjects unknowingly participate in the study due to their daily routines, their interest in the content, or the decision task. Moreover, in experimental psychology, student subjects sometimes need to take part in experiments as part of their course requirements.

The second task of the researcher is to motivate subjects during the experiment and implement incentives, which often entail strategic elements. In a typical experiment, most notably in the laboratory, participants are confronted with decision tasks. People do not decide haphazardly but have a motivation to make a particular decision. Given that motivations are internal to the subject, it is impossible for researchers to observe them. In experimental research, there are two approaches to deal with this problem, differing in whether they view individual motivations as a methodological nuisance or as drivers of behavior that participants bring into the laboratory and that are of substantive interest to the researcher. On the one hand, variation in motivation is regarded as a nuisance that potentially undermines the validity of findings. Therefore, in experimental economics, it is standard practice to use monetary incentives. The main reason for doing so relates to the economists' core interest in the allocation of scarce resources, and money provides such a scarce resource. The size of the payoff, thus, usually depends on own decisions as well as on the behavior of other subjects, which creates strategic incentives and is assumed to induce subjects to maximize their payoff. For example, in the beauty contest game (Nagel 1995), subjects are asked to guess a number between 0 and 100 that comes closest to the mean of the numbers chosen by all participants multiplied by a factor p ranging between zero and one. While the game-theoretic solution of this game is straightforward – according to backward induction, it is zero – solving this game requires analytic skills and mental effort. In order to motivate subjects to at least invest in the latter, the subject that comes closest to the true value receives a monetary reward.

On the other hand, psychologists are interested in and focus on motivations that subjects themselves bring into the laboratory as a predisposition to behavior (Hilton 2001), cognitive biases developed to navigate the world (Gil-White 2001), and decision domains for which external criteria to evaluate performance cannot be objectively determined (Betsch & Haberstroh 2001). Moreover, an influential literature – mainly in psychology, but also in the other social and behavioral sciences – is interested in the way in which the presentation of the decision problem – the frame – affects the decision (Kahneman & Tversky 1979). As a result, it is common in experimental psychology that subjects do not receive any monetary rewards for participating or for their behavior. Instead, psychologists sometimes put more trust in the intrinsic motivation of subjects to participate in experiments and use other means to keep the experiment interesting and entertaining. For example, group tasks with related social dynamics and normative expectations can secure a high involvement of individuals. From this perspective, monetary incentivization would, on the one hand, override intrinsic motivations and, on the other hand, undermine concealed experimentation with unobtrusive treatments and measures. These problems basically rule out monetary incentives for experiments interested in intrinsic motivations (Tyler & Amodio 2015). This reasoning equally applies to concealed field experiments. For example, in their broken windows experiments (see Chapter 7), Keizer, Lindenberg, and Steg (2008) prepared a local environment in which passers-by unwittingly participated in the experiment in an orderly and a disorderly condition and observed littering behavior in the respective contexts.

Sociological research takes elements from both perspectives and emphasizes institutional, cultural, and social determinants of human behavior. For example, Berger (2015) considers experiments as a social process embedded in a temporal and socio-spatial environment that influences the selection and responses of subjects. Experimental sociology is thus located between those two poles of the continuum – sometimes, especially in game-theoretic applications, leaning more toward experimental economics, and sometimes, especially in sociological investigations of group processes, putting more emphasis on nonmonetary incentives, framing, and social determinants. In this chapter, we outline these perspectives of experimental sociology in more detail. First, we present the traditional approach to framing as it is used in psychological and economic research. Then, we introduce an analytical framework developed in sociology for the integration of this traditional approach in a theory of action, which we finally use to discuss the working of incentives.

11.2 MONETARY AND NONMONETARY INCENTIVES IN EXPERIMENTAL RESEARCH

Framing is perhaps the most well-known concept of how the presentation of a decision problem affects behavior and illustrates the complex interplay between monetary and nonmonetary incentives. On the one hand, the use of monetary incentives can crowd out nonmonetary motives of action (Titmuss 1970; Frey 1997; Bowles 2016). A classic example is the donation of blood, where intrinsic motivation (donating for a good reason) is crowded out by extrinsic motivation (donating for money). As research shows, the overall number of blood donations does not increase, despite the introduction of monetary incentives (for a systematic review and meta-analysis, see Niza, Tung, & Marteau 2013). Similarly, Gneezy and Rustichini (2000a) have shown that introducing a fine for late pickup of children at a day care center induced even more parents to be late.

On the other hand, framing can also modify the effects of monetary incentives. As outlined in prospect theory (Kahneman & Tversky 1979), framing monetary incentives as gains or losses can make a large difference. Prospect theory suggests that losses loom larger than gains of equal size.[1] Individuals tend to be risk-averse in risky choices involving gains, whereas they become risk-seeking in risky choices involving losses. Based on the so-called Asian disease problem, Tversky and Kahneman (1981) highlighted that people prefer different programs against fighting the outbreak of an unusual disease depending on whether the programs are presented in terms of people saved or dying. Hence, depending on the social phenomenon

---

[1] Consistent with this, Neumann et al. (2018) find that players in dictator and ultimatum games behave somewhat less generously in games over losses than in games over gains.

experimenters want to study, they need to carefully decide whether they frame incentives in terms of gains or losses.

But frames also influence behavior in more general ways. For example, Liberman, Samuels, and Ross (2004) have shown that labeling the very same task once as the "Wall Street Game" and once as the "Community Game" had substantial effects on subjects' willingness to cooperate with each other. In the study, subjects played the prisoner's dilemma in which mutual cooperation with the other player is the collectively desirable outcome, while incentives to free-ride were in place. Nonetheless, about 70 percent of the subjects cooperated when the game was labeled as a "Community Game," whereas only about 30 percent were willing to cooperate in the very same game labeled as a "Wall Street Game."[2] While framing effects are often not as strong as in this example and cannot be completely avoided, the main takeaway is that the presentation of a decision task deserves careful consideration, especially when taking into account the unwanted effects of labeling and framing.

However, framing effects do not always need to be treated as a nuisance but can be actively used as an experimental manipulation to test social theories. In factorial survey experiments, the exact description of a decision situation is varied in the vignette text. For instance, Auspurg, Hinz, and Sauer (2017) asked respondents whether they perceive the earnings of hypothetical men and women as unfairly low, fair, or unfairly high (for details, see Chapter 8). Since this evaluation may depend on the specific context, they varied the occupation of the hypothetical employee as one dimension in their vignette study. Analyzing the gender gap in fairness judgments by occupation, they find discrimination against females both in management and in gender-neutral occupations (Auspurg, Hinz, & Sauer 2017, 196). Experimentally manipulating the situation at hand can thus shed light on the nature of gender stereotypes at work and can provide deeper insights into the social mechanisms structuring the labor market.

Likewise, framing also plays an important role in field experiments and can help answer the substantive research question. A frequently used type of framing in sociological and psychological research relies on normative appeals and social influence. For example, Goldstein, Cialdini, and Griskevicius (2008) examined the effects of towel-rack messages on towel reuse in hotels. In the baseline condition, the message "Help save the

---

[2] In a similar experiment using a dictator game, Bocca, Romanò, and Barrera (2021) manipulated the frame combined with three types of incentives (money, chocolate, and no incentive) in a full factorial design. The prosocial frame significantly increased donations in all incentive conditions, without significant differences between the types of incentive.

environment" emphasized the social norm of pro-environmental behavior, whereas the message "Join your fellow guests in helping to save the environment" in the treatment condition added a social influence component by establishing a descriptive norm of towel reuse.[3] As expected by the authors, social influence was indeed much more effective than the simple normative appeal, increasing the percentage of towel reuse by 9 percentage points.

11.3 GOALS, FRAMES, AND SCRIPTS OF ACTION – A SOCIOLOGICAL PERSPECTIVE

While the examples in the previous section highlight the moldability of human behavior by manipulating the decision situation and the description of the task, the results also show that subjects take into account more than one aspect when assessing their options. Instead of assuming that monetary payoffs override any other human motivation (Smith 1976), experimental researchers usually make the more realistic assumption that subjects can be incentivized by monetary payoffs but are also motivated by nonmonetary incentives such as other-regarding preferences, reciprocity, and other social norms. From a sociological perspective, these nonmonetary incentives can be more or less activated by situational cues in the experimental situation. In the following, we will introduce this perspective.

Sociological theory is a multi-paradigmatic field that has not developed a commonly agreed framework for understanding and explaining social behavior. Nevertheless, a common starting point of many sociological analyses is the concept of the definition of the situation. The basic idea of this concept is that each situation and decision context involves a code of behavior that is shaped by social norms and expectations (Thomas & Thomas 1928). One and the same behavior can thus be socially acceptable in one situation but not in another. Encountering a decision context, individuals will thus first try to make sense of the present situation, that is, to analyze and define the situation and activate certain scripts of action according to the salience of social cues.

---

[3] The complete messages read "HELP SAVE THE ENVIRONMENT. You can show your respect for nature and help save the environment by reusing your towels during your stay". and "JOIN YOUR FELLOW GUESTS IN HELPING TO SAVE THE ENVIRONMENT. Almost 75% of guests who are asked to participate in our new resource savings program do help by using their towels more than once. You can join your fellow guests in this program to help save the environment by reusing your towels during your stay" (Goldstein, Cialdini, & Griskevicius 2008, 473).

Building on this sociological concept, especially the work of Alfred Schütz on the definition of the situation, Esser (1993) has introduced a "model of frame selection," which tries to integrate sociological rational choice with insights on the importance of framing and situational cues (see also Esser & Kroneberg 2015). The starting point of this theoretical framework is that actors activate mental frames and scripts when faced with a certain decision situation. Thereby, frames are mental models of types of situations that are informed by previous experiences and are identified by means of situational objects. Scripts are routines of action that appear appropriate in the kind of situation identified. For example, a large building with a tower, with Christian signs on the wall and benches facing an altar, is quickly identified as a church. Individuals familiar with Christian culture know that certain kinds of behavior are appropriate and others inappropriate when entering such a building. According to the model of frame selection, individuals will rely on such scripts and switch to a so-called automatic, spontaneous mode of action if the script is mentally easily accessible and fits the situation at hand sufficiently well. Otherwise, they rely on the so-called reflective–calculating mode, which is mainly driven by subjective expected utility maximization.

Closely related to this model of frame selection is the theory of goal framing developed by Lindenberg (2013). While sharing the basic idea that the framing of a situation based on situational cues matters for human decision-making, the advantage of goal-framing theory is that it does not require the assumption of different modes of action. Instead, goal-framing theory posits that human decision-making is guided by three overarching goals: the "hedonic," "gain," and "normative goal frame." While the hedonic goal frame is "oriented toward the here and now," and its "criterion for goal realization is an improvement in the way one feels," the gain frame makes "people very sensitive to changes in their personal resources" and the normative frame makes "people focus on being members of a group" and raises the importance of "appropriateness" of behavior (Lindenberg 2013, 82–83). These goals become more or less important depending on the activated goal frame, with the hedonic goal frame being the most basic one. Importantly, situational cues in the environment can cause shifts in overarching frames and the relative weight of the overarching goals.

For example, interpreting the experiment on towel usage from the perspective of goal-framing theory, the reference to social influence moved the normative goal to the forefront of the hotel guests.[4] Similarly, the

---

[4] The experiment by Goldstein, Cialdini, and Griskevicius (2008) is also a good example of a more recent trend in behavioral experimental research that uses

broken windows experiments presented in Chapter 7 have also been designed in a way to vary descriptive norms and to strengthen the normative goal frame by leaving visible traces of norm violations.[5]

What has all this to do with sociological experiments? The main point is that the design of the experiment and the ways in which behavior is incentivized have important implications for experimental results, as well as for their interpretation and, thus, the consequences for theory testing. In the following section, we will illustrate how changes in incentivization have implications for theory testing in more detail.

11.4 MONETARY INCENTIVES, REAL-EFFORT TASKS, AND STAKE SIZES

There are different ways to incentivize behavior. As said before, it is standard practice in experimental economics to use monetary incentives; in fact, many economists criticize experiments without such incentivization because subjects might not put sufficient effort into the experimental task (Hertwig & Ortmann 2001a, b). The methodological basis for such an approach is induced-value theory (Smith 1976). Induced-value theory assumes that monetary payoffs override any other human motivation in laboratory economic experiments: "[C]ontrol can be achieved by using a reward structure to induce prescribed monetary value on actions" (Smith 1976, 275). This assumption rests on the postulate of non-satiation; that is, utility is thought to increase monotonously with monetary reward.[6] From a sociological perspective, monetary incentives signal to experimental subjects that the

---

so-called nudges to influence human behavior (Thaler & Sunstein 2008; see Campos-Mercade et al. 2021 for a randomized control trial study comparing the effects of monetary incentives and nudges on vaccination rates). An easy and frequently used way to change the framing of a situation and to manipulate non-monetary incentives is the choice of a default option. For example, in two field studies with energy suppliers in Switzerland, Liebe, Gewinner, and Diekmann (2021) presented renewable energy to existing customers as the standard option in order to encourage pro-environmental behavior. This seemingly small stimulus had a large default effect; that is, a substantial share of the households and business sector customers stayed with this default option.

[5] A descriptive norm is a social norm that can be inferred from observing how other people behave in a certain context, as opposed to an injunctive norm, which is a formally stated rule prescribing what behavior is expected or forbidden in a certain context.

[6] Smith (1976, 276) acknowledges perceived subjective costs related to the effort involved in market transactions, which may distort experimenter control over induced values.

goal of the situation in which they find themselves is to earn money. The reason is that paying somebody for a certain action fundamentally changes the definition of the situation and the activated mental frames and scripts. Thus, it is assumed that the situation generates a mindset that activates the "gain frame" (Lindenberg, 2013).

While economic incentives potentially strengthen the gain frame in subjects' minds and weaken the hedonic and normative frame, the latter do not completely disappear. Indeed, economic games like the dictator game and the ultimatum game have highlighted that the behavior of a substantial share of the subjects is not purely driven by monetary self-interest (Engel 2011; Güth & Kocher 2014). Despite the use of monetary incentives, social motives like prosociality, solidarity, and reciprocity seem to play an important role, at least for a relevant subset of individuals. In order to reconcile these empirical results with the theoretical foundation of self-interested income-maximizing actors, several efforts have been made to modify the experimental design in a way as to strengthen the "gain frame" in subjects' minds.

One important way to reach this goal, frequently used in applied research, is to let subjects work for the money distributed in the experimental game, for example, by requiring them to complete some simple tasks or to answer a quiz (for a literature review, see Carpenter & Huet-Vaughn 2019). The underlying motivation for using such real efforts tasks is that making decisions on money that one "earned" is different from "playing" with a bestowed endowment. In particular, one might suspect that the extent of prosocial behavior and risk-taking is higher with such "Casino" money (Thaler & Johnson 1990). Empirical studies suggest that this indeed makes a difference. For example, in a now well-known study, Cherry, Frykblom, and Shogren (2002) compared subjects' behavior with earned versus unearned wealth in a dictator game with a $10 endowment. The results showed that dictators acted much more selfishly in the case of an effort task via a quiz (79% offering $0) than in the baseline condition with windfall gains (19% offering $0).[7] While follow-up studies did not always find equally strong effects of real-effort tasks (see Carpenter & Huet-Vaughn 2019), such effort-based designs are certainly one important way to strengthen the gain frame in an experiment.

A second possibility to accomplish the goal of strengthening the gain frame is to increase the size of the stakes in the experiment (Gneezy &

---

[7] Moreover, Cherry, Frykblom, and Shogren (2002) varied the degree of anonymity in the experiment and also found more selfish behavior in the double blind than in the baseline condition. Similar results have been found by Franzen and Pointner (2012). While these experiments were not informed by the proposed sociological perspective on framing, their empirical results are well in line with it.

Rustichini 2000b). However, existing evidence is not clearly supporting the effectiveness of this measure. For example, the study by Cherry, Frykblom, and Shogren (2002) compared the commonly used low-stakes condition ($10) with a higher-stakes condition ($40). The percentage of dictators offering $0 was even slightly lower with high stakes in both conditions – with unearned money (79% vs. 70%) and with earned money (19% vs. 15%). Results from studies using much larger stakes have also revealed that while offers in ultimatum games with higher stakes are less likely to be rejected (Karagözoglu & Urhan 2016), the extent of offers in dictator and ultimatum games is remarkably robust toward this variation in experimental conditions (for a meta-analysis, see Larney, Rotella, & Barlay 2019).

Finally, another potential way to move incentives in the direction of the gain frame is to purposefully generate an experimenter demand effect by explicitly instructing subjects to "... set out to maximize your winnings" (Binmore, Shaked, & Sutton 1985)[8] to "be concerned only with winning as much as you possibly can" (Ofshe & Ofshe 1970, 341), to "assume a pro-self orientation" (Willer et al. 2014, 204), or to "earn as many points as they can" (Willer & Emanuelson 2008, 182). A variant of this procedure is to rule out the possibility of taking others' outcomes into account by restricting the pool of subjects who are allocated some share of a resource. For example, in experiments typical of the network exchange school, subjects can bargain over the distribution of a common endowment, but, despite the presence of other subjects, the endowment can only be allocated within the negotiating dyad (Cook et al. 2013; Molm 2014). Schwaninger, Neuhofer, and Kittel (2019) have shown that subjects do indeed opt for more prosocial behavior if the pool of subjects to whom resources can be allocated also includes other individuals whose consent is not required for the conclusion of an agreement.

11.5 EXPERIMENTAL DESIGN AND INCENTIVE STRUCTURE

Monetary incentives are useful for experiments that focus on structural conditions of behavior because they homogenize the behavioral motivations of subjects and thus reduce variation in behavior that interferes with the focused structural effects implemented in different treatments. Questions such as "How does the design of institutions affect individual behavior in social interactions?," "How does a norm influence individual behavior?,"

---

[8] Although the experimental instructions of Binmore, Shaked, and Sutton's (1985) article seems to be no longer available online, they are quoted in several other papers (e.g., Suleiman 2001, 429; Stahl & Haruvy 2008, 293).

or "Which social mechanism is effective in a particular situation?" are examples of this kind of research interest.

In a broader sense, however, monetary incentives may be viewed as one factor in the experimental design among others that influence subjects' responses to treatments. The behavior of subjects is potentially influenced by the design of the experiment, as well as by their experiences in the laboratory. All these factors can be regarded as part of an incentive structure. A first example of such a broader incentive structure relates to the distinction between within- and between-subjects designs. A design that sequentially confronts one and the same subject with different treatments (within-subjects design) can be contrasted with a design in which treatments are varied across subjects, and each subject just makes a single decision in one treatment (between-subjects design) (see Chapter 5). The two designs have advantages and disadvantages. A big advantage of the within-subjects design is that one can compare the behavior of the same subject in different treatments and, thus, rule out that differences in behavior are due to differences between subjects. The comparison of treatments is thus independent of the allocation of subjects to treatments. A second methodological advantage is that a large number of observations can be produced in one experimental session. Each session requires considerable time spans before and after the experiment proper for seating subjects, reading instructions, familiarizing them with the task, finishing the session, and paying subjects. Hence, collecting several data points per subject is more efficient than a single data point.

However, these advantages may be counterbalanced by a potentially big disadvantage. When subjects repeatedly play a game with small variations, they may learn how to play the game to generate individually optimal payoffs. For some research questions, this effect may be desirable. For example, Fudenberg (2006, 700) argues that the first rounds of an experiment should not be used to test game theoretic predictions because it usually takes some experience for subjects to find the equilibrium strategy. In the same vein, Hertwig and Ortmann (2001a, 390) argue that reasoning competence increases after several trials of the same decision problem. It is a well-known stylized fact in the experimental social sciences that people who cooperate in the beginning tend to become less cooperative as they experience exploitation of their cooperation by others, for example, in experiments on public goods (Fehr & Gächter 2000) and common pool resources (Ostrom, Walker, & Gardner 1992).

A second example relates to sequence effects, which appear in several forms. For example, outcomes of earlier treatments may affect the attitudes of subjects in later treatments. Losses may induce changes in risk attitudes, anger about others' egoistic behavior may affect social values, or the experience of nice behavior may influence the willingness to cooperate, pointing to the possibility of the development of reciprocal relationships or a generally more cooperative atmosphere in a session. Subjects may also infer the aim of the experiment from the variations between the treatments, which may affect their behavior in treatments that are administered at a later point in a session. These so-called experimenter-demand effects invalidate results because subjects do not respond to treatments but to their expectations about the expectations of the experimenter (see Chapter 12). Like social desirability effects in surveys, experimenter-demand effects produce confounded results because of the researcher's intervention. The two differ in that, in the former, survey respondents give answers that they believe to be socially appropriate, whereas in the latter, experimental subjects behave in certain ways because they believe that this is what they are intended to do.

To some extent, these disadvantages can be minimized by counterbalancing the treatments, that is, varying the sequence of treatments such that possible systematic differences between the placement of treatments in the sequence can be tested and potentially controlled (see Chapter 5). The development of direct reciprocity can be prevented by randomly reallocating subjects to groups after every round of the experiment. But indirect reciprocity, which involves potentially all participants in a session, is more difficult to control. It is also more difficult to contain the effects of individual moods on the way people respond to treatments.

For one-shot experiments, the advantages and disadvantages are inverse to repeated play. The biggest advantage is that the comparison of behavior between subjects is "clean" in the sense of being void of any sequence effects because all subjects obtain their single treatment at the same moment in the course of an experimental session. Thus, subjects' experiences from the moment that they enter the laboratory until the treatment is administered are held constant as much as possible. The major disadvantage is that in such designs, all inferences rest on differences between treatments, which rely on the random allocation of subjects to treatments. Moreover, subjects cannot learn to understand the demands of the experiment by experiences in the early rounds. Experimenters have to ensure that the explanation of the behavioral options in the instructions is sufficiently clear; at the same time, the instructions should minimize conveying or hinting at the aim of the experiment in order to circumvent experimental demand effects. By testing the subjects' perception of the tasks and the implications of different strategies and by administering inconsequential test rounds before the real experiment starts, the understanding of the experiment can be improved. But subjects differ in the speed at which they understand what is asked of them.

A problem that may appear in repeated play designs is that subjects may lose concentration because of a lack of interest or boredom. This phenomenon occurs in particular when an experiment consists of several rounds of the same treatment, which are experienced by subjects as repetitive tasks. Subjects lacking concentration may start playing around and, for example, test the effect of different strategies, which invalidates the outcome of the experiment. If earnings grow incrementally in every round, the effect of inattentive, that is, erratic or arbitrary behavior on the final earnings, may be limited because some rounds will yield higher and other rounds lower payoffs, resulting in an average level of overall earnings that may be satisfactory to a subject. Thus, typically the design of an experiment will include means to maintain a high salience of the outcome throughout all rounds of a session. A popular strategy is to randomly select a single round or a small subset of rounds for the payoff. This design widens the range of expectable earnings because the final payoff then depends on a single round or a small number of rounds, which raises the individual stakes because very low and very high final earnings are more likely. As a result, payoffs of every single round are salient, and subjects have an incentive to remain alert until the end of the experiment.

A third example of the incentive structure concerns the context in which participants make decisions. What do subjects know, and what do they experience before they make their decisions? Apart from previous rounds, the experimental design affects these decisions by the timing at which the decision is to be taken. Two major alternatives are employed in laboratory experiments, the direct-response method and the strategy method. In the direct-response method, subjects make decisions as they move through the stages of a treatment representing the game tree. That means that at the moment of decision, they are informed about the earlier behavior of other subjects, and they respond to that behavior. In the strategy method, in turn, subjects have to determine their choices for every possible action of the other subject before the game starts. Because the strategy method consists of hypothetical questions covering all potential decision situations at the beginning of the experiment, while in the direct response method, subjects are confronted with the single outcome of previous decisions, one might expect a more rational behavior that is not influenced by emotions raised in the course of the game. Using an ultimatum game, Rauhut and Winter (2010) demonstrate that offers do not differ between the two methods, but responses are more strongly motivated by normative principles in the strategy method as respondents more often reject unfair offers, whereas in the direct-response method, they accept more offers. Likewise, in a survey of studies on differences between the two methods, Brandts and Charness (2011) find evidence consistent with Rauhut and Winter's (2010) results. Overall, the two methods do not seem to produce substantial differences in treatment effects.

12 Ethics and Deception

12.1 INTRODUCTION

In the 1960s, Robert Rosenthal conducted a series of studies on the role of expectations, including one study in which twelve research assistants purportedly conducted an experiment comparing the performances of "maze-bright" and "maze-dull" rats (Rosenthal & Fode 1963). The rats were, in fact, all just ordinary laboratory rats, but the research assistants were told that they had been selectively bred from rats that performed better and worse in mazes. Accordingly, the assistants reported better performances for the "maze-bright" rats and poorer ones for the "maze-dull" rats. In this case, the biased results were entirely caused by the assistants' expectations because rats are unlikely to produce a compliance bias.

In social science experimental research that involves humans, there are more potential sources of biases because participants' behavior during an experiment can affect the results in ways that are difficult to predict. Unlike rats, participants may correctly guess the hypothesis of the study in which they are partaking and try to prove it right, or they may correctly guess the research hypothesis and try to prove it wrong, or they may incorrectly guess the research hypothesis and alter their behavior trying to support or falsify what they erroneously think is the research hypothesis (Willer & Walker 2007).

Experimental research aims at creating conditions that isolate the treatment effect, ensuring that the behavior under investigation is as much as possible unaffected by the setting where the experiment takes place or by minor details of the experimental protocol. When deciding the amount of information that goes into the experimental instructions, full disclosure of the research design, including the hypotheses, is not a realistic option for two reasons. First, participants do not possess sufficient knowledge of the problem under inquiry to fully understand the research design and procedures. Second, and most importantly, revealing the research hypotheses would certainly lead to behavioral biases, such as participants trying to comply with the researchers' expectations. Since the information that experimental participants receive has to be necessarily incomplete, structuring the interaction between researchers and experimental participants potentially poses two types of problems: ethical and practical. How much information should be provided to research participants for an experiment to be ethically acceptable? And how accurate should this information be to ensure that risks to the validity of the experimental results are minimized?

Although they are clearly related, the ethical and the practical problem have different solutions and raise different controversies. The ethical problem has led to the development of formal regulations and institutions to which all scientific organizations and agencies funding research must conform nowadays. By contrast, different scientific disciplines developed different solutions to the practical problem, leading to much disagreement concerning which procedure should be followed to protect the validity of experimental results. The most controversial issue related to experimental practices is the use of deception, that is, the provision of false or crucially incomplete information to the research participants (Hey 1998; McDaniel & Starmer 1998). Although ethical considerations are also relevant, this controversy focused primarily on the practical consequences of deceiving participants. Before turning to the deception debate, we try to contextualize it in the next section by briefly summarizing the history of contemporary ethics in experimental research.

12.2 THE DEVELOPMENT OF MODERN ETHICAL PRINCIPLES REGULATING EXPERIMENTAL RESEARCH

The foundations of modern ethical restrictions concerning the protection of human research subjects were established shortly after the end of World War II. An American military tribunal opened proceedings against several Nazi doctors for atrocities and experiments that they conducted on their prisoners inside German and Austrian concentration camps and psychiatric clinics. Two American doctors, Andrew Ivy and Leo Alexander, who had worked with the prosecution team, wrote a memorandum that provided a list of ten principles defining permissible medical experiments. These principles later became known as the Nuremberg Code.[1] The importance of the Nuremberg Code is that, for the first time, an international document introduced the principle of informed consent, stating that participation in experiments must be voluntary. In addition, the Code stated that those who initiate, direct, or engage in the experiment bear the responsibility to inform

---

[1] Some controversy exists over the paternity of the code, as some years after the Nuremberg trial both Ivy and Alexander claimed sole authorship (Gaw 2014).

participants about the nature, duration, purpose, and methods of the study, as well as about all inconveniences and risks associated with participation (Weindling 2001). These principles were expanded in 1964 when the World Medical Association published the Declaration of Helsinki, which established that all research protocols involving human participants should be reviewed by independent ethical committees, prior to the initiation of data collection. The Declaration of Helsinki inspired the regulations of ethics and research that were later adopted by many countries.

In 1972, the US Public Health Service Syphilis Study at Tuskegee became public. In this study, 600 African-American males, 400 of whom had contracted syphilis, were monitored for 40 years (1932–1972). The researchers offered them free medical examinations, but they did not inform the diseased participants that they were infected with syphilis nor did they offer treatment, even when an effective cure had become available in 1950. In the social sciences, ethical concerns had already been raised shortly after the publication of Stanley Milgram's (1963) famous obedience studies (Baumrind 1964). The Tuskegee study and other ethically deplorable, inhumane research projects led to the establishment of the National Commission for the Protection of Human Subjects of Biomedical and Behavioral Research in 1974. Institutional Review Boards (IRBs) were also established in the same year.

In 1979, the National Commission published the Belmont Report, outlying the ethical guidelines for conducting scientific research that involves humans. The Belmont Report indicated three main ethical principles: respect for persons, beneficence, and justice. These principles were linked to three areas of application: informed consent, assessment of risk and benefits, and selection of subjects. In a nutshell, the principles imply that (1) subjects must be given all relevant information in a comprehensible format and participation must be voluntary, (2) risks and benefits must be assessed systematically, and (3) the selection of research participants must be the result of a procedure that distributes risks and benefits justly among the participants (Fischer 2006).

In 1981, the US Department of Health and Human Services issued a set of rules for conducting research involving humans, which was largely based on the Belmont Report. Subsequently, this set of rules became known in the United States as the "common rule" and was adopted by most university departments and agencies that sponsor or conduct research involving humans. Among other things, the common rule includes procedures regulating the composition, tasks, and objectives of Institutional Review Boards (Fischer 2006). Boards or committees with similar functions have been established in most countries. In Europe, they are generally referred to as ethics committees, though they often have local names in different European countries.

The Belmont Report and the subsequent federal regulations addressed ethical issues concerning both biomedical and social science research. However, strict enforcement of these regulations would create severe limitations for procedures and practices that are relatively common in behavioral research. For example, a strict interpretation of the principles regulating informed consent would imply that research participants need to receive full information, including even the research hypotheses of the study in which they are set to participate. The use of deception in experimental research would be impossible, and the same holds for covert observation in ethnographic research. Accordingly, the National Science Foundation provided guidelines that allow Institutional Review Boards some flexibility, especially with respect to informed consent in behavioral research involving deception.[2]

Next to these general institutional regulations, most professional associations provide their members with ethical codes that, among many other aspects, provide rules for the use of deception for those disciplines where deception is contemplated. For example, the use of deception is regulated in the Code of Ethics of the American Sociological Association (see ASA 11.04) as well as in the Code of Conduct of the American Psychological Association (see APA 8.07). In both codes, the rules concerning deception are articulated around three principles: (1) Deception is permitted when it is justified by a study's prospective scientific, educational, or applied value and when alternative procedures to conduct the same study without using deception are not available; (2) deception is permitted when it is reasonably expected that it will not cause physical harm or severe emotional distress to the research participants; (3) when deception is used, researchers must inform the participants as early as possible of all features concerning the study in which they participated. In addition, psychologists developed a specific procedure called debriefing (see APA 8.0) to ensure that participants are adequately informed about the study and offered the possibility to withdraw their data. The ASA code also specifies that researchers may need to conceal their identity under specific circumstances, provided that the study does not involve any risk for the participants. Finally, both codes stipulate that the use of any form of deception is subject to ethical approval by an Institutional Review Board.

The code of conduct of the American Economic Association (AEA), adopted in 2018, does not explicitly address the relationship between

---

[2] See the Frequently Asked Questions about the Common Rule for Behavioral and Social Science Research on the NSF Website (www.nsf.gov/bfa/dias/policy/human.jsp, Reference GPG chapter II.D.6).

researchers and research participants nor does it forbid or regulate deception. Nevertheless, economists have developed a strict social norm against the use of deception in experimental research. This policy is enforced by all major journals publishing experimental research in economics. However, the economists' ban on deception is hardly ever attributed to ethical concerns, but rather to reputational concerns. Economists strongly oppose the use of deception because they believe that the experience of deception leads participants to distrust the researchers, potentially undermining the validity of data garnered from experiments that employ participants who have been deceived in the past (Hertwig & Ortmann 2001a).

Conversely, deception is typically associated with experimental social psychology. The experimental method became paramount in psychology in the first thirty years of the twentieth century, contributing to the establishment of psychology as a science. Social psychologists developed the use of deception to exert control over the experimental stimulus, which, in their field, typically consisted of other people's behavior. Historically, the use of deception was rare before 1930 and limited to less than 10 percent of the studies published by the major social psychology journals between 1930 and 1945. However, experiments using deception became much more popular during the 1950s and 1960s, eventually leveling off in the 1970s, when about 50 percent of the articles published by the most prominent journal in the field – the Journal of Personality and Social Psychology – used deception (Korn 1997). The rapid increase in the publication of studies using deception that started in the 1950s was accompanied by a change in the quality of the deception used in psychological research. Following the influential work of Kurt Lewin and Leon Festinger, social psychologists began to design complex experiments in which they used increasingly elaborate forms of deceptions involving confederates, complicated scripts, and cover stories.

Experimental sociologists do not follow a common norm concerning the use of deception. The American community of experimental sociologists is generally close to the social psychology tradition; their research focuses on group processes, and many of them use deception in experimental research and regularly publish on both sociology and social psychology outlets. The flagship journal of the American community of experimental sociologists is Social Psychology Quarterly, published by the American Sociological Association. By contrast, many European experimental sociologists adhere to the rational choice school, which is theoretically close to experimental economics. In addition, European laboratories and subject pools are often hosted by or shared with economists, who impose a strict "no-deception" policy.[3] Therefore, in general, European sociologists frequently enforce the "no-deception" rule for the same reputational reasons used by economists.

12.3 THE DECEPTION DEBATE

Generally speaking, deception is considered an important methodological tool by experimental social psychologists as well as sociologists of the group processes school (e.g., Korn 1997; Bröder 1998; Kimmel 1998; Weiss 2001; Ariely & Norton 2007; Cook & Yamagishi 2008), while deception is a taboo and has to be avoided at all costs according to experimental economists (e.g., Davis & Holt 1993; Ledyard 1995; Hey 1998; McDaniel & Starmer 1998; Hertwig & Ortmann 2001a, b). However, while the two camps of the debate are clear, what precisely defines deception remains far from trivial. As a consequence, it is difficult to find a consensus regarding what should be permitted or forbidden, even within each of the two camps.

On the one hand, deception is formally permitted in social psychology experiments, according to both ASA and APA codes of conduct, as stated earlier. Yet, both codes posit quite strong restrictions to its use. In particular, the APA code standard 8.07, paragraph a, states that "[p]sychologists do not conduct a study involving deception unless they have determined that the use of deceptive techniques is justified by the study's significant prospective scientific, educational, or applied value and that *effective nondeceptive alternative procedures are not feasible*" (emphasis added).

Many experiments employing deception involve the use of confederates or simulated agents since most experiments are nowadays conducted using computers. Some of the most famous cases of ethically questionable use of deception in social psychological research have been claimed not to have been possible otherwise. For example, it has been argued that if Stanley Milgram (1974) had informed the participants that they were confronted with an actor, he would not have been able to reveal the extent of obedience to authority. Yet, in many experiments that use deception, a nondeceptive alternative would be feasible. In studies using simulated agents, deception is often used to ensure control over the variation of the stimuli. In such cases, deception could be avoided by replacing

---

[3] For example, currently the "Experimental Laboratory for Sociology and Economics" (ELSE) at Utrecht University, the "Center for Experimental Social Sciences" (CESS) at Nuffield College, University of Oxford, the "Decision Science Lab" (DeSciL) at ETH Zurich, the "Bologna Laboratory for Experiments in Social Science" (BLESS) at the University of Bologna, and the Center for LabOratory Simulations and Experimental Research (CLOSER), at the University of Turin have facilities and subject pools shared among sociologists and economists.

simulated agents with real participants. However, more participants would probably be necessary to achieve the required statistical power, not only because each simulated agent has to be replaced by a real person but also because the behavior of real people varies. Thus, the ethics committee approving an experimental research project needs to weigh the moral and psychological costs of deception against both the scientific value of the study and the potential extra costs (usually in public funds) of recruiting many more participants in order to conduct the same study without deception. There is a large gray area, including experiments of high scientific value that should be conducted either without deception, if the ethics committee applies a strict interpretation of the "feasibility of nondeceptive procedure" clause, or with deception, if the committee chooses to give priority to saving public research funds.[4]

On the other hand, banning deception altogether, as agreed upon by the majority of experimental economists, seems an easier solution to the dilemma. However, even among economists, there is not a complete consensus on what precisely should be banned (see Cooper 2014; Hersch 2015; Krawczyk 2019; Ortmann 2019; Charness, Samek, & van de Veen 2021). The earliest and most cited definitions of deception typically refer to explicit and intentional acts of deception. For example, Hey (1998, 398) wrote, "There is a world of difference between not telling participants things and telling them the wrong things. The latter is deception, the former is not." Substantively similar definitions can be found in McDaniel and Starmer (1998) and Hertwig and Ortmann (2001a), and they are consistent with the psychologists' point of view on the matter (e.g., Baumrind 1985). Thus, there is some consensus across disciplines that acts of commission constitute deception, but acts of omission do not.

Nevertheless, as pointed out by Hersch (2015), providing participants with incomplete information about the experimental setting or procedure may lead them to form erroneous beliefs (Hersch refers to this practice as "implicit deception"). When, at the end of the experiment, the participants discover that the experimental instructions induced them to believe something that later turned out to be false, they could feel deceived. Therefore, the effects of implicit deception on trust in researchers and on suspicion in future experiments are arguably not different from the effects of explicit deception (Hersch 2015). Yet, implicit deception is more acceptable in all experimental laboratories, including those in economics.

---

[4] On rare occasions, deception was used in the past by economists for the same reason, i.e., to avoid the need to recruit a number of participants that would have made the experiment prohibitively expensive (e.g., Kim & Walker 1984).

Of course, not all implicit deception is equally problematic. The magnitude of the problem must depend on the severity of the feeling of deception experienced; pro-deception experimentalists would argue that the same holds for explicit deception, but anti-deception ones would disagree. Several scholars have contributed to this debate by analyzing and classifying types of deception according to their severity (e.g., Krawczyk 2019; Charness, Samek, & van de Veen 2021). These typologies include explicit forms of deception – such as the use of confederates, simulated agents, and false cover stories – as well as implicit forms of deception, such as unannounced endogenous matching (e.g., matching participants in a trust game according to the cooperation level that they displayed in a previous interaction) or unannounced restart of an experiment (e.g., after one series of repeated interaction ends, a second series starts, without being announced at the beginning of the experiment). While an experimental study using explicit deception would be rejected by most economics journals, reaching a consensus on implicit deception seems to be more difficult. Some scholars may agree with Cooper (2014, 113), who stated that "only an extremist would claim that experimenters (or economists in general) should never use (implicit) deception." However, others maintain that weakening the no-deception norm is a slippery slope and "only a minimal set of acts of omission (such as dividing a group of participants into matching groups without telling them)" (Ortmann 2019, 36) should be allowed.

12.4 RESEARCH ON CONSEQUENCES OF DECEPTION

As argued previously, the use of deception is inextricably linked to the ethical principles regulating scientific research and, in particular, to the interpretation and implementation of the principle of informed consent. Deception lies at the edge between the information that participants need to receive for their consent to be truly "informed" and details of the design that should rather be omitted for the experimental manipulation to be effective. Interestingly, however, there is relatively little interdisciplinary disagreement on ethical principles. The strongest ethical objections to the use of deception originated within the field of psychology (e.g., Baumrind 1964, 1985, 2015), but the contemporary debate between experimental social psychology and experimental economics is generally of a pragmatic nature and concerns the validity of experimental data obtained from subjects who experienced deception. For many research questions that concern economists, deception spoils the internal validity of experimental data because if participants distrust the information they receive during the experiment, their behavior is no longer a valid response for the research problem under investigation. By contrast, for many questions studied by psychologists, internal validity rests on the use of deception because social psychologists are especially interested in spontaneous behavior, unaffected by concerns for self-presentation. Disguising the true purpose of an experiment, by means of deception, is the strategy psychologists use to prevent participants from acting in accordance with the image of themselves they want to project (Tyler & Amodio 2015).

While possible ethical concerns related to the use of deception fall in the normative domain, potential reputational effects, such as those feared by the majority of scholars opposing deception, are amenable to empirical investigation. Thus, empirical research on the consequences of deception proliferated, starting in the years when the use of deception in social psychology was at its peak. Broadly speaking, early empirical studies of deception addressed two basic issues: whether deceived participants are subsequently more likely to harbor negative feelings or attitudes toward experimental research (e.g., Cook et al. 1970; Christensen 1988) and whether suspicion resulting from the actual experience of deception (e.g., Willis & Willis 1970; Stang 1976) or from warnings that deception may be used (e.g., Fillenbaum 1966; Cook et al. 1970) affects the behaviors of participants during the course of a single experiment. Hertwig and Ortmann (2008) extensively reviewed these studies and concluded that the evidence about the consequences of deception on suspicion and behavior in the experiments is inconclusive.

After the revival of the deception debate that followed the development of experimental economics, two experimental studies (Jamison, Karlan, & Schechter 2008; Barrera & Simpson 2012) explicitly investigated the effects of experiencing deception in one experiment on the participants' behavior in subsequent experiments. Both deceived participants in the first part of the study and conducted the second part a couple of weeks later to collect the dependent variables. Jamison, Karlan, and Schechter (2008) found a partial negative effect (i.e., only significant among females) on the probability of returning for the second part of the experiment after experiencing deception and a small effect in one of the control variables (i.e., more erratic behavior among deceived subjects in a lottery designed to study risk aversion). However, Jamison, Karlan, and Schechter (2008) did not control for history effects related to what happened in the first part of their experiment, which consisted of a trust game repeated five times. Barrera and Simpson (2012) replicated this study but simplified the design, using a one-shot prisoner's dilemma in part one to eliminate potential confounds that may arise when a repeated and asymmetric game is used, as in Jamison, Karlan, and Schechter (2008). They found a significant effect on the subjects' beliefs, that is, deceived subjects believed that social psychologists used deception more often, but they found no effects of deception on the subjects' behavior in part two, which consisted of several one-shot games. In addition, Barrera and Simpson (2012) conducted a second experiment to test the hypothesis that indirect exposure to deception (i.e., reading a description of an experiment employing deception) affects experimental behavior or beliefs but found no effects.

Finally, a few empirical studies investigated attitudes and beliefs about deception by conducting surveys among students or researchers (or both) (Krawczyk 2019; Krasnow, Howard, & Eisenbruch 2020; Charness, Samek, & van de Veen 2021). Krawczyk (2019) interviewed 143 researchers recruited from the Economic Science Association and about 360 students recruited from the subject pool of the laboratory of experimental economics at the University of Warsaw. Respondents were asked to rate various experimental scenarios on deceptiveness. According to the results of the survey, both students and experts have highly heterogeneous opinions, but the two groups tend to order the different deceptive techniques in similar ways. For example, explicit deception (lying) is consistently rated worse than implicit deception (omitting crucial information). Students have a more favorable view of deception than experts, but even experts turn out to be more tolerant of deception than it was expected. Charness, Samek, and van de Veen (2021) conducted a similar survey to Krawczyk (2019), but they asked researchers to rate the scenarios on more dimensions and also to recommend alternatives for each deceptive practice. Charness and colleagues recruited their researchers from IDEAS, a large bibliographic database dedicated to economics, whereas students were recruited from the laboratory subject pools of two American universities and one British university. Seven hundred and fifty-six experts completed the researchers' survey, and 445 students completed the students' survey. The results showed high heterogeneity in the ratings. Students are less concerned than researchers by the possibility that deception is present, and most students are not even aware of the no-deception policy in their laboratory. Mild (implicit) deception is generally considered acceptable when the scientific importance of the research is high and no alternative is available. Krasnow, Howard, and Eisenbruch (2020) surveyed attitudes of both psychologists and economists. In addition, they measured suspicion levels and compared that with behavior in four economic tasks. They found no correlation between suspicion in subjects who had experienced deception and behavior in the economic tasks and concluded that a ban on deceptive studies cannot be justified on pragmatic grounds (Krasnow, Howard, & Eisenbruch 2020, 1185). All in all, none of these empirical studies can claim to provide conclusive evidence on the matter. However, they have contributed to the development of evidence-based policies that may help regulate the use of deception and the management of laboratories and subject pools in the future.

13 Experimental Sociology – Quo Vadis?

Experimental sociology can be understood both as a century-long endeavor in sociology and as a new subfield in the discipline. Although sociology has a tradition of experimentation of its own, modern experimental sociology has been primarily inspired by methodological approaches that have initially been developed in psychology and economics. To the extent that psychology and economics disagree on particular questions, most notably the issue of deception, experimental sociologists – often leaning either toward psychology or economics – tend to replicate these disagreements within their discipline. Besides deception, the use of monetary and other incentives to motivate experimental participants and the particular approach to validity constitute core methodological debates in experimental sociology.

Our view in this volume is that given this state of the art, it is difficult to formulate universal norms of what is considered scientifically sound in experimental sociology beyond some general quality standards for social research. Instead, sociological work has to confront ambivalences, ambiguities, and trade-offs upfront and elaborate on the conditions under which it seems better to apply the methodological standards of one discipline or the other or to develop its own standards altogether. Hereby, it is essential to first consider the particular features that result from the specific perspective that sociologists take on social reality emphasizing the interrelatedness of individual behavior and socially emergent phenomena. In fact, one of our conclusions is that the defining feature of sociological experiments is not a unique set of methodological standards per se but the focus on genuine sociological explanations, which in turn defines the boundaries of research questions, theoretical conceptualizations, and experimental operationalizations. In this sense, whereas many research questions in (behavioral) economics and psychology are formulated at the level of individual dispositions, the relevant questions in sociology are considered properties of the social situation. If these differences matter, it may be legitimate to imagine disciplines as "centers of gravitation" of specific perspectives on and conceptions of the social world.

Recent reviews of the state of experimental methods in the social sciences show a slow increase of experimental research published in the flagship mainstream journals in sociology as compared to those in neighboring disciplines. As we argued at various points in the book, the initial resistance to adopting the experimental method in sociology is largely due to a misconception of the method itself, combined with an excessive emphasis on the importance of statistical generalizability as a validity criterion. Whereas quantitative empirical research in sociology tends to be associated primarily with classical survey research based on general population random samples, experimental research is mostly identified with laboratory experiments and convenience samples.

Yet, we envision a continuation, if not an increase, of the slow trend toward more experimental research in sociology, for two main reasons. First, as highlighted in Part I of the book, the most important contribution that experiments can bring to sociological research is their unique focus on the causal mechanisms linking characteristics of a social situation with certain behavioral outcomes. This contribution is by no means a prerogative of laboratory experiments only. In a nutshell, experiments are often defined as consisting of a three-step strategy: randomize, manipulate, and look for differences across experimental groups in the outcome variable(s). If laboratory experiments can be considered as the prototypical application of this strategy, in Part II of the book, we show how the same strategy can be adopted in a wide range of different applications and used to investigate very different phenomena. It is precisely the expansion of the several types of experiments discussed in the second part of the book that provides us with a second reason for predicting an increase in experimental research published in sociological mainstream journals.

Generally speaking, in the other experimental types described in Part II, the researcher sacrifices some of the advantages of the laboratory setting to improve on some of its limitations. Thus, different types of experiments should not be seen as competing but as complementary designs. In field experiments, the three-step strategy is applied in natural settings, whereby the researcher relinquishes some control over potential confounds in order to gain in empirical realism. In addition, participants may not be aware that they are taking part in an experimental study. Therefore, in field experiments, the researcher can observe spontaneous behavior unaffected by potential reactivity biases that are difficult to exclude in laboratory experiments. For this reason, field experiments can be a more suitable tool for studying socially undesirable behavior, such as discrimination or norm infractions.

In vignette experiments, the researcher renounces the possibility of observing actual behavior but applies the same three-step strategy to investigate beliefs, judgments, and intentions. This allows studying treatments that would be difficult to implement in real-world settings and varying a large number of experimental treatments and treatment conditions simultaneously. In addition, vignette designs can be incorporated into surveys and administered to random samples of the population or tailored subgroups, thereby ensuring statistical power, improving the statistical generalizability of the results, and enabling tests of theories for different social groups.

Finally, natural experiments and quasi-experiments demonstrate that the three-step strategy can be bent to investigate naturally occurring phenomena *as if* they were the product of an experiment. Many natural events resemble randomization because they affect some groups and spare other comparable groups. Accordingly, in natural experiments ensuring comparability between treated and control groups can be challenging, but natural experiments can be used to investigate the effects of factors or events that could never be directly manipulated by the researchers. By contrast, in quasi-experiments, manipulation is present, but randomization is missing. Thus, quasi-experiments allow for the investigation of the effects of human intervention in natural settings, but as the interventions do not target random individuals or groups, finding a comparable control group can be even more challenging than in natural experiments.

The field of experimental sociology is becoming more diverse, and experiments conducted outside of the laboratory are increasingly gaining popularity due to the perception of their higher generalizability. As it is also happening in other disciplines, like political science, vignette experiments embedded in surveys as well as experiments conducted digitally, are alternative types of experiments that are currently growing particularly fast. The traditional relevance of survey methodology in sociology combined with the relative ease of experimental implementation in such surveys, either in the field or online, makes us believe that survey and digital field experiments will be the most frequently used experimental approaches in sociology in the near future.

Yet, a word of caution is warranted. While new and creative experimental approaches should be embraced, we would like to emphasize the importance of theory in ensuring the overall validity of experimental findings. For most sociologically relevant questions, the understanding of causal processes through experiments is only possible when experimental designs are informed by an appropriate theory of human action and mechanism-based explanations. As argued in this volume, the robustness and replicability of what we learn from the data beyond the case under investigation are guarded under the conditions of a theory-based experiment. What is generalized is not a single experimental result to other empirical settings but a theoretical mechanism that would eventually inform new experiments, including intuition-driven experiments.

In fact, the best direction to go is to combine the theoretical approach with empirical cross-validation. Theory condenses what is known about a research question and allows the researcher to derive new expectations. In turn, surprising empirical findings help to push forward creative and innovative thinking about the phenomenon studied. This combination involves guidance from theory and implementation of complementary research designs to cross-validate (i) results from laboratory, field, and survey experiments; (ii) experimental results with observational findings; and (iii) all these with more nascent approaches such as digital field experiments. To make this possible, it is important to further advance theoretical approaches to validity for rigorous sociological research. For example, as we have elaborated in this book, many misunderstandings about the concept of external validity exist among sociologists, which have led them to reject the experimental approach. However, if one follows the theoretical approach to validity, no single result can be directly generalized to other populations, contexts, experimental settings, and times. Thus, simply rejecting experiments in sociology because they are conducted in the laboratory or rely on student samples is hard to justify.

Moreover, in the face of declining public trust in science caused by the spread of "alternative facts" and fake news, reports about academic misconduct, and the replication crisis in the behavioral sciences, experimental sociology should push efforts to advance transparent and reproducible research. Replications of published results should be established as a standard practice of academic research, where both junior and senior researchers are proactively involved. An important precondition to facilitate such a replication culture is open access to experimental materials, design, data, and analysis code, as well as the establishment of reporting standards (e.g., reporting manipulation checks, balance tests, and measures of uncertainty such as confidence bands) in academic journals. Likewise, it is important to facilitate the publication of successful replications, failed replications, and insignificant or null results because each replication adds to the number of observations on which a theory has been tested and eventually improved.

A recent development is the preregistration of research aims. This procedure, which has already become a mandatory step for publishing in an increasing number of journals, implies that the researcher uploads a brief description of the theory and the hypotheses that are tested in empirical studies to a public server before the study itself is conducted. In some cases, details are required on how to test the theory, including the exact model specification and the statistical tests that will be used. We strongly support the underlying aim of making assumptions and theoretical arguments explicit, avoiding ex post rationalizations, and fostering academic honesty. At the same time, there needs to be room for exploratory analysis of the data, which would allow for generating new and challenging research questions. Many new developments started with unexpected findings after meticulous scrutiny of the data, which instigated an intellectual search for the causes of the deviation from the expected outcome.

All things considered, we strongly support the advancement of recent trends toward more transparent and reproducible research in sociology and the social sciences altogether. Like any other methodological tool, experiments have their strengths and weaknesses. Yet, we believe that their particular advantage in affordable and accurate replication should make experiments a frontrunner in pushing this trend forward. Overall, we hope to have shown through this volume that there are numerous reasons to join this vibrant community of experimental sociology.

References

Abell, P. (2003). On the prospects for a unified social science: Economics & sociology. *Socio-Economic Review*, 1(1), 1–26.

Abraham, M., Auspurg, K., & Hinz, T. (2010). Migration decisions within dual-earner partnerships: A test of bargaining theory. *Journal of Marriage and Family*, 72(4), 876–892.

Aguiar, F., Brañas, P., & Miller, L. (2008). Moral distance in dictator games. *Judgment and Decision Making*, 3(4), 344–354.

Alfano, G. & Marwell, G. (1980). Experiments on the provision of public goods by groups III: Nondivisibility and free riding in "real" groups. *Social Psychology Quarterly*, 43(3), 300–309.

Alferes, V. R. (2012). *Methods of Randomization in Experimental Designs*. Thousand Oaks, CA: Sage.

Allison, P. D. (2001). *Missing Data*. Thousand Oaks, CA: Sage.

Allison, P. D. (2009). *Fixed Effects Regression Models*. London: Sage.

Alonso, F. M. (2017). Reductive views of shared intention. In: M. Jankovic & K. Ludwig, eds., *The Routledge Handbook of Collective Intentionality*. London: Routledge, pp. 34–44.

Al-Ubaydli, O. & List, J. (2015). On the generalizability of experimental results in economics. In: G. Frechette & A. Schotter, eds., *Handbook of Experimental Economic Methodology*. Oxford: Oxford University Press, pp. 420–462.

Álvarez-Benjumea, A. & Winter, F. (2018). Normative change and culture of hate: An experiment in online environments. *European Sociological Review*, 34(3), 223–237.

Anderson, J., Burks, S., Carpenter, J., et al. (2013). Self-selection and variations in the laboratory measurement of other-regarding preferences across subject pools: Evidence from one college student and two adult samples. *Experimental Economics*, 16(2), 170–189.

Angell, R. C. (1932). The difficulties of experimental sociology. *Social Forces*, 11(2), 207–210.

Angrist, J. D., Imbens, G. W., & Rubin, D. B. (1996). Identification of causal effects using instrumental variables. *Journal of the American Statistical Association*, 91(434), 444–455.

References

Angrist, J. D. & Krueger, A. B. (1992). Estimating the payoff to schooling using the Vietnam-era draft lottery. *NBER Working Paper 4067*.

Angrist, J. D. & Pischke, J. S. (2009). *Mostly Harmless Econometrics*. Princeton, NJ: Princeton University Press.

Angrist, J. D. & Pischke, J. S. (2015). *Mastering Metrics: The Path from Cause to Effect*. Princeton, NJ: Princeton University Press.

Ariely, D. & Norton, M. I. (2007). Psychology and experimental economics: A gap in abstraction. *Current Directions in Psychological Science*, 16(6), 336–339.

Auspurg, K. & Brüderl, J. (2022). How to increase reproducibility and credibility of sociological research. In: K. Gërxhani, N. D. de Graaf, & W. Raub, eds., *Handbook of Sociological Science: Contributions to Rigorous Sociology*. Cheltenham: Edward Elgar, pp. 512–527.

Auspurg, K. & Hinz, T. (2015a). *Factorial Survey Experiments*. London: Sage.

Auspurg, K. & Hinz, T. (2015b). Multifactorial experiments in surveys: Conjoint analysis, choice experiments, and factorial surveys. In: M. Keuschnigg & T. Wolbring, eds., *Experimente in den Sozialwissenschaften: Soziale Welt. Sonderband 22*. Baden-Baden: Nomos, pp. 291–315.

Auspurg, K., Hinz, T., & Sauer, C. (2017). Why should women get less? Evidence on the gender pay gap from multifactorial survey experiments. *American Sociological Review*, 82(1), 179–210.

Azmat, G. & Iriberri, N. (2010). The importance of relative performance feedback information: Evidence from a natural experiment using high school students. *Journal of Public Economics*, 94(7-8), 435–452.

Bader, F., Baumeister, B., Berger, R., & Keuschnigg, M. (2021). On the transportability of laboratory results. *Sociological Methods and Research*, 50(3), 1452–1481.

Balcells, L. & Torrats-Espinosa, G. (2018). Using a natural experiment to estimate the electoral consequences of terrorist attacks. *Proceedings of the National Academy of Sciences*, 115(42), 10624–10629.

Baldassarri, D. & Abascal, M. (2017). Field experiments across the social sciences. *Annual Review of Sociology*, 43, 41–73.

Bales, R. F. (1950). *Interaction Process Analysis*. Cambridge, MA: Addison-Wesley.

Balliet, D., Li, N. P., Macfarlan, S. J., & Van Vugt, M. (2011). Sex differences in cooperation: A meta-analytic review of social dilemmas. *Psychological Bulletin*, 137(6), 881–909.

Barabas, J. & Jerit, J. (2010). Are survey experiments externally valid? *American Political Science Review*, 104(02), 226–242.

References

Bardsley, N., Cubitt, R., Loomes, et al. (2010). *Experimental Economics: Rethinking the Rules*. Princeton, NJ: Princeton University Press.

Barker Bausell, R. & Li, Y.-F. (2002). *Power Analysis for Experimental Research: A Practical Guide for the Biological, Medical and Social Sciences*. Cambridge: Cambridge University Press.

Barr, A., Miller, L., & Ubeda, P. (2016). Moral consequences of becoming unemployed. *Proceedings of the National Academy of Sciences*, 113(17), 4676–4681.

Barr, A., Miller, L., & Ubeda, P. (2023). Is the acknowledgment of earned entitlement effect robust across experimental modes and populations? *Sociological Methods and Research*, 52(1), 209–230.

Barrera, D. (2014). Mechanisms of cooperation. In: G. Manzo, ed., *Analytical Sociology, Actions and Networks*. New York: John Wiley & Sons, pp. 172–195.

Barrera, D. & Buskens, V. (2007). Imitation and learning under uncertainty: A vignette experiment. *International Sociology*, 22(3), 366–395.

Barrera, D. & Buskens, V. (2009). Third-party effects. In: K. Cook, C. Snijders, V. Buskens, & C. Cheshire, eds., *eTrust*. New York: Russell Sage Foundation, pp. 37–72.

Barrera, D., Buskens, V., & Raub, W. (2015). Embedded trust: The analytical approach in vignettes, laboratory experiments and surveys. In: F. Lyon, G. Möllering, M. Saunders, & T. Hatzakis, eds., *Handbook of Research Methods on Trust*, 2nd ed. Cheltenham: Edward Elgar, pp. 251–264.

Barrera, D. & Simpson, B. (2012). Much ado about deception: Consequences of deceiving research participants in the social sciences. *Sociological Methods & Research*, 41(3), 383–413.

Baumrind, D. (1964). Some thoughts on ethics of research: After reading Milgram's "Behavioral study of obedience." *American Psychologist*, 19(6), 421–423.

Baumrind, D. (1985). Research using intentional deception: Ethical issues revisited. *American Psychologist*, 40(2), 165–174.

Baumrind, D. (2015). When subjects become objects: The lies behind the Milgram legend. *Theory & Psychology*, 25(5), 690–696.

Beck, M. & Opp, K.-D. (2001). Der faktorielle Survey und die Messung von Normen. *Kölner Zeitschrift für Soziologie und Sozialpsychologie*, 53(2), 283–306.

Bellemare, C., Kröger, S., & van Soest, A. (2008). Measuring inequity aversion in a heterogeneous population using experimental decisions and subjective probabilities. *Econometrica*, 76(4), 815–839.

References

Belot, M., Duch, R., & Miller, L. (2015). A comprehensive comparison of students and non-students in classic experimental games. *Journal of Economic Behavior & Organization*, 113, 26–33.

Berg, J., Dickhaut, J., & McCabe, K. (1995). Trust, reciprocity, and social history. *Games and Economic Behavior*, 10(1), 122–142.

Berger, J., Conner, T. L., & Fişek, M. H. (1974). *Expectation States Theory: A Theoretical Research Program*. Cambridge, MA: Winthrop Publishers.

Berger, J., Fişek, M. H., Norman, R. Z., & Zelditch, Jr., M. (1977). *Status Characteristics and Social Interaction: An Expectations States Approach*. New York: Elsevier.

Berger, J., Ridgeway, C., & Zelditch M. (2002). Construction of status and referential structures, *Sociological Theory*, 20(2), 157–179.

Berger, J., Zelditch, Jr., M., & Anderson, B. (1966). *Sociological Theories in Progress*, Boston: Houghton Mifflin.

Berger, R. (2015). Das Laborexperiment als sozialer Prozess. In: M. Keuschnigg & T. Wolbring, eds., *Experimente in den Sozialwissenschaften, Soziale Welt Sonderband 22*. Baden-Baden: Nomos, pp. 58–81.

Bergstrom, T. C. (2003). Vernon Smith's insomnia and the dawn of economics as an experimental science. *Scandinavian Journal of Economics*, 105(2), 181–205.

Betsch, T. & Haberstroh, S. (2001). Financial incentives do not pave the road to good experimentation. *Behavioral and Brain Sciences*, 24(3), 404–404.

Binmore, K., Shaked, A., & Sutton, J. (1985). Testing non-cooperative game theory: A preliminary study. *American Economic Review*, 75(5), 1178–1180.

Blau, P. M. (1964). *Exchange and Power in Social Life*. New Brunswick, NJ: Transaction Publishers.

Bloom, H. S., Bos, J. M., & Lee S.-W. (1999). Using cluster random assignment to measure program impacts: Statistical implications for the evaluation of education programs. *Evaluation Review*, 23(4), 445–469.

Blossfeld, H. P. (2017a). Evidence of causation – The contribution of life course research, part I: Dominant models of causal inference and their limitations in life course research. In: R. A. Scott & S. M. Kosslyn, eds., *Emerging Trends in the Social and Behavioral Sciences*. Wiley Online Library. https://doi.org/10.1002/9781118900772.etrds0442.

Blossfeld, H. P. (2017b). Evidence of causation – The contribution of life course research, part II: Causation as generative process. In: R. A. Scott & S. M. Kosslyn, eds., *Emerging Trends in the Social and Behavioral*

Sciences. Wiley Online Library. https://doi.org/10.1002/978111890 0772.etrds0443.
Bocca, G., Romanò, S., & Barrera, D. (2021). Come stimolare la prosocialità: effetti di incentivi e frame in laboratorio. *Polis*, 36(2), 271–299.
Bolton, G. E. & Ockenfels, A. (2000). ERC: A theory of equity, reciprocity, and competition. *American Economic Review*, 90(1), 166–193.
Bond R. M., Fariss C. J., Jones J. J., et al. (2012). A 61-million-person experiment in social influence and political mobilization. *Nature*, 489, 295–298.
Boots, D. P., Cochran, J. K., & Heide, K. M. (2003). Capital punishment preferences for special offender populations. *Journal of Criminal Justice*, 31(6), 553–565.
Bowles, S. (2016). *The Moral Economy: Why Good Incentives Are No Substitute for Good Citizens.* New Haven, CT: Yale University Press.
Bowles, S. & Polania-Reyes, S. (2012). Economic incentives and social preferences: Substitutes or complements? *Journal of Economic Literature*, 50(2), 368–425.
Braga, A. A. & Bond, B. J. (2008). Policing crime and disorder hot spots: A randomized controlled trial. *Criminology*, 46(3), 577–607.
Brandts, J. & Charness, G. (2011). The strategy vs. the direct-response method: A first review of experimental comparisons. *Experimental Economics*, 14(3), 375–398.
Brearley, H. C. (1931). Experimental sociology in the United States. *Social Forces*, 10(2), 196–199.
Breen, R. (2022). Causal inference with observational data. In: K. Gërxhani, N. D. de Graaf. & W. Raub, eds., *Handbook of Sociological Science: Contributions to Rigorous Sociology.* Cheltenham: Edward Elgar, pp. 272–286.
Brehm, S. S., Kassin, S. M., & Fein, S. (1990). *Social Psychology.* Boston: Houghton Mifflin.
Bröder, A. (1998). Deception can be acceptable. *American Psychologist*, 53(7), 805–806.
Brugarolas, P. & Miller, L. (2021). The causal effect of polls on turnout intention: A local randomization regression discontinuity approach. *Political Analysis*, 29(4), 554–560.
Bunge, M. (2004). How does it work? The search for explanatory mechanisms. *Philosophy of the Social Sciences*, 34(2), 182–210.
Burhans, D. T. (1977). Coalition game research: A reexamination. *American Journal of Sociology*, 79(2), 389–408.

Buskens, V. & Raub, W. (2002). Embedded trust: Control and learning, *Advances in Group Processes*, 19, 167–202.

Buskens, V. & Raub, W. (2013). Rational choice social research on social dilemmas: Embeddedness effects on trust. In: R. Wittek, T. A. B. Snijders, & V. Nee, eds., *Handbook of Rational Choice Social Research*. Stanford, CA: Stanford University Press, pp. 113–150.

Buskens, V., Raub, W., & van der Veer, J. (2010). Trust in triads: An experimental study. *Social Networks*, 32(4), 301–312.

Buskens, V. & Weesie, J. (2000). An experiment on the effects of embeddedness in trust situations: Buying a used car. *Rationality and Society*, 12(2), 227–253.

Camerer, C. (2015). The promise and success of lab-field generalizability in experimental economics: A critical reply to Levitt and List. In: G. Frechette & A. Schotter, eds., *Handbook of Experimental Economic Methodology*. Oxford: Oxford University Press, pp. 249–295.

Camerer, C., Dreber, A., Forsell, E., et al. (2016). Evaluating replicability of laboratory experiments in economics. *Science*, 351, 1433–1436.

Campbell, D. T. (1957). Factors relevant to the validity of experiments in social settings. *Psychological Bulletin*, 54(4), 297.

Campbell, D. T. (1986). Relabeling internal and external validity for applied social scientists. In: W. M. K. Trochim, ed., *Advances in Quasi-experimental Design and Analysis*. San Francisco: Jossey-Bass, pp. 67–77.

Campbell, D. T. & Russo, M. J. (1999). *Social Experimentation, vol. 1*. New York: Sage.

Campbell, D. T. & Stanley, J. C. (1966). *Experimental and Quasi-experimental Designs for Research*. Chicago: Rand McNally.

Campos-Mercade, P., Meier, A. N., Schneider, F. H., et al. (2021). Monetary incentives increase COVID-19 vaccinations. *Science*, 374(6569), 879–882.

Caplow T. (1956). A theory of coalitions in the triad. *American Sociological Review*, 21(4), 489–493.

Caplow, T. (1959). Further development of a theory of coalitions in the triad. *American Sociological Review*, 64(5), 488–493.

Card, D. & Krueger, A. B. (1994). Minimum wages and employment: A case study of the fast-food industry in New Jersey and Pennsylvania. *The American Economic Review*, 84(4), 772–793.

Carpenter, J., Burks, S., & Verhoogen, E. (2005). Comparing students to workers: The effects of social framing on behavior in distribution games. *Research in Experimental Economics*, 10, 261–290.

References

Carpenter, J., Connolly, C., & Myers, C. (2008). Altruistic behavior in a representative dictator experiment. *Experimental Economics*, 11(3), 282–298.

Carpenter, J. & Huet-Vaughn, E. (2019). Real-effort tasks. In: A. Schram & A. Ule, eds., *Handbook of Research Methods and Applications in Experimental Economics*. Cheltenham: Edward Elgar, pp. 368–383.

Carr, L. J. (1929). Experimental sociology: A preliminary note on theory and method. *Social Forces*, 8(1), 63–74.

Castilla, E. J., Lan, G. J., & Rissing, B. A. (2013). Social networks and employment: Outcomes (Part 2). *Sociology Compass*, 7(12), 1013–1026.

Cattaneo, M. D., Idrobo, N., & Titiunik, R. (2020). *A Practical Introduction to Regression Discontinuity Designs: Foundations*. Cambridge: Cambridge University Press.

Centola, D. (2010). The spread of behavior in an online social network experiment. *Science*, 329, 1194–1197.

Centola, D., Willer, R., & Macy, M. W. (2005). The emperor's dilemma: A computational model of self-enforcing norms. *American Journal of Sociology*, 110(4), 1009–1040.

Chamberlin, E. H. (1948). An experimental imperfect market. *Journal of Political Economy*, 56(2), 95–108.

Chapin, F. S. (1917a). The experimental method and sociology. *The Scientific Monthly*, 4(2), 133–144.

Chapin, F. S. (1917b). The experimental method and sociology II. *The Scientific Monthly*, 4(3), 238–247.

Chapin, F. S. (1931). The problem of controls in experimental sociology. *Journal of Educational Sociology*, 4(9), 541–551.

Chapin, F. S. (1932). The advantages of experimental sociology in the study of family group patterns. *Social Forces*, 11(2), 200–207.

Chapin, F. S. (1936). Social theory and social action. *American Sociological Review*, 1(1), 1–11.

Chapin, F. S. (1938). Design for social experiments. *American Sociological Review*, 3(6), 786–800.

Chapin, F. S. (1940a). An experiment on the social effects of good housing. *American Sociological Review*, 5(6), 868–879.

Chapin, F. S. (1940b). A study of social adjustment using the technique of analysis by selective control. *Social Forces*, 18(4), 476–487.

Chapin, F. S. (1947). *Experimental Designs in Sociological Research*. New York: Harper & Brothers.

Chapin, F. S. (1950). Experimental design in sociology: Limitations and abuses. *Social Forces*, 29(1), 25–28.

Charness, G., Gneezy, U., & Kuhn, M. A. (2012). Experimental methods: Between-subject and within-subject design. *Journal of Economic Behavior & Organization*, 81(1), 1–8.

Charness, G. & Rabin, M. (2002). Understanding social preferences with simple tests. *The Quarterly Journal of Economics*, 117(3), 817–869.

Charness, G., Samek, A., & van de Veen, J. (2021). What is considered deception in experimental economics? *Experimental Economics*, 25(2), 385–412.

Chen, J. & Tam, T. (2020). Uses of artificial and composite treatments in experimental methods: Reconsidering the problem of validity and its implications for stratification research. *Research in Social Stratification and Mobility*, 65, 100443.

Cherry, T. L., Frykblom, P., & Shogren, J. F. (2002). Hardnose the dictator. *American Economic Review*, 92(4), 1218–1221.

Chmielewski, M. & Kucker, S. C. (2019). An MTurk crisis? Shifts in data quality and the impact on study results. *Social Psychological and Personality Science*, 11(4), 464–473.

Chong, D. & Druckman, J. N. (2007). Framing theory. *Annual Review of Political Science*, 10, 103–126.

Christensen, L. (1988). Deception in psychological research: When is its use justified? *Personality and Social Psychology Bulletin*, 14(4), 664–675.

Clampet-Lundquist, S. & Massey, D. S. (2008). Neighborhood effects on economic self-sufficiency: A reconsideration of the moving to opportunity experiment. *American Journal of Sociology*, 114(1), 107–143.

Cleave, B. L., Nikiforakis, N., & Slonim, R. (2013). Is there selection bias in laboratory experiments? The case of social and risk preferences. *Experimental Economics*, 16(3), 372–382.

Cohen, J. (1988). *Statistical Power Analysis for the Behavioral Sciences*, 2nd ed. Hillsdale, NJ: Lawrence Erlbaum Associates.

Coleman, J. S. (1986). Social theory, social research, and a theory of action. *American Journal of Sociology*, 91(6), 1309–1335.

Coleman, J. S. (1990). *Foundations of Social Theory*. Cambridge: Belknap.

Comte, A. (1875). *The Positive Philosophy of Auguste Comte*. Freely Translated and Condensed by Harriet Martineau. London: Trübner & Co.

Conley, D. & Heerwig, J. (2012). The long-term effects of military conscription on mortality: Estimates from the Vietnam-era draft lottery. *Demography*, 49(3), 841–855.

Cook, K. S. & Cheshire, C. (2013). Social exchange, power, and inequality in networks. In: R. Wittek, T. A. B. Snijders, & V. Nee, eds., *The Handbook of Rational Choice Social Research*. Stanford, CA: Stanford Social Sciences, pp. 185–219.

References

Cook K. S., Cheshire, C., Rice, E. R. W., et al. (2013). Social exchange theory. In: J. DeLamater & A. Ward, eds., *Handbook of Social Psychology*. Berlin: Springer, pp. 61–88.

Cook K. S. & Emerson, R. M. (1978). Power, equity and commitment in exchange networks. *American Sociological Review*, 43(5), 721–739.

Cook, K. S. & Hegtvedt, K. A. (1983). Distributive justice, equity, and equality. *Annual Review of Sociology*, 9(1), 217–241.

Cook, K. S. & Yamagishi, T. (2008). A defense of deception on scientific grounds. *Social Psychology Quarterly* 71(3), 215–221.

Cook K. S., Yamagishi, T., Cheshire, C., et al. (2005). Trust building via risk taking: A cross-societal experiment. *Social Psychology Quarterly*, 68(2), 121–142.

Cook, T. D., Bean, J. R., Calder, B. J., et al. (1970). Demand characteristics and three conceptions of the frequently deceived subjects. *Journal of Personality and Social Psychology*, 14(3),185–194.

Cook, T. D. & Campbell, D. T. (1979). *Quasi-Experimentation: Design & Analysis Issues for Field Settings*. Boston: Houghton Mifflin Company.

Cooper, D. J. (2014). A note on deception in economic experiments. *Journal of Wine Economics*, 9(2), 111–114.

Cooper D. J. & Kagel, J. H. (2016). Other-regarding preferences: A selective survey of experimental results. In: J. H. Kagel & A. E. Roth, eds., *The Handbook of Experimental Economics*, vol. 2. Princeton, NJ: Princeton University Press, pp. 217–289.

Coppock, A. (2018). Generalizing from survey experiments conducted on mechanical Turk: A replication approach. *Political Science Research and Methods*, 7(3), 1–16.

Coppock, A. & Green, D. P. (2015). Assessing the correspondence between experimental results obtained in the lab and field: A review of recent social science research. *Political Science Research and Methods*, 3(01), 113–131.

Coppock, A., Leeper, Th., & Mullinix, K. J. (2018). Generalizability of heterogeneous treatment effect estimates across samples. *Proceedings of the National Academy of Sciences*, 115(49), 12441–12446.

Corman, H. & Mocan, N. (2005). Carrots, sticks, and broken windows. *The Journal of Law and Economics*, 48(1), 235–266.

Corra, M. & Willer, D. (2002). The gatekeeper. *Sociological Theory*, 20(2), 180–207.

Correll, S. J., Benard, S., & Paik, I. (2007). Getting a job: Is there a motherhood penalty? *American Journal of Sociology*, 112(5), 1297–1338.

Correll, S. J. & Ridgeway, C. L. (2006). Expectation states theory. In: J. Delamater, ed., *Handbook of Social Psychology*. Boston: Springer, pp. 29–51.

Crawford, V. P. (2002). Introduction to experimental game theory. *Journal of Economic Theory*, 104(1), 1–15.

Cronbach, L. J. & Meehl, P. E. (1955). Construct validity in psychological tests. *Psychological Bulletin*, 52(4), 281–302.

Cunningham, S. (2021). *Causal Inference: The Mixtape*. New Haven, CT & London: Yale University Press.

Dafoe, A., Zhang, B., & Caughey, D. (2018). Information Equivalence in Survey Experiments. *Political Analysis*, 26(4), 399–416.

Davis, D. D. & Holt, C. A. (1993). *Experimental Economics*. Princeton, NJ: Princeton University Press.

Dawid, A. P. & Musio, M. (2022). Effects of causes and causes of effects. *Annual Review of Statistics and its Application*, 9, 261–287.

Deaton, A. & Cartwright, N. (2018). Understanding and misunderstanding randomized controlled trials. *Social Science & Medicine*, 210, 2–21.

Denk, C. E., Benson, J. M., Fletcher, J. C., & Reigel, T. M. (1997). How do Americans want to die? A factorial vignette survey of public attitudes about end-of-life medical decision-making. *Social Science Research*, 26(1), 95–120.

De Rooij, E. A., Green, D. P., & Gerber, A. S. (2009). Field experiments on political behavior and collective action. *Annual Review of Political Science*, 12, 389–395.

De Silva, D. G., McComb, R. P., Moh, Y. K., et al. (2010). The effect of migration on wages: Evidence from a natural experiment. *American Economic Review*, 100(2), 321–326.

De Souza Briggs, X., Popkin, S. J., & Goering, J. (2010). *Moving to Opportunity: The Story of an American Experiment to Fight Ghetto Poverty*. Oxford: Oxford University Press.

Diekmann, A. (1985). Volunteer's dilemma. *Journal of Conflict Resolution*, 29(4), 605–610.

Diekmann, A. (1986). Volunteer's dilemma: A social trap without a dominant strategy and some empirical results. In: A. Diekmann & P. Mitter, eds., *Paradoxical Effects of Social Behavior: Essays in Honor of Anatol Rapoport*. Heidelberg/Wien: Physica, pp. 187–197.

Diekmann, A. (1993). Cooperation in an asymmetric volunteer's dilemma game: Theory and experimental evidence. *International Journal of Game Theory*, 22, 75–85.

Diekmann, A. (2008). Soziologie und Ökonomie: Der Beitrag experimenteller Wirtschaftsforschung zur Sozialtheorie. *Kölner Zeitschrift für Soziologie und Sozialpsychologie*, 60(3), 528–550.

Diekmann, A. (2022). Rational choice sociology: Heuristic potential, applications and limitation. In: K. Gërxhani, N. D. de Graaf, & W. Raub, eds., *Handbook of Sociological Science: Contributions to Rigorous Sociology*. Cheltenham: Edward Elgar, pp. 100–119.

Diekmann, A., Dittrich, R., Hatzinger, R., et al. (1981). 'Diktator'. Hypothesen und Design für ein experimentelles Vierpersonenspiel. Arbeitskreis Experimentelle Spiele. Institutsarbeit 150. Wien: Institut für Höhere Studien.

Diekmann, A. & Przepiorka, W. (2016). "Take one for the team!" Individual heterogeneity and the emergence of latent norms in a volunteer's dilemma. *Social Forces*, 94(3), 1309–1333.

Diekmann, A., Przepiorka, W., & Rauhut, H. (2015). Lifting the veil of ignorance: An experiment on the contagiousness of norm violations. *Rationality and Society*, 27(3), 309–333.

Diekmann, A. & Voss, T. (2016). Rational-Choice-Rezeption in der deutschsprachigen Soziologie. In: S. Moebius & A. Ploder, eds., *Handbuch Geschichte der deutschsprachigen Soziologie. Band 1: Geschichte der Soziologie im deutschsprachigen Raum*. Wiesbaden: Springer VS, pp. 663–682.

Di Stasio, V. & Gërxhani, K. (2015). Employers' social contacts and their hiring behavior in a factorial survey. *Social Science Research*, 51(1), 93–107.

Dodd, S. C. (1934). *A Controlled Experiment on Rural Hygiene in Syria*. Beirut: Publications of the American University in Beirut.

Dohmen, T., Falk, A., Huffman, D., et al. (2011). Individual risk attitudes: Measurement, determinants, and behavioral consequences. *Journal of the European Economic Association*, 9(3), 522–550.

Druckman, J. N., Kuklinski, J. H., & Sigelman, L. (2009). The unmet potential of interdisciplinary research: Political psychology approaches to voting and public opinion. *Political Behavior*, 31(4), 485–510.

Dülmer, H. (2007). Experimental plans in factorial surveys: Random or quota design? *Sociological Methods & Research*, 35(3), 382–409.

Dunning, T. (2012). *Natural Experiments in the Social Sciences. A Design-Based Approach*. Cambridge: Cambridge University Press.

Durkheim, E. (1982 [1895]). *The Rules of Sociological Method*. New York: The Free Press.

Duvendack, M, Palmer-Jones, R., & Reed, W. R. (2017). What is meant by "replication" and why does it encounter resistance in economics? *American Economic Review*, 107(5), 46–51.

Eifler, S. (2010). Validity of a factorial survey approach to the analysis of criminal behavior. *Methodology*, 6(3), 139–146.

Eifler, S. & Petzold, K. (2019). Validity aspects of vignette experiments. Expected 'what-if' differences between reported and actual behavior.

In: P. J. Lavrakas, M. W. Traugott, C. Kennedy, et al., eds., *Experimental Methods in Survey Research: Techniques that Combine Random Sampling with Random Assignment*. Hoboken, NJ: John Wiley & Sons, pp. 393–416.

Elster, J. (2007). *Explaining Social Behavior: More Nuts and Bolts for the Social Sciences*. Cambridge: Cambridge University Press.

Emerson, R. M. (1962). Power-dependence relations. *American Sociological Review*, 9(1), 217–241.

Emerson, R. M. (1964). Power-dependence relations: Two experiments. *Sociometry*, 27(3), 282–298.

Emerson, R. M. (1972a). Exchange theory, part I: A psychological basis for social exchange. In: J. Berger, M. Zelditch, Jr., & B. Anderson, eds., *Sociological Theories in Progress*, vol. 2. Boston: Houghton Mifflin, pp. 38–57.

Emerson, R. M. (1972b). Exchange theory, part II: Exchange relations and networks. In: J. Berger, M. Zelditch, Jr., & B. Anderson, eds., *Sociological Theories in Progress*, vol. 2. Boston: Houghton Mifflin, pp. 58–87.

Emerson R. M. (1976). Social exchange theory. *Annual Review of Sociology*, 2, 335–362.

Enders, C. K. (2022). *Applied Missing Data Analysis*. New York: Guilford Publications.

Erikson, R. S., & Stoker, L. (2011). Caught in the draft: The effects of Vietnam draft lottery status on political attitudes." *American Political Science Review*, 105(2), 221–237.

Eriksson, K., Strimling, P., Gelfand, M., et al. (2021). Perceptions of the appropriate response to norm violation in 57 societies. *Nature Communication*, 12, 1481.

Esser, H. (1993). The rationality of everyday behavior. A rational choice reconstruction of the theory of action by Alfred Schütz. *Rationality and Society*, 5(1), 7–31.

Esser, H. (1999). *Soziologie. Allgemeine Grundlagen*. Frankfurt/M.: Campus.

Esser, H. & Kroneberg, C. (2015). An integrative theory of action: The model of frame selection. In: E. J. Lawler, S. R. Thye, & J. Yoon, eds., *Order on the Edge of Chaos: Social Psychology and the Problem of Social Order*. New York: Cambridge University Press, pp. 63–85.

Exadaktylos, F., Espín, A. M., & Brañas-Garza, P. (2013). Experimental subjects are not different. *Scientific Reports*, 3, 1213.

Faas, T. & Huber, S. (2010). Experimente in der Politikwissenschaft: Vom Mauerblümchen zum Mainstream. *Politische Vierteljahresschrift*, 51(4), 721–749.

References

Falk, A., Becker, A., Dohmen, T., Enke, B., Huffman, D., & Sunde, U. (2018). Global evidence on economic preferences. *The Quarterly Journal of Economics*, 133(4), 1645–1692.

Falk, A., Fehr, E., & Fischbacher, U. (2008). Testing theories of fairness: Intentions matter. *Games and Economic Behavior*, 62(1), 287–303.

Falk, A. & Fischbacher, U. (2006). A theory of reciprocity. *Games and Economic Behavior*, 54(2), 293–315.

Falk, A. & Heckman, J. J. (2009). Lab experiments are a major source of knowledge in the social sciences. *Science*, 326(5952), 535–538.

Falk, A., Meier, S., & Zehnder, C. (2013). Do lab experiments misrepresent social preferences? The case of self-selected student samples. *Journal of the European Economic Association*, 11(4), 839–852.

Fehr, E. & Gächter, S. (2000). Cooperation and punishment in public goods experiments. *American Economic Review*, 90(4), 980–994.

Fehr, E. & Gächter, S. (2002). Altruistic punishment in humans. *Nature*, 415, 137–140.

Fehr, E. & Gintis, H. (2007). Human motivation and social cooperation: Experimental and analytical foundations. *Annual Review of Sociology*, 33, 43–64.

Fehr, E. & Schmidt, K. M. (1999). A theory of fairness, competition, and cooperation. *The Quarterly Journal of Economics*, 114(3), 817–868.

Fillenbaum, S. (1966). Prior deception and subsequent experimental performance: The "faithful" subject. *Journal of Personality and Social Psychology*, 4(5), 532–537.

Fischer, B. A., IV (2006). A summary of important documents in the field of research ethics. *Schizophrenia Bulletin*, 32(1), 69–80.

Fisher, R. A. (1971 [1935]). *The Design of Experiment*. New York: Hafner.

Frank, R. H., Gilovich, T., & Regan, D. T. (1993). Does studying economics inhibit cooperation? *Journal of Economic Perspectives*, 7(2), 159–171.

Franzen, A. & Pointner S. (2012). Anonymity in the dictator game revisited. *Journal of Economic Behavior & Organization*, 81, 74–81.

Franzen, A. & Pointner, S. (2013). The external validity of giving in the dictator game: A field experiment using the misdirected letter technique. *Experimental Economics*, 16(2), 155–169.

Fréchette, G. R. (2012). Session-effects in the laboratory. *Experimental Economics*, 15(3), 485–498.

Fréchette, G. R. (2015). Laboratory experiments: Professionals versus students. In: G. Fréchette & A. Schotter, eds. *Handbook of Experimental Economic Methodology*. Oxford: Oxford University Press, pp. 360–390.

Freese, J. & Peterson, D. (2017). Replication in social science. *Annual Review of Sociology*, 43, 147–165.

Frey, B. (1997). *Not Just for the Money*. Cheltenham: Edward Elgar.

Fudenberg, D. (2006). Advancing beyond advances in behavioral economics. *Journal of Economic Literature*, 44(3), 694–711.

Gaddis, S. M. (2018). An introduction to audit studies in the social sciences. In: S. M. Gaddis, ed., *Audit Studies: Behind the Scenes with Theory, Method, and Nuance*. Cham: Springer, pp. 3–44.

Galizzi, M. & Navarro-Martinez, D. (2018). On the external validity of social preference games: A systematic lab-field study. *Management Science*, 65(3), 976–1002.

Gallop, M. & Weschle, S. (2019). Assessing the impact of non-random measurement error on inference: A sensitivity analysis approach. *Political Science Research and Methods*, 7(2), 367–384.

Gamson, W. A. (1961a). An experimental test of a theory of coalition formation. *American Sociological Review*, 26(4), 565–573.

Gamson, W. A. (1961b). A theory of coalition formation. *American Sociological Review*, 26(3), 373–382.

Gangl, M. (2010). Causal inference in sociological research. *Annual Review of Sociology*, 36, 21–47.

Gaw, A. (2014). Reality and revisionism: New evidence for Andrew C Ivy's claim to authorship of the Nuremberg Code. *Journal of the Royal Society of Medicine*, 107(4), 138–143.

Gerber, A. S. & Green, D. P. (2012). *Field Experiments: Design, Analysis, and Interpretation*. New York: W. W. Norton & Company.

Gerrig, R. J. (2013). *Psychology and Life*, 20th ed. Upper Saddle River: Pearson.

Gerring, J. (2001). *Social Science Methodology: A Criterial Framework*. Cambridge: Cambridge University Press.

Gertler, P. J., Martinez, S., Premand, P., Rawlings, L. B., & Vermeersch, C. M. (2011). *Impact Evaluation in Practice*. Washington, DC: The World Bank.

Gërxhani, K. (2020). Status ranking and gender inequality: A cross-country experimental comparison. *Research in Social Stratification and Mobility*, 65, 100474.

Gërxhani, K., Brandts, J., & Schram, A. (2023). Competition and gender inequality: A comprehensive analysis of effects and mechanisms. *American Journal of Sociology*, 129(3), 715–752.

Gërxhani, K., de Graaf, N. D., & Raub, W., eds. (2022). *Handbook of Sociological Science: Contributions to Rigorous Sociology*. Cheltenham: Edward Elgar.

Gërxhani, K. & Kosyakova, Y. (2022). The effect of co-ethnic social capital on immigrants' labor market integration: A natural experiment. *Comparative Migration Studies*, 10(1), 1–20.

Gërxhani, K. & Miller, L. (2022). Experimental sociology. In: K. Gërxhani, N. D. de Graaf, & W. Raub, eds., *Handbook of Sociological Science: Contributions to Rigorous Sociology*. Cheltenham: Edward Elgar, pp. 309–323.

Gërxhani, K. & Schram, A. (2006). Tax evasion and income source: A comparative experimental study. *Journal of Economic Psychology*, 27(3), 402–422.

Gërxhani, K., Volker, B., & van Breemen, J. (2021). Who will do it? Volunteering to change cooperation rules in a heterogeneous population. *European Sociological Review*, 37(3), 482–496.

Gillespie, G. (1991). *Manufacturing Knowledge: A History of the Hawthorne Experiments*. Cambridge, MA: Cambridge University Press.

Gil-White, F. J. (2001). A good experiment of choice behavior is a good caricature of a real situation. *Behavioral and Brain Sciences*, 24(3), 409–410.

Gintis, H. (2014). *The Bounds of Reason. Game Theory and the Unification of the Social Sciences*, Princeton, NJ: Princeton University Press.

Gneezy, U. & List, J. (2013). *The Why Axis: Hidden Motives and the Undiscovered Economics of Everyday Life*. New York: Public Affairs Books.

Gneezy, U., Niederle, M., & Rustichini, A. (2003). Performance in competitive environments: Gender differences. *The Quarterly Journal of Economics*, 118(3), 1049–1074.

Gneezy, U. & Rustichini, A. (2000a). A fine is a price. *The Journal of Legal Studies*, 29(1), 1–17.

Gneezy, U. & Rustichini, A. (2000b). Pay enough or don't pay at all, *The Quarterly Journal of Economics*, 115(3), 791–810.

Golder, S. & Macy, M. (2014). Digital footprints: Opportunities and challenges for online social research. *Annual Review of Sociology*, 40, 129–152.

Goldstein, N. J., Cialdini, R. B., & Griskevicius, V. (2008). A room with a viewpoint: Using social norms to motivate environmental conservation in hotels. *Journal of Consumer Research*, 35(3), 472–482.

Goldthorpe, J. H. (2001). Causation, statistics, and sociology. *European Sociological Review*, 17(1), 1–20.

González, L. (2013). The effect of a universal child benefit on conceptions, abortions, and early maternal labor supply. *American Economic Journal: Economic Policy*, 5(3), 160–188.

Gosnell, H. F. (1927). *Getting out the Vote: An Experiment in the Stimulation of Voting*. Chicago: University of Chicago Press.

Granovetter, M. (1985). Economic action and social structure: The problem of embeddedness. *American Journal of Sociology*, 91(3), 481–510.

Green, P. E. & Rao, V. R. (1971). Conjoint measurement-for quantifying judgmental data. *Journal of Marketing Research*, 8(3), 355–363.

Greenberg, D. & Shroder, M. (2004). *The Digest of Social Experiments*, 3rd ed. Washington, DC: Urban Institute Press.

Greenwald, A. (1976). Within-subjects designs: To use or not to use. *Psychological Bulletin*, 83(2), 314–320.

Greenwood, E. (1945). *Experimental Sociology: A Study in Method*. New York: King's Crown Press.

Guala, F. (2005). *The Methodology of Experimental Economics*. Cambridge: Cambridge University Press.

Guala, F. (2006). Paradigmatic experiments: The ultimatum game from testing to measurement device. *Philosophy of Science*, 75(5), 658–669.

Guala, F. (2012). Reciprocity: Weak or strong? What punishment experiments do (and do not) demonstrate. *Behavioral and Brain Sciences*, 35(1), 1–59.

Güth, W. & Kocher, M. G. (2014). More than thirty years of ultimatum bargaining experiments: Motives, variations, and a survey of the recent literature. *Journal of Economic Behavior & Organization*, 108, 396–409.

Güth, W., Schmittberger, R., & Schwarze, B. (1982). An experimental analysis of ultimatum bargaining. *Journal of Economic Behavior & Organization*, 3(4), 367–388.

Hainmueller, J., Hangartner, D., & Pietrantuono, G. (2017). Catalyst or crown: Does naturalization promote the long-term social integration of immigrants? *American Political Science Review*, 111(2), 256–276.

Hainmueller, J., Hangartner, D., & Yamamoto, T. (2015). Validating vignette and conjoint survey experiments against real-world behavior. *Proceedings of the National Academy of Sciences*, 112(8), 2395–2400.

Hainmueller, J., Hopkins, D. J., & Yamamoto, T. (2014). Causal inference in conjoint analysis: Understanding multidimensional choices via stated preference experiments. *Political Analysis*, 22(1), 1–30.

Halaby, Charles N. (2004). Panel models in sociological research: Theory into practice. *Annual Review of Sociology*, 30, 507–544.

Happé, F., Cook, J. L., & Bird, G. (2017). The structure of social cognition: In(ter)dependence of sociocognitive processes. *Annual Review of Psychology*, 68, 243–267.

Harcourt, B. E. & Ludwig, J. (2006). Broken windows: New evidence from New York City and a five-city social experiment. *University of Chicago Law Review*, 73(1), 271–320.

Harrison, G. W. & List, J. A. (2004). Field experiments. *Journal of Economic Literature*, 42(4), 1009–1055.

Heckman, J. J. & Smith, J. A. (1995). Assessing the case for social experiments. *Journal of Economic Perspectives*, 9(2), 85–110.

Hedström, P. (2005). *Dissecting the Social: On the Principles of Analytical Sociology*. Cambridge: Cambridge University Press.

Hedström, P. & Bearman, P., eds. (2009). *The Oxford Handbook of Analytical Sociology*. Oxford: Oxford University Press.

Hedström, P. & Swedberg, R. (1998). Social mechanisms: An introductory essay. In P. Hedström & R. Swedberg, eds., *Social Mechanisms. An Analytical Approach to Social Theory*, Cambridge, UK: Cambridge University Press, pp. 1–31.

Henrich, J., Bowles, S., Boyd, R., et al. (2004). *Foundations of Human Sociality: Economic Experiments and Ethnographic Evidence from Fifteen Small-Scale Societies*. New York: Oxford University Press.

Henrich, J., Heine, S. J., & Norenzayan, A. (2010). The weirdest people in the world? *Behavioral and Brain Science*, 33(2–3), 61–83.

Hersch, G. (2015). Experimental economics' inconsistent ban on deception. *Studies in History and Philosophy of Science*, 52, 13–19.

Hertwig, R. & Ortmann, A. (2001a). Experimental practices in economics: A methodological challenge for psychologists? *Behavioral and Brain Sciences*, 24(3), 383–403.

Hertwig, R. & Ortmann, A. (2001b). Money, lies, and replicability: On the need for empirically grounded experimental practices and interdisciplinary discourse. *Behavioral and Brain Sciences*, 24(3), 433–444.

Hertwig, R. & Ortmann, A. (2008). Deception in experiments: Revisiting the argument in its defense. *Ethics and Behavior*, 18(1), 59–92.

Hey, J. D. (1998). Experimental economics and deception: A comment. *Journal of Economic Psychology*, 19(3), 397–401.

Hikichi H., Sawada, Y., Tsuboya, T., et al. (2017). Residential relocation and change in social capital: A natural experiment from the 2011 Great East Japan Earthquake and Tsunami. *Science Advances*, 3(7), e1700426.

Hilton, D. J. (2001). Is the challenge for psychologists to return to behaviourism? *Behavioral and Brain Sciences*, 24(3), 415–416.

Hogarth, R. M. (2005). The challenge of representative design in psychology and economics, *Journal of Economic Methodology*, 12(2), 253–263.

Holland, P. W. (1986). Statistics and causal inference. *Journal of the American Statistical Association*, 81(396), 945–960.

Holland, P. W. (1988). Causal inference, path analysis, and recursive structural equation models. *Sociological Methodology*, 18, 449–484.

Homans, G. (1961). *Social Behavior: Its Elementary Forms*. New York: Harcourt Brace.

Horne, C. (2003). The internal enforcement of norms. *European Sociological Review*, 19(4), 335–343.

Horne, C. & Mollborn, S. (2020). Norms: An integrated framework. *Annual Review of Sociology*, 46, 467–487.

Hummell, H. J. (1972a). Zur Problematik der Ableitung in sozialwissenschaftlichen Aussagesystemen. Ein Plädoyer for Formalisierung (Teil 1). *Zeitschrift für Soziologie*, 1(1), 31–46.

Hummell H. J. (1972b). Zur Problematik der Ableitung in sozialwissenschaftlichen Aussagesystemen. Ein Plädoyer for Formalisierung (Teil 2). *Zeitschrift für Soziologie*, 1(2), 118–138.

Imbens, G. W. & Rubin, D. B. (2015). *Causal Inference for Statistics, Social and Biomedical Sciences: An Introduction*. New York: Cambridge University Press.

Jackson, M. & Cox, D. R. (2013). The principles of experimental design and their application in sociology. *Annual Review of Sociology*, 39, 27–49.

Jamison, J., Karlan, D., & Schechter, L. (2008). To deceive or not to deceive: The effects of deception on behavior in future laboratory experiments. *Journal of Economic Behavior & Organization*, 68(3), 477–88.

Jankovic, M. & Ludwig, K., eds. (2017). *The Routledge Handbook of Collective Intentionality*. New York: Routledge.

Jann, B. & Przepiorka, W., eds. (2017). *Social Dilemmas, Institutions, and the Evolution of Cooperation*. München: De Gruyter Oldenbourg.

Jasso, G. (2006). Factorial survey methods for studying beliefs and judgments. *Sociological Methods & Research*, 34(3), 334–423.

Jasso, G. & Opp, K.-D. (1997). Probing the character of norms: A factorial survey analysis of the norms of political action. *American Sociological Review*, 62(6), 947–964.

Jasso, G. & Rossi, P. H. (1977). Distributive justice and earned income. *American Sociological Review*, 42(4), 639–651.

Jimenez-Buedo, M. & Miller, L. (2010). Why a trade-off? The relationship between the internal and external validity of experiments. *Theoria*, 18(3), 271–282.

Jones, Stephen R. G. (1992). Was there a Hawthorne effect? *American Journal of Sociology*, 98(3), 451–468.

Kahneman, D. (2011). *Thinking Fast and Slow*. New York: Farrar, Straus and Giroux.

Kahneman, D. & Tversky, A. (1979). Prospect theory: An analysis of decision under risk. *Econometrica*, 47(2), 263–292.

Kalkhoff, W. & Thye, S. R. (2006). Expectation states theory and research: New observations from meta-analysis. *Sociological Methods & Research*, 35(2), 219–249.

Kalwitzki, T., Kittel, B., Luhan, W., & Peuker, B. (2015). Strategische Wort-Wahl in der Politik: Ein qualitativer Ansatz zur Analyse experimenteller Gremienwahlen. In: A. Bächtiger, S. Shikano, & E. Linhart, eds., *Jahrbuch für Handlungs- und Entscheidungstheorie, Band 9: Deliberation und Aggregation*. Wiesbaden: Springer VS, pp. 65–92.

Kalwitzki, T., Luhan, W. J., & Kittel, B. (2012). Experimental chats: Opening the black box of group experiments. In: B. Kittel, W. J. Luhan, & R. B. Morton, eds., *Experimental Political Science: Principles and Practices*. London: Palgrave-Macmillan, pp. 178–205.

Karagözoglu, E. & Urhan, Ü. B. (2016). The effect of stake size in experimental bargaining and distribution games: A survey. *Group Decision and Negotiation*, 26(2), 285–325.

Keele, L. J. & Titiunik, R. (2015). Geographic boundaries as regression discontinuities. *Political Analysis*, 23(1), 127–155.

Keizer, K., Lindenberg, S., & Steg, L. (2008). The spreading of disorder. *Science*, 322 (5908), 1681–1685.

Keizer K., Lindenberg S., & Steg L. (2014). Doing field studies. What is it all about? *Group Processes and Intergroup Relations*, 17(3), 404–410.

Kelling, G. L. & Sousa, W. H. (2001). *Do Police Matter? An Analysis of the Impact of New York City's Police Reforms*. CCI Center for Civic Innovation at the Manhattan Institute.

Kennedy, R., Clifford, S., Burleigh, T., et al. (2020). The shape of and solutions to the MTurk quality crisis. *Political Science Research and Methods*, 8(4), 614–629.

Kerr, N. L. & Tindale, R. S. (2004). Group performance and decision making. *Annual Review of Psychology*, 55, 623–655.

Keuschnigg, M. & Wolbring, T. (2015a). *Experimente in den Sozialwissenschaften. Soziale Welt, Sonderband 22*. Baden-Baden: Nomos.

Keuschnigg, M. & Wolbring, T. (2015b). Disorder, social capital, and norm violation: Three field experiments on the broken windows thesis. *Rationality & Society*, 27(1), 96–126.

Kim, O. & Walker, M. (1984). The free rider problem: Experimental evidence. *Public Choice*, 43(1), 3–24.

Kimmel, A. J. (1998). In defense of deception. *American Psychologist*, 53(7), 803–805.

Kirk, D. S. (2009). A natural experiment on residential change and recidivism: Lessons from hurricane Katrina. *American Sociological Review*, 74(3), 484–505.

Kirk, D. S. (2015). Geographic concentration of former prisoners. *Proceedings of the National Academy of Sciences*, 112(22), 6943–6948.

Kittel, B. (2006). A crazy methodology? On the limits of macroquantitative social science research. *International Sociology*, 21(5), 647–677.

Kittel, B. (2015). Experimente in der Wirtschaftssoziologie: Ein Widerspruch? In: M. Keuschnigg & T. Wolbring, eds., *Experimente in den Sozialwissenschaften, Soziale Welt, Sonderband 22*. Baden-Baden: Nomos, pp. 79–104.

Kittel, B. & Marcinkiewicz, K. (2012). Voting behavior and political institutions: An overview of challenging questions in theory and experimental research. In: B. Kittel, W. J. Luhan, & R. B. Morton, eds., *Experimental Political Science: Principles and Practices*. London: Palgrave-Macmillan, pp. 17–53.

Klasnja, M. & Titiunik, R. (2017). The incumbency curse: Weak parties, term limits, and unfulfilled accountability. *American Political Science Review*, 111(1), 129–148.

Konow, J. (2003). Which is the fairest one of all? A positive analysis of justice theories. *Journal of Economic Literature*, 41(4), 1188–1239.

Korn, J. H. (1997). *Illusions of Reality: A History of Deception in Social Psychology*. New York: SUNY Press.

Krasnow, M. M., Howard, R. M., & Eisenbruch, A. B. (2020). The importance of being honest? Evidence that deception may not pollute social science subject pools after all. *Behavior Research Methods*, 52(3), 1175–1188.

Krawczyk, M. (2019). What should be regarded as deception in experimental economics? Evidence from a survey of researchers and subjects. *Journal of Behavioral and Experimental Economics*, 79, 110–118.

Kroher, M. & Wolbring, T. (2015). Social control, social learning, and cheating. Evidence from lab and online experiments on dishonesty. *Social Science Research*, 53, 311–324.

Kroneberg, C. & Kalter, F. (2012). Rational choice theory and empirical research: Methodological and theoretical contributions in Europe. *Annual Review of Sociology*, 38, 73–92.

Krosnick, J. A., Judd, C. M., & Wittenbrink, B. (2014). The measurement of attitudes. In: D. Albarracín & B. T. Johnson, eds., *The Handbook of Attitudes, Volume 1: Basic Principles*. New York: Routledge, pp. 45–105.

Kuhfeld, W. F., Tobias, R. D., & Garratt, M. (1994). Efficient experimental design with marketing research applications. *Journal of Marketing Research*, 31(4), 545–557.

References

Larney, A., Rotella, A., & Barclay, P. (2019). Stake size effects in ultimatum game and dictator game offers: A meta-analysis. *Organizational Behavior and Human Decision Processes*, 151, 61–72.

Lavrakas, P. J., Traugott, M. W., Kennedy, C., et al. (2019). *Experimental Methods in Survey Research: Techniques That Combine Random Sampling with Random Assignment*. New York: Wiley.

Lazarsfeld, P. F. & Menzel, H. (1961). On the relationship between individual and collective properties. In: A. Etzioni, ed., *Complex Organizations: A Sociological Reader*. New York: Holt, Rinehart & Winston, pp. 499–516.

Ledyard J. O. (1995). Public goods: A survey of experimental research. In: J. H. Kagel & A. E. Roth, eds., *The Handbook of Experimental Economics*. Princeton, NJ: Princeton University Press, pp. 253–348.

Lefebvre, P. & Merrigan, P. (2008). Child-care policy and the labor supply of mothers with young children: A natural experiment from Canada. *Journal of Labor Economics*, 26(3), 519–548.

Legewie, J. (2013). Terrorist events and attitudes toward immigrants: A natural experiment. *American Journal of Sociology*, 118(5), 1199–1245.

Levitt, S. D. (2004). Understanding why crime fell in the 1990s: Four factors that explain the decline and six that do not. *Journal of Economic Perspectives*, 18(1), 163–190.

Levitt, S. D. & List, J. A. (2007). Viewpoint: On the generalizability of lab behaviour to the field. *Canadian Journal of Economics*, 40(2), 347–370.

Levitt, S. D. & List, J. A. (2009). Field experiments in economics: The past, the present, and the future. *European Economic Review*, 53(1), 1–18.

Levitt, S. D. & List, J. A. (2011). Was there really a Hawthorne effect at the Hawthorne plant? An analysis of the original illumination experiments. *American Economic Journal: Applied Economics*, 3(1), 224–38.

Lewis, P. D. & Willer, D. (2017). Does social value orientation theory apply to social relations? *Sociological Science*, 3, 249–262.

Liberman, V., Samuels, S. M., & Ross, L. (2004). The name of the game: Predictive power of reputations versus situational labels in determining prisoner's dilemma game moves. *Personality and Social Psychology Bulletin*, 30(9), 1175–1185.

Liebe, U., Gewinner, J., & Diekmann, A. (2021). Large and persistent effects of green energy defaults in the household and business sectors. *Nature Human Behavior*, 5, 576–585.

References

Liebe, U. & Meyerhoff, J. (2021). Mapping potentials and challenges of choice modelling for social science research. *Journal of Choice Modelling*, 38, 100270.

Lindemann, G. (2010). Die Emergenzfunktion des Dritten – Ihre Bedeutung für die Analyse der Ordnung einer funktional differenzierten Gesellschaft. *Zeitschrift für Soziologie*, 39(6), 493–511.

Lindenberg, S. (1977). The direction of ordering and its relation to social phenomena. *Zeitschrift für Soziologie*, 6(2), 203–221.

Lindenberg, S. (1997). Grounding groups in theory: Functional, cognitive, and structural interdependencies. *Advances in Group Processes*, 14, 281–331.

Lindenberg, S. (2013). Social rationality, self-regulation, and well-being: The regulatory significance of needs, goals, and the self. In: V. Nee, R. Wittek, & T. A. B. Snijders, eds., *The Handbook of Rational Choice Social Research*. Stanford, CA: Stanford University Press, pp. 72–112.

Lindenberg, S. (2015). The sociology of groups. In: J. D. Wright, ed., *International Encyclopedia of the Social & Behavioral Sciences*. Amsterdam: Elsevier, pp. 434–440.

Little, R. J. & Rubin, D. B. (2002). Bayes and multiple imputation. In: R. J. Little & D. B. Rubin, eds., *Statistical Analysis with Missing Data*. Hoboken: Wiley, pp. 200–220.

Lockwood, D. (1964). Social integration and system integration. In: G. K. Zollschan & W. Hirsch, eds., *Social Change: Explorations, Diagnosis and Conjectures*. London: Routledge & Paul, pp. 244–257.

Loewenstein, G. (1999). Experimental economics from the vantage-point of behavioural economics. *The Economic Journal*, 109(453), F25–F34.

Lorenz, J., Rauhut, H., Schweitzer, F., & Helbing, D. (2011). How social influence can undermine the wisdom of crowd effect. *Proceedings of the National Academy of Sciences*, 108(22), 9020–9025.

Lovaglia, M. J., Lucas, J. W., & Thye, S. R. (1998). Status processes and mental ability test scores. *American Journal of Sociology*, 104(1), 195–228.

Luhan, W. J., Kocher, M. G., & Sutter, M. (2009). Group polarization in the team dictator game reconsidered. *Experimental Economics*, 12(1), 26–41.

Lynn, P., ed. (2009). *Methodology of Longitudinal Surveys*. New York: Wiley.

Mankiw, N. G. & Taylor, M. P. (2006). *Economics*. London: Thomson Learning.

Martin, M. W. & Sell, J. (1979). The role of the experiment in the social sciences. *Sociological Quarterly*, 20(4), 581–590.

References

Marwell, G. & R. E. Ames (1979). Experiments on the provision of public goods. I. Resources, interest, group size, and the free-rider problem. *American Journal of Sociology*, 84(6), 1335–1360.

Marwell, G. & Ames, R. A. (1980). Experiments on the provision of public goods. II. Provision points, stakes, experience, and the free-rider problem. *American Journal of Sociology*, 85(4), 926–937.

Marwell, G. & Oliver, P. (1993). *The Critical Mass in Collective Action: A Micro-Social Theory*. Cambridge: Cambridge University Press.

Maxwell, S. E. & Delaney, H. D. (1990). *Designing Experiments and Analyzing Data: A Model Comparison Approach*. Pacific Grove, CA: Brooks/Cole.

McDaniel, T. & Starmer, C. (1998). Experimental economics and deception: A comment. *Journal of Economic Psychology*, 19(3), 403–409.

Meeker, B. F. & Leik, R. K. (2007). Experimentation in sociological social psychology. In M. Webster & J. Sell, eds., *Laboratory Experiments in the Social Sciences*. London: Elsevier, pp. 630–649.

Messick, D. M. & McClintock, C. G. (1968). Motivational bases of choice in experimental games. *Journal of Experimental Social Psychology*, 4(1), 1–25.

Milgram, S. (1963). Behavioral study of obedience. *The Journal of Abnormal and Social Psychology*, 67(4), 371–378.

Milgram, S. (1974). *Obedience to Authority: An Experimental View*. New York: Harper & Row.

Mills, T. M. (1954). The coalition pattern in three person groups. *American Sociological Review*, 19(6), 657–667.

Mitchell, G. (2012). Revisiting truth or triviality: The external validity of research in the psychological laboratory. *Perspectives on Psychological Science*, 7(2), 109–117.

Mize, T. D. & Manago, B. (2022). The past, present, and future of experimental methods in the social sciences. *Social Science Research*, 108, 102799.

Molm, L. D. (2010). The structure of reciprocity. *Social Psychology Quarterly*, 73(2), 119–131.

Molm, L. D. (2014). Experiments on exchange relations and exchange networks in sociology. In M. Webster, Jr. & J. Sell, eds., *Laboratory Experiments in the Social Sciences*, 2nd ed. Amsterdam: Elsevier, pp. 199–224.

Molm, L. D., Collett, J. L., & Schaefer, D. R. (2007). Building solidarity through generalized exchange: A theory of reciprocity. *American Journal of Sociology*, 113(1), 205–242.

Molm, L. D. & Cook, K. S. (1995). Social exchange and exchange networks. In: K. S. Cook, G. A. Fine, & J. House, eds., *Sociological*

Perspectives on Social Psychology. Needham Heights, MA: Allyn & Bacon, pp. 209–235.

Morgan, S. L. & Winship, C. (2015). *Counterfactuals and Causal Inference. Methods and Principles for Social Research*, 2nd ed. Cambridge, MA: Cambridge University Press.

Morton, R. B. & Williams, K. C. (2010). *Experimental Political Science and the Study of Causality. From Nature to the Lab.* Cambridge: Cambridge University Press.

Mouw, T. (2006). Estimating the causal effect of social capital: A review of recent research. *Annual Review of Sociology*, 32(1), 79–102.

Mueller, D. C. (2003). *Public Choice III.* Cambridge: Cambridge University Press.

Mullinix, K. J., Leeper, Th., Druckman, J. N., & Freese, J. (2016). The generalizability of survey experiments. *Journal of Experimental Political Science*, 2(02), 109–138.

Mummolo, J., & Peterson, E. (2019). Demand effects in survey experiments: An empirical assessment. *American Political Science Review*, 113(2), 517–529.

Munger K. (2016). Tweetment effects on the tweeted: Experimentally reducing racist harassment. *Political Behavior*, 39, 629–649.

Muñoz, J., Falcó-Gimeno, A., & Hernández, E. (2020). Unexpected event during survey design: Promise and pitfalls for causal inference. *Political Analysis*, 28(2), 186–206.

Murphy, R. O. & Ackermann, K. A. (2014). Social value orientation: Theoretical and measurement issues in the study of social preferences. *Personality and Social Psychology Review*, 18(1), 13–41.

Murphy, R. O., Ackermann, K. A., & Handgraaf, M. J. J. (2011). Measuring social value orientation. *Judgment and Decision Making*, 6(8), 771–781.

Mutz, D. C. (2011). *Population-Based Survey Experiments.* Princeton, NJ: Princeton University Press.

Nagel, R. (1995). Unraveling in guessing games: An experimental study. *American Economic Review*, 85(5), 1313–1326.

Neuhofer, S. (2021). Let's chat about justice in a fair distribution experiment. *FOR2104 Working Paper 2021-03.*

Neuhofer S., Reindl, I., & Kittel, B. (2015). Social exchange networks: A review of experimental studies. *Connections*, 35(2), 34–51.

Neumann, T., Kierspel, S., Windrich, I., Berger, R., & Vogt, B. (2018). How to split gains and losses? Experimental evidence of dictator and ultimatum games. *Games*, 9(4), 78.

Niederle, M. (2015). Intelligent design: The relationship between economic theory and experiments: Treatment-driven experiments.

In: G. R. Fréchette & A. Schotter, eds., *Handbook of Experimental Economic Methodology*, Oxford: Oxford University Press, pp. 104–131.

Niederle, M. & Vesterlund, L. (2007). Do women shy away from competition? Do men compete too much? *The Quarterly Journal of Economics*, 122(3), 1067–1101.

Niza, C., Tung, B., & Marteau, T. M. (2013). Incentivizing blood donation: Systematic review and meta-analysis to test Titmuss' hypotheses. *Health Psychology*, 32(9), 941.

Nosek, B. A. & Lakens, D. (2014). Registered reports: A method to increase the credibility of published results. *Social Psychology*, 45(3), 137–141.

Nullmeier, F. & Pritzlaff, T. (2010). The implicit normativity of political practices. Analyzing the dynamics and power relations of committee decision making. *Critical Policy Studies*, 3(3–4), 357–374.

Oakley, A. (1998). Experimentation and social interventions: A forgotten but important history. *British Medical Journal*, 317(7167), 1239–1242.

Ofshe, R. & Ofshe, S. L. (1970). Choice behavior in coalition games. *Behavioral Science*, 15(4), 337–349.

Oliver, P. E. (1980). Selective incentives in an apex game: An experiment in coalition formation. *Journal of Conflict Resolution*, 24(1), 113–141.

Oliver, P. E. (1984). Rewards and punishments as selective incentives: An apex game. *Journal of Conflict Resolution*, 28(1), 123–148.

Olson, M. (1965). *The Logic of Collective Action: Public Goods and the Theory of Groups*. Cambridge, MA: Harvard University Press.

Open Science Collaboration (2015). Estimating the reproducibility of psychological science. *Science*, 349, aac4716.

Opp, K.-D. (1970). *Methodologie der Sozialwissenschaften: Einführung in Probleme ihrer Theorienbildung*. Reinbek bei Hamburg: Rowohlt.

Opp, K.-D. (2002). When do norms emerge by human design and when by the unintended consequences of human action? The example of the no-smoking norm. *Rationality and Society*, 14(2), 131–158.

Opp, K.-D. (2015). Norms. In: J. D. Wright, ed., *International Encyclopedia of the Social and Behavioral Sciences*. Amsterdam: Elsevier, pp. 5–10.

Ortmann, A. (2019). Deception. In: A. Schram & A. Ule, eds., *Handbook of Research Methods and Applications in Experimental Economics*. Cheltenham: Edward Elgar, pp. 28–38.

Ostrom, E., Walker, J., & Gardner, R. (1992). Covenants with and without a sword: Self-governance is possible. *American Political Science Review*, 86(2), 404–417.

Pager, D., Bonikowski, B., & Western, B. (2009). Discrimination in a low-wage labor market: A field experiment. *American Sociological Review*, 74(5), 777–789.

Palfrey, T. R. (2009). Laboratory experiments in political economy. *Annual Review of Political Science*, 12, 379–388.

Parsons, T. & Shils, E. (1951). *Toward a General Theory of Action*. Cambridge, MA: Harvard University Press.

Pearl, J. & Mackenzie, D. (2018). *The Book of Why: The New Science of Cause and Effect*. New York: Basic Books.

Persson, T. & Tabellini, G. E. (2000). *Political Economics: Explaining Economic Policy*. Cambridge, MA: MIT Press.

Petzold, K. & Wolbring, T. (2019). What can we learn from factorial surveys about human behavior? A validation study comparing field and survey experiments on discrimination. *Methodology*, 15(1), 19–30.

Phan, T. Q. & Airoldi, E. M. (2015). Social network formation and dynamics. *Proceedings of the National Academy of Sciences*, 112 (21), 6595–6600.

Przepiorka, W. & Diekmann, A. (2013). Temporal embeddedness and signals of trustworthiness: Experimental tests of a game theoretic model in the United Kingdom, Russia, and Switzerland. *European Sociological Review*, 29(5), 1010–1023.

Raub, W. (2017). *Rational Models. Expanded Version of Farewell Lecture as Dean of Social and Behavioral Sciences at Utrecht University*. Utrecht: Utrecht University.

Raub, W., de Graaf, N. D., & Gërxhani, K. (2022). Rigorous sociology. In: K. Gërxhani, N. D. de Graaf, & W. Raub, eds., *Handbook of Sociological Science: Contributions to Rigorous Sociology*. Cheltenham: Edward Elgar, pp. 2–19.

Raub, W. & Keren, G. (1993). Hostages as a commitment device: A game-theoretic model and an empirical test of some scenarios. *Journal of Economic Behavior & Organization*, 21(1), 43–67.

Raub, W. & Voss, T. (1986). Conditions for cooperation in problematic social situations. In: A. Diekmann & P. Mitter, eds., *Paradoxical Effects of Social Behavior. Essays in Honor of Anatol Rapoport*. Heidelberg/Wien: Physica, pp. 85–103.

Raub, W. & Voss, T. (2017). Micro-macro models in sociology: Antecedents of Coleman's diagram. In: B. Jann & W. Przepiorka, eds., *Social Dilemmas, Institutions, and the Evolution of Cooperation*. Berlin: de Gruyter, pp. 11–36.

Raub, W. & Weesie, J. (1993). The management of matches: Decentralized mechanisms for cooperative relations with applications

References

to organizations and households. *ISCORE Papers 1*. Utrecht: Utrecht University.

Rauhut, H. (2013). Beliefs about lying and spreading of dishonesty: Undetected lies and their constructive and destructive social dynamics in dice experiments. *PLoS ONE*, 8(11), e77878.

Rauhut, H. & Winter, F. (2010). A sociological perspective on measuring social norms by means of strategy method experiments. *Social Science Research*, 39(6), 1181–1194.

Regan, D. T. (1971). Effects of a favor and liking on compliance. *Journal of Experimental Social Psychology*, 7(6), 627–639.

Reilly, T., Carpenter, S., Dul, V., Bartlett, K., & Brewer, M. B. (1982). The factorial survey: An approach to defining sexual harassment on campus. *Journal of Social Issues*, 38(4), 99–110.

Reindl, I., Hoffmann, R., & Kittel, B. (2019) Let the others do the job: Comparing public good contribution behavior in the lab and in the field. *Journal of Behavioral and Experimental Economics*, 81, 73–83.

Rieken, H. W. & Boruch, R. F. (1978). Social experiments. *Annual Review of Sociology*, 4, 511–532.

Roethlisberger, F. J. & Dickson, W. J. (1939). *Management and the Worker*. Oxford: Harvard University Press.

Romanò, S. & Barrera, D. (2021). The impact of market-oriented reforms on inequality in transitional countries: New evidence from Cuba. *Socio-Economic Review*, 19(2), 765–787.

Rosenthal R. & Fode K. L. (1963). The effect of experimenter bias on the performance of the albino rat. *Behavioral Science*, 8(3), 183–189.

Roskin, M. G. (2020). Political science. www.britannica.com/topic/political-science, Accessed 1 May 2021.

Rossi, P. H. (1979). Vignette analysis: Uncovering the normative structure of complex judgments. In: R. K. Merton, J. Coleman, & P. H. Rossi, eds., *Qualitative and Quantitative Social Research. Papers in Honor of Paul F. Lazarsfeld*. New York: Free Press, pp. 176–185.

Roth, A. E. (1995). Introduction to experimental economics. In: J. H. Kagel & A. E. Roth, eds., *The Handbook of Experimental Economics*. Princeton, NJ: Princeton University Press, pp. 3–109.

Rubin, D. B. (1974). Estimating causal effects of treatments in randomized and nonrandomized studies. *Journal of Educational Psychology*, 66(5), 688–701.

Rubin, D. B. (1980). Randomization analysis of experimental data: The Fisher randomization test. *Journal of the American Statistical Association*, 75(371), 591–593.

Salganik, M. J. (2018). *Bit by Bit: Social Research in the Digital Age*. Princeton, NJ: Princeton University Press.

Salganik, M. J., Dodds, P. S., & Watts, D. J. (2006). Experimental study of inequality and unpredictability in an artificial cultural market. *Science*, 311, 854–856.

Sampson, R. J. (2008). Moving to inequality: Neighborhood effects and experiments meet social structure. *American Journal of Sociology*, 114(1), 189–231.

Sauer, C., Auspurg, K., & Hinz, T. (2020). Designing multi-factorial survey experiments: Effects of presentation style (text or table), answering scales, and vignette order. *mda: methods, data, analyses*, 14(2), 195–214.

Sauermann, H. & Selten, R. (1959). Ein Oligopolexperiment. *Zeitschrift für die gesamte Staatswissenschaft*, 115(3), 427–471.

Schram, A. (2005). Artificiality: The tension between internal and external validity in economic experiments. *Journal of Economic Methodology*, 12(2), 225–237.

Schram, A., Brandts, J., & Gërxhani, K. (2019). Status ranking: A hidden channel to gender inequality under competition. *Experimental Economics*, 22(2), 396–418.

Schutz, A. (1967 [1932]). *The Phenomenology of the Social World*. Evanston, IL: Northwestern University Press.

Schwaninger, M., Neuhofer, S., & Kittel, B. (2019). Offers beyond the negotiating dyad: Including the excluded in a network exchange experiment. *Social Science Research*, 79, 258–271.

Scott, J. T., Matland, R. E., Michelbach, P. A., & Bornstein, B. H. (2001). Just deserts: An experimental study of distributive justice norms. *American Journal of Political Science*, 45(4), 749–767.

Shadish, W. R., Cook, T. D., & Campbell D. T. (2002). *Experimental and Quasi-experimental Designs for General Causal Inference*. Boston: Houghton Mifflin.

Shamon, H., Dülmer, H., & Giza, A. (2022). The factorial survey: The impact of the presentation format of vignettes on answer behavior and processing time. *Sociological Methods & Research*, 51(1), 396–438.

Sherif, M., Harvey, O. J., White, J. B., & Sherif, C. W. (1961). *Intergroup Conflict and Co-operation: The Robber's Cave Experiment*. Norman, OK: University Book Exchange.

Shikano, S., Bräuninger, T., & Stoffel, M (2012). Statistical analysis of experimental data. In: B. Kittel, W. J. Luhan, & R. B. Morton, eds., *Experimental Political Science: Principles and Practices*, Basingstoke: Palgrave-Macmillan, pp. 163–177.

Simmel, G. (1950 [1908]). *The Sociology of Georg Simmel*. Glencoe: The Free Press.

Simpson, B., McGrimmon, T., & Irwin, K. (2007). Are blacks really less trusting than whites? Revisiting the race and trust question. *Social Forces*, 86(2), 525–552.

Simpson, B. & Willer, D. (2015). Beyond altruism: Sociological foundations of cooperation and prosocial behavior. *Annual Review of Sociology*, 41, 43–63.

Simpson, B., Willer, D., & Ridgeway, C. L. (2012). Status hierarchies and the organization of collective action. *Sociological Theory*, 30(3), 149–166.

Smith, E. & Mackie, D. (1999). *Social Psychology*. Philadelphia: Psychology Press.

Smith, V. (1962). An experimental study of competitive market behavior. *Journal of Political Economy*, 70(2), 111–137.

Smith, V. (1976). Experimental economics: Induced value theory. *American Economic Review*, 66(2), 274–279.

Snowberg, E. & Yariv, L. (2021). Testing the waters: Behavior across participant pools. *American Economic Review*, 111(2), 687–719.

Sorokin, P. A. (1928a). Arbeitsleistung und Entlohnung. *Kölner Vierteljahresschrift für Soziologie*, 7(2), 186–198.

Sorokin, P. A. (1928b). Experimente zur Soziologie. *Zeitschrift für Völkerpsychologie und Soziologie*, 4(1), 1–10.

Sorokin, P. A. (1931). Sociology as a science. *Social Forces*, 10(1), 21–27.

Sorokin, P. A. (1936). Is accurate social planning possible? *American Sociological Review*, 1(1), 12–25.

Sorokin, P. A, Tanquist, M., Parten, M., et al. (1930). An experimental study of efficiency of work under various specified conditions. *American Journal of Sociology*, 35(5), 765–782.

Spadaro, G., Graf, C., Jin, S., et al. (2022a). Cross-cultural variation in cooperation: A meta-analysis. *Journal of Personality and Social Psychology*, 123(5), 1024–1088.

Spadaro G., Tiddi, I., Columbus, S., et al. (2022b). The Cooperation Databank: Machine-readable science accelerates research synthesis. *Perspectives on Psychological Science*, 17(5), 1472–1489.

Spears, R. (2021). Social influence and group identity. *Annual Review of Psychology*, 72, 367–390.

Stahl, D. O. & Haruvy, E. (2008). Subgame perfection in ultimatum bargaining trees. *Games and Economic Behavior*, 63(1), 292–307.

Stang, D. J. (1976). Ineffective deception in conformity research: Some causes and consequences. *European Journal of Social Psychology*, 6(3), 353–367.

Stasser, G. & Abele, S. (2020). Collective choice, collaboration, and communication. *Annual Review of Psychology*, 71, 589–612.

References

Strodtbeck, F. L. (1954). The family as a three-person group. *American Sociological Review*, 19(1), 23–29.

Suleiman, R. (2001). Different perspectives of human behavior entail different experimental practices. *Behavioral and Brain Sciences*, 24(3), 429–429.

Tam, A. (2020). The legitimacy of groups: Toward a we-reasoning view. *Analyse & Kritik*, 42(2), 343–367.

Taves, M. (1953). An experimental design to preserve randomization in social experiments. *American Sociological Review*, 18(1), 90–96.

Teele, D. L., ed. (2014). *Field Experiments and Their Critics: Essays on the Uses and Abuses of Experimentation in the Social Sciences*. New Haven, CT: Yale University Press.

Thaler, R. H. & Johnson, E. J. (1990). Gambling with the house money and trying to break even: The effects of prior outcomes on risky choice. *Management Science*, 36(6), 643–660.

Thaler, R. H. & Sunstein, C. R. (2008). *Nudge: Improving Decisions about Health, Wealth, and Happiness*. New Haven, CT: Yale University Press.

Thistlewaite, D. L. & Campbell, D. T. (1960). Regression-discontinuity analysis: An alternative to the ex post facto experiment. *Journal of Educational Psychology*, 51(6), 309–317.

Thomas, W. I. & Thomas, D. D. S. (1928). *The Child in America: Behavior, Problems and Programs*. New York: A. A. Knopf.

Thye, S. (2000). Reliability in experimental sociology. *Social Forces* 78(4), 1277–1309.

Thye, S. (2014). Logical and philosophical foundations of experimental research in the social sciences. In: M. Webster & J. Sell, eds., *Laboratory Experiments in the Social Sciences*. London: Elsevier, pp. 53–82.

Titiunik, R. (2021). Natural experiments. In: J. Druckman & D. Green, eds., *Advances in Experimental Political Science*. New York: Cambridge University Press, pp. 103–129.

Titmuss R. (1970). *The Gift Relationship: From Human Blood to Social Policy*. London: George Allen and Unwin.

Traub, S., Schwaninger, M., Paetzel, F., & Neuhofer, S. (2023). Evidence on need-sensitive giving behavior: An experimental approach to the acknowledgment of needs. *Journal of Behavioral and Experimental Economics*, 105, 102028.

Treischl, E. & Wolbring, T. (2022). The past, present and future of factorial survey experiments: A review for the social sciences. *mda: methods, data, analyses*, 16(2), 141–170.

Tuomela, R. (2017). Non-reductive views of shared intention. In: M. Jankovic & K. Ludwig, eds., *The Routledge Handbook of Collective Intentionality*. London: Routledge, pp. 25–33.

Tversky, A. & Kahneman, D. (1981). The framing of decision and the psychology of choice. *Science*, 21(4481), 453–458.

Tyler, T. R. & Amodio, D. M. (2015). Psychology and economics: Areas of convergence and difference. In: G. R. Fréchette & A. Schotter, eds., *Handbook of Experimental Economic Methodology*. Oxford: Oxford University Press, pp. 181–196.

van de Rijt, A., Kang, S. M., Restivo, M., & Patil, A. (2014). Field experiments of success-breeds-success dynamics. *Proceedings of the National Academy of Sciences*, 111(19), 6934–6939.

Van Lange, P. A. M., Balliet, D., Parks, C., & Van Vugt, M. (2013). *Social Dilemmas: Understanding Human Cooperation*. New York: Oxford University Press.

Vinacke, W. E. & Arkoff, A. (1957). An experimental study of coalitions in the triad. *American Sociological Review*, 22(4), 406–414.

Vogt, S., Zaid, N. A. M., Ahmed, H. E. F., Fehr, E., & Efferson, C. (2016). Changing cultural attitudes on female genital cutting. *Nature*, 538(7726), 506–509.

von Neumann, J. & Morgenstern, O. (1944). *Theory of Games and Economic Behavior*. Princeton, NJ: Princeton University Press.

Wagstaff, G. F., Huggins, J. P., & Perfect, T. J. (1993). Equity, equality, and need in the adult family. *The Journal of Social Psychology*, 133(4), 439–443.

Wallander, L. (2009). 25 years of factorial surveys in sociology: A review. *Social Science Research*, 38(3), 505–520.

Webb, E., Campbell, D. T., Schwartz, R., & Sechrest, L., eds. (2000 [1965]). *Unobtrusive Measures*, rev. ed. Thousand Oaks, CA: Sage.

Weber, M. (1978 [1921/22]). *Economy and Society. An Outline of Interpretive Sociology*. Berkeley: University of California Press.

Webster, M., Jr. & Sell, J., eds. (2014a). *Laboratory Experiments in the Social Sciences*, 2nd ed. San Diego, CA: Academic Press.

Webster, M., Jr. & Sell, J. (2014b). Why do experiments? In: M. Webster, Jr. & J. Sell, eds., *Laboratory Experiments in the Social Sciences*, 2nd ed. San Diego, CA: Academic Press, pp. 5–21.

Weimann, J. & Brosig-Koch, J. (2019). *Methods in Experimental Economics*. Berlin: Springer.

Weinberg, J., Freese, J., & McElhattan, D. (2014). Comparing data characteristics and results of an online factorial survey between a population-based and a crowdsource-recruited sample. *Sociological Science*, 1(19), 292–310.

Weindling, P. (2001). The origins of informed consent: The international scientific commission on medical war crimes, and the Nuremberg Code. *Bulletin of the History of Medicine*, 75(1), 37–71.

Weiss, D. J. (2001). Deception by researchers is necessary and not necessarily evil. *Behavioral and Brain Sciences*, 24(3), 431–432.

Wicherts, J. M. & Bakker, M. (2014). Broken windows, mediocre methods, and substandard statistics. *Group Processes and Intergroup Relations*, 17(3), 388–403.

Willer, D. (1967). *Scientific Sociology: Theory and Method*. Englewood Cliffs: Prentice-Hall.

Willer, D. (1992). A comment on developed theory and theory development. *Sociological Theory*, 10(1), 106–110.

Willer, D., ed. (1999). *Network Exchange Theory*. Westport, CT: Praeger.

Willer, D. & Emanuelson, P. (2008). Testing ten theories. *Journal of Mathematical Sociology*, 32(3), 165–203.

Willer, D., Emanuelson, P., Lovaglia, et al. (2014). Elementary Theory: 25 years of expanding scope and increasing precision. In: S. R. Thye & E. J. Lawler, eds., *Advances in Group Processes*, vol. 31. Bingley, UK: Emerald, pp. 175–217.

Willer, D., Gladstone, E., & Berigan, N. (2013). Social values and social structure. *Journal of Mathematical Sociology*, 37(2), 113–130.

Willer, D. & Walker, A. (2007). *Building Experiments*. Stanford, CA: Stanford University Press.

Willer, R. Kuwabara, K., & Macy, M. (2009). The false enforcement of unpopular norms. *American Journal of Sociology*, 115(2), 451–490.

Willis, R. H. & Willis, Y. A. (1970). Role playing versus deception: An experimental comparison. *Journal of Personality and Social Psychology*, 16(3), 472–477.

Wilson, J. Q. & Kelling, G. L. (1982). Broken windows: The police and neighborhood safety. *The Atlantic Monthly*, 127(2), 29–38.

Winter, F., Rauhut, H., & Helbing, D. (2012). How norms can generate conflict: An experiment on the failure of cooperative micro-motives on the macro-level. *Social Forces*, 90(3), 919–946.

Wolbring, T. & Keuschnigg, M. (2015). Feldexperimente in den Sozialwissenschaften. Grundlagen, Herausforderungen, Beispiele. In: M. Keuschnigg & T. Wolbring, eds. *Experimente in den Sozialwissenschaften, Soziale Welt Sonderband 22*. Baden-Baden: Nomos, pp. 219–245.

Woodward, J. (2003). *Making Things Happen: A Theory of Causal Explanation*. Oxford: Oxford University Press.

References

Yamagishi, T., Cook, K. S., & Watabe, M. (1998). Uncertainty, trust, and commitment formation in the United States and Japan. *American Journal of Sociology*, 104(1), 165–194.

Yoon, J., Thye, S. R., & Lawler, E. J. (2013). Exchange and cohesion in dyads and triads: A test of Simmel's hypothesis. *Social Science Research*, 42, 1457–1466.

Zelditch, M. (2014a). Thirty years of advances in group processes: A review essay. In: S. Thye & E. J. Lawler, eds., *Advances in Group Processes: 30th Anniversary Edition*, Bingley: Emerald, pp. 1–20.

Zelditch, M. (2014b). Laboratory experiments in sociology. In: M. Webster & J. Sell, eds., *Laboratory Experiments in the Social Sciences*. Amsterdam: Elsevier, pp. 517–531.

Zelditch, M. (2014c). The external validity of experiments that test theories. In: Webster, M. & Sell, J., eds. *Laboratory Experiments in the Social Sciences*. Amsterdam: Elsevier, pp. 87–112.

Index

ABA design 59
accumulation 127
   empirical 127
   knowledge 48, 129
action
   collective 26–27, 32, 37, 41, 73
   individual 5, 16, 30–31
agent 1–2, 5, 34
   behavior 38
   individual 2, 5
   simulated 149–151
agent-based model 54
aggregation
   level of 30, 39
   logic of 33
   parametric 31
   strategic 31
altruism 15, 32–33, 54
always-taker 87–88
American Economic Association (AEA) 147
American Psychological Association (APA) 147, 149
American Sociological Association (ASA) 23, 147–149
Ames, Ruth E. 41
analysis
   exploratory 158
   unit of 75
approach
   counterfactual 43–48, 57
   empirical 122, 124, 126, 129
   experimental 82, 156–157
   factorial 60, 104
   methodological 48, 154

   psychological 34
   sociological 29, 34
   statistical 88
   theoretical 122, 127, 129, 157
   traditional 134
   unobtrusive 81, 87
Arkoff, Abe 22–24
artificiality 8, 65, 70, 124, 126
Asian disease problem 133
attrition 8, 65, 92, 126
audit study 81
Auspurg, Katrin 97, 100, 102–103, 135
average treatment effect (ATE) 45–46, 88
average treatment effect on the treated (ATT) 45–46

balance test 110, 115, 157
Bales, Robert 22, 26
Barr, Abigail 129–131
Barrera, Davide 54, 111, 152
baseline condition 57, 83, 89, 93, 135, 139
beauty contest game 133
belief 17, 24, 26, 31–32, 35, 60, 96, 98, 103, 150, 152, 156
Belmont Report 146–147
bias, reactivity 155
Blossfeld, Hans-Peter 49, 52
Brandts, Jordi 77, 143
Breen, Richard 40, 49
broken windows theory 56, 82, 85, 89, 91–92
Brugarolas, Pablo 109, 112–113

Index

Buskens, Vincent ix, 54, 74, 96, 99–101, 103, 129
bystander effect 27

Camerer, Colin 124–127
Campbell, Donald T. 46, 110, 119, 122
Card, David 107
carryover effect 59
Cartwright, Nancy 48, 50, 127
causal inference 3, 40, 44, 65, 81, 87, 121
   fundamental problem 44–45, 47, 56, 58
   resulting bias 90
central limit theorem 61, 63, 79
ceteris paribus clause 1, 3, 97
Chamberlin, Edward H. 21
Chapin, Frank Stuart 14, 16–21, 23
characteristic, unobserved 46, 114
choice 6, 9, 23, 31, 34, 37–38, 41, 65–66, 74, 93, 95–96, 98, 100–101, 104, 131, 134, 143
   behavior 95
   binary 102
   experiment 65
   friendship 41
   methodological 4
   psychology of 32
   rational 27, 29, 41, 50, 53, 83, 137, 148
coalition, theory of 4, 23
code of conduct 147
common rule 146
communication channel 25, 69, 79
comparability 8, 43, 66, 83, 86, 90, 110, 156
competition 21–22, 63, 77–78, 155
compliance 37, 55, 58, 82, 87, 144
complier 87
Comte, Auguste 13, 21
condition, structural 71, 75, 140
confederate 22, 27, 39, 148–149, 151

confidence, level of 62
confound 8, 15, 42, 45–46, 64, 90, 103, 109, 123, 142, 152, 155
conjoint analysis 65, 95, 101–103
consent, informed 86–87, 94, 145–147, 151
construct, theoretical 120, 127, 129
continuum 52, 55–56, 74, 121, 127, 134
control 1, 3, 6–7, 14, 17–20, 25, 38, 42–43, 46–47, 54, 57–58, 65, 69, 74, 83, 85–86, 89–90, 99–100, 109, 111, 114, 119, 121–122, 124, 148–149, 155–156
condition 18, 39, 42, 44, 47, 57, 59–60
   effect 54, 59
   limit 58
   precision 20
   selective 19
   situation 48
   strict 64
   treatment 20, 44
   variable 152
Cook, Karen 25
counterbalance 59–61, 64, 141–142
counterfactual model 43–47
countries, WEIRD 75
covariate, pre-determined 8, 110, 114
critical threshold 54, 56
cross-validation 129, 131, 157
crowdsource-recruited sample 105

Deaton, Angus 48, 50, 127
deception 8–9, 15, 25, 145, 147–154
Declaration of Helsinki 146
D-efficient design 101–102
defier 87–88
design
   between-subject 45, 57, 64–65, 141
   complementary 155

design (cont.)
  complementary research 51
  complex factorial 65, 94
  factorial 32, 42, 60–61, 100
  fractionalized factorial 101
  full factorial 42, 60, 101
  orthogonal 102
  quota 98, 101
  random 101
  random, clustered 101
  within-subject 44, 58–59, 61, 80, 141
dictator game 53, 55, 139–140
Diekmann, Andreas ix, 24, 27, 50, 54, 61, 71
Difference-in-difference (DID) 114
digital field experiment 82, 92–94, 156
direct-response method 143
disorder, spreading of 82
Dodds, Peter Sheridan 93
Durkheim, Émile 16
dyadic learning 99

economic psychology 55
edge 25, 151
effect
  causal 1, 3, 17, 21, 41, 45, 50, 66, 82, 91, 106, 109–110, 113–114, 124
  demand 8, 126, 140, 142
  session 79
election forecast 109, 112–113
embeddedness 5, 29–30, 33, 61
emergence 9, 31–32, 35, 70–72
Emerson, Richard M. 25
endowment effect 55
error 86
  type I 62
  type II 62
  variance 46
Esser, Hartmut 30–31, 137

ethic 8
  code of 147
  committee 146, 150
  contemporary 145
  regulations of 146
exchange theory 4–5, 24–25, 27, 53
exogeneity 108–109
experiment
  as-if 8, 110, 113–114
  complement, laboratory 124
  different types of 6, 8, 78, 129, 155
  embedded natural 104
  empirically driven 49–50, 52, 55
  field 81–82, 84–94, 133, 157
  intuition-driven 55–56, 157
  laboratory, prerogative of 155
  model-driven 53–55, 57
  multifactorial 6, 65
  opportunity 85, 87–88
  other types of 3, 7, 76, 81, 85–86, 93, 126
  population-based survey 66
  protocol 2, 74, 80, 144
  quasi 7, 14, 43, 106, 110–112, 114, 156
  social psychology 9, 148–149, 151
  survey ix, 3–4, 6, 27, 65, 126, 129, 131, 157
  theoretically based 156
  theory-driven 50, 53, 56, 78
  vignette 7, 86, 95–99, 104–105
explanation, mechanism-based 50, 156
ex post facto experiment 18, 110
external force 8, 38, 109, 111–113
extrapolation 121, 123

falsification test 115
filler task 57
Fisher, Ronald A. 20
formal theoretical model 54, 98
frame selection, model of 137
framing theory 9

Index

freeriding 26, 73, 135
frontrunner 158

Gamson, William 23–24
gender pay gap 97, 100
gender stereotype 135
generalizability, statistical 155–156
Gërxhani, Klarita 32, 77, 108
goal 5, 7, 34–35, 40, 49, 77, 90, 112, 121, 124–125, 128, 137, 139
  common 17
  group 30, 36
  normative 137
Goldthorpe, John 41
Greenwood, Ernest 20
group
  comparison 46, 81, 88, 107, 114
  control 18, 20, 57–58, 66, 87–89, 92, 94, 107, 109–112, 114–115, 156
  experimental 46–47, 65, 87, 89–90, 110–111, 113, 155
  level 37, 58, 63, 75, 79–80
  member 22, 37, 43, 72, 79, 130
  phenomena 26, 34, 37
  process 34–35, 94, 134, 148–149
  size 26–27, 41–42
  small 21, 25, 36, 42, 63, 89, 114
  social 30, 33, 35, 75, 81, 156
  specific 104
  task 130, 133
  treatment 8, 61, 87–88, 94, 107, 109, 112, 115
  untreated 46
Guala, Francesco 55

Hawthorne effect 19, 91
Henrich, Joseph 54
Hersch, Gil 150
Hertwig, Ralph 141, 150, 152
heterogeneity 2, 63, 85, 91, 114, 153
hierarchy, status 37
Hinz, Thomas 97

history 3, 8, 93, 145, 152
honesty, academic 158
hostage game 28
hypothesis 23, 26, 28, 52, 97, 144
  alternative 22
  null 58, 62
  research 91, 144
  test 26, 49, 54, 79, 153

identification 42–44, 66, 91, 108–109, 114, 121
incentive 3, 6, 8, 15, 23, 27, 34, 76, 83, 86–88, 92, 132, 134–135, 140, 143, 154
  broader 141
  economic 139
  homogeneous 3
  implement 132
  monetary 9, 22, 76, 83, 86, 93, 132–134, 138–140
  non-monetary 134, 136
  strategic 133
incentivization 2–3, 76, 133, 138
independence 2, 16, 18–19, 31, 46, 58, 62, 64, 70, 79, 101, 130, 141, 146
  behavior 37, 76
  decision 80
  observation 80
  social 93
independently and identically distributed (iid) 62
individual treatment effect (ITE) 44
induced-value theory 9, 138
institutional review board 146–147
intentionality, collective 35, 37
intention-to-treat (ITT) analysis 88
interaction effect 61, 94, 101
interdependent 36
  cognitive 35
  functional 35
  structural 35
interrelatedness 29, 154

intervention 13–14, 19, 41–43, 47–48, 66, 81, 86, 88–91, 93, 110, 112, 114, 128, 142, 156
  experimental 42, 49, 89
  human 156
  policy 58, 106, 110, 128
  potential 66
  random 112

Jamison, Julian 152
Jasso, Guillermina 32, 96, 102
judgment 7, 30, 95–96, 98, 100, 102, 135, 156
justice, distributive 32, 130

Kahneman, Daniel 55, 134
Karlan, Dean 152
Keizer, Keith 56, 83–84, 86–87, 91–92, 133
Keuschnigg, Marc 56, 83–84
Kirk, David S. 107
Kittel, Bernhard 32, 125
knowledge claim 48, 119, 128–129
Krueger, Alan B. 107

Lazarsfeld, Paul 20
Lindenberg, Siegwart 26, 35–36, 56, 92, 137
List, John 123
lottery 104, 108–109, 152

macro-level phenomena 56
macro-micro-macro model 30
Marwell, Gerald 26–27, 41
match
  partner 74
  stranger 72
measure, unobtrusive 7, 65, 81, 87–88, 91, 93–94
measurement error 48
Mechanical Turk 104–105
mechanism, causal 40, 49, 155
mental frame 137, 139

meta-analysis 125, 129, 134, 140
Milgram, Stanley 146, 149
Mill, John Stuart 20
Miller, Luis ix, 48, 109, 112–113, 129
Mills, Theodore M. 22
minimum wage 107
model, formal 3, 29, 52–55, 73
Molm, Linda 25, 32, 38
motivation 3, 9, 34, 74, 86, 132
  behavior 140
  extrinsic 134
  group-level 36–37
  human 9, 136, 138
  individual 132
  intrinsic 76, 86, 133–134
  non-material 33
  underlying 139
  unitary 17
multilevel data structure 80
music lab 93

natural disaster 107–109
naturalness 81, 94, 103
network exchange theory 24, 53
never-taker 87–88
Neyman-Rubin model 43
nonresponse 126
norm, social 6, 37, 40, 70–72, 136, 148
Nuremberg Code 145

observation, covert 147
Oliver, Pamela 26–27
one-shot 152
  experiment 142
  game 71, 153
  interaction 54, 73
open access 157
Opp, Karl-Dieter 32, 95
opportunity costs 132
order effect 23, 59, 61
orthogonality 43, 101–102

Index

Ortmann, Andreas 141, 150, 152
outcome, potential 43–45, 47
oversocialized 30

participant 1–3, 9, 15, 17, 19, 22, 24, 27, 33, 39, 42–48, 53–54, 59, 69–71, 74–76, 78–80, 86, 91, 93–94, 96, 100, 106, 125–126, 130, 132, 142–144, 146–147, 149–151, 155
  behavior 69, 79, 152
  deceived 152
  deceiving 145
  decision to 76
  diseased 146
  employ 148
  experimental 48, 145, 152, 154
  future 89
  human 146
  inform 146
  lead 148
  potential 76, 106
  recruiting 104
  research 145–148
  semi-professional 105
  survey 65, 104
  volunteer 126
participation, repeated 86
phenomenon, social 15–16, 18, 22, 28, 30–31, 33, 35–38, 134
placebo test 8, 110, 113–115
political science 16, 30, 34, 95, 113, 130, 156
post-randomization bias 47
posttest 58, 60
power 22, 25, 37, 51, 80
  imbalanced 27
  pattern 23
  relation 34, 75
  statistical 58, 60, 62, 94, 102, 150, 156
  structure 25
power analysis 62

predictability 39
prediction, point 52, 54, 131
preregistration 157
presentation 95, 103, 133–135, 152
pretest 58–60
prisoner dilemma 28, 53, 135, 152
process, generative 51
product, Cartesian 100
prosocial behavior 33, 84, 131, 139–140
prospect theory 32, 134
Przepiorka, Wojtek ix, 54, 61, 71–72
public good 42, 47, 59, 71–72, 141

questionnaire 48, 77

randomization
  assignment 42–43
  crucial 45
  ex ante 109
  failure 86
  process 112
  solution 20
  test 58, 115
  treatment 62
randomized controlled trials (RCTs) 18, 49, 66, 84, 110, 123, 126
ranking 77–78, 102
rating 93, 102, 153
Raub, Werner 28
reactivity 65–66, 81, 85, 90–91
real-effort task 139
realism 103, 121–122, 155
recidivism 107, 112
reciprocity 9, 32, 38–39, 73, 80, 136, 139, 142
regularity, empirical 7, 40, 49, 52, 56, 77–78
representativeness 120–122
reputation 28, 30, 33, 35, 94, 99, 148–149, 152
respondent, multiple 101
result, insignificant 64, 157

reward, monetary 76, 130, 133, 138
risk aversion 152
robustness 22, 28, 64, 83–85, 119, 131, 156
Rossi, Peter H. 95–96
Roth, Alvin 53, 55
Rubin, Donald 115

Salganik, Matthew J. 93
sample
  convenience 7, 85, 98, 104–105, 125
  small 46, 114
sample size 60, 62, 114
Sauer, Carsten 97, 103
scalability 92
Schechter, Laura 152
Schram, Arthur 77, 124
selection 8, 20, 45, 86, 102, 107, 110, 112, 122, 124, 126, 133, 146
  logic of 31–32
sequence effect 141–142
setting, natural 65, 70, 74–75, 123–124, 155–156
Shadish, William R. 120
shock, unexpected 106
show-up fee 132
similarity, proximal 120
Simmel, Georg 22
Simpson, Brent 30, 152
situation, definition of 5, 136, 139
situational cues 136–137
Smith, Vernon L. 21, 76
social contagion 89
social desirability bias 81, 142
social influence 93, 136–137
  affect 93
  condition 93
social mechanism 33, 36, 135, 141
social media 92
social psychology 4, 24, 34–35, 38–39, 55, 58, 73, 76, 148–149, 152
  deception in 152
social status
  ranking 77
  study of 95
social-status ranking 77–78
social structure 25, 30, 39, 69
  dimension of 73
  existence of 34
social value orientation 32, 120
sociology, rigorous 5, 157
Sorokin, Pitirim Alexandrovich 14–16, 22–23
spillover effect 65, 89–90
stability, temporal 44
stable unit treatment value assumption (SUTVA) 89
standard, gold 122–123, 126
Stanley, Julian 122
static, comparative 54, 125
Steg, Linda 56, 92
strategy method 143
stress test 127–128
student sample 75, 124–125, 131, 157
subject pool 64, 66, 70, 76, 104, 121, 125, 148, 153
subject, recruitment of 85
survey, factorial 4, 32, 64–66, 95, 100, 135
symmetry 71–73, 152

tabular format 103
theory, sociology 21, 24, 26, 29, 51, 66, 69, 94, 136
three-step strategy 155
thumb, rule of 62, 90
tie 25, 35
trade-off 34, 78, 121–122, 154
transience, causal 44, 59
transparent 75, 157–158
transportability 84, 121
treatment, asymmetric 71–73
treatment effect, direction of 124
trust game 54, 61, 151–152

Index

Tuskegee study 146
Tversky, Amos 134

Ubeda, Paloma 129
ultimatum game 53, 64, 75, 139–140, 143
unannounced endogenous matching 151
unannounced restart 151
unbiased estimate 48
undersocialized 30
utility 22, 32–34, 137–138

validity
  external 8, 78, 103, 105, 119–122, 124–125, 127, 129, 157
  internal 8, 21, 46, 61, 91, 119–120, 122, 151–152
variable 1, 18, 30, 41, 43–47, 59, 62, 76, 79, 85, 89, 99, 102, 108, 112–113, 124, 127
  binary 62
  causal 119
  control 76, 97
  dependent 1, 30–31, 41, 46, 59, 64, 102, 112, 124, 128, 152
  dummy 46, 80, 100
  group-level 75
  independent 1, 41, 46–47, 54, 60, 112, 124
  intervening 109
  manipulated 41–42, 97
  ordinal 100
  outcome 38, 41, 106, 108, 124, 155
  relation 6
  standardized 102
  system 30
  theoretical 1
  treatment 57
vignette 130, 135
  design 100–101, 156
  example 96–98
  experiment 95–96, 156
  selection 101–102
  study 102–105, 129, 135
  universe 97, 100–101
Vinacke, W. Edgar 22–24
Vogt, Sonja 60
volunteer dilemma 27, 50, 71–73

Walker, Henry A. 4, 20
Wallander, Lisa 95–96
Watts, Duncan J. 93
Weber, Max 5, 29, 49
Weesie, Jeroen 28, 96, 99–101, 103
Willer, David 30, 32, 35, 52–53, 55
Wolbring, Tobias 56, 83–84, 86, 129
World Wide Web 92

For EU product safety concerns, contact us at Calle de José Abascal, 56–1°, 28003 Madrid, Spain or eugpsr@cambridge.org.

www.ingramcontent.com/pod-product-compliance
Lightning Source LLC
LaVergne TN
LVHW010258260326
834688LV00044B/1345